A Gathering of Brilliant Moons

A Gathering of Brilliant Moons

Practice Advice from the Rimé Masters of Tibet

Edited by

Holly Gayley and Joshua Schapiro

Wisdom Publications
199 Elm Street
Somerville, MA 02144 USA
wisdompubs.org

Library of Congress Cataloging-in-Publication Data
Names: Gayley, Holly, editor. | Translating Buddhist Luminaries Conference (2013: University of Colorado Boulder)
Title: A gathering of brilliant moons: practice advice from the Rimé masters of Tibet / edited by Holly Gayley and Joshua Schapiro.
Description: Somerville: Wisdom Publications, 2017. | "Translating Buddhist Luminaries Conference . . . at the University of Colorado Boulder in April 2013 . . . a conference on Ecumenism and Tibetan translation" —ECIP galley. |
Identifiers: LCCN 2017018050 (print) | LCCN 2017034492 (ebook) | ISBN 9781614292173 (ebook) | ISBN 1614292175 (ebook) | ISBN 9781614292005 (pbk.: alk. paper) | ISBN 1614292000 (pbk.: alk. paper)
Subjects: LCSH: Buddhist literature—Translations into English—Congresses.
Classification: LCC BQ1012 (ebook) | LCC BQ1012 .G38 2017 (print) | DDC 294.3/444—dc23
LC record available at https://lccn.loc.gov/2017018050

ISBN 978-1-61429-200-5   ebook ISBN 978-1-61429-217-3

21 20 19 18 17   5 4 3 2 1

Cover design by Tim Holtz. Cover Image: Jamgon Kongtrul Lodro Thaye (1813-1899) Tibet; late 19th century. Pigments on cloth. Courtesy of the Rubin Museum of Art. C2003.25.2 (HAR 65265) Interior design by Partners Composition. Set in DGP 10.5 pt./12.5 pt.

Wisdom Publications' books are printed on acid-free paper and meet the guidelines for permanence and durability of the Production Guidelines for Book Longevity of the Council on Library Resources.

♻ This book was produced with environmental mindfulness. For more information, please visit wisdompubs.org/wisdom-environment.

Printed in the United States of America.

Please visit fscus.org

This anthology is dedicated to E. Gene Smith,
whose indefatigable efforts to collect and preserve
Tibetan literature in ecumenical fashion continues the
legacy of the rimé masters celebrated within these pages.

Contents

Foreword

This book contains heart advice from Buddhist masters in eastern Tibet who promoted an ecumenical, or *rimé*, approach. Their advice comes from the depth of their own spiritual experience and addresses the genuine needs of practitioners.

Translating this type of text can be challenging. It is not a matter of finding equivalences for words but of understanding a way of seeing the world and then translating that way of seeing into another language and cultural context. Like poetry and prayers, spiritual advice is meant to inspire, and so the language of the translation needs to be inspiring. This is what the translators in this anthology have contributed.

The rimé approach is actually the Buddhist approach. From its founding, Buddhism has encouraged an ecumenical attitude that appreciates diversity and difference. The Buddha is said to have given 84,000 different teachings for myriad types of sentient beings. Various spiritual paths—within Buddhism and beyond—have the purpose to benefit humanity; it is important to respect all of them. We can learn a great deal from different spiritual teachings and practices.

I am happy that this book is dedicated to E. Gene Smith, who did so much to preserve Tibetan literature. He had a special interest in the ecumenical approach of the Buddhist masters whose works are translated here.

May these profound teachings bring benefit and contribute to lasting and true happiness.

Ringu Tulku Rinpoche
November 11, 2015

Preface

For generations, Buddhist masters in Tibet have composed poetic and poignant instructions, tailored to the needs of their disciples, in the form of short works of advice. Due to their brevity, translations of these works can be difficult to find in publication. For this reason, we have compiled this anthology of personal advice and practice instructions, focusing on an influential and inspiring generation of Buddhist teachers: the nineteenth-century rimé masters of eastern Tibet. The reader will encounter figures well known for their writings on philosophical and tantric topics, such as Jamgön Kongtrul, Patrul Rinpoché, and Ju Mipham. Yet they are only the best known among a larger circle of associates with an expressed interest in ecumenism, clustered in the kingdom of Degé and its surrounding areas. To broaden awareness about this larger circle, *A Gathering of Brilliant Moons* presents translated works by a range of figures representing a diverse set of lineages. While contemporary practitioners commonly associate rimé with Kongtrul, Jamyang Khyentsé Wangpo, and Patrul, and therefore with the Kagyü, Sakya, and Nyingma practice lineages, we intentionally include works representing the Jonang, Bön, and Geluk traditions as well.

The translations in this anthology emerged from a conference at the University of Colorado Boulder in April 2013, titled "Translating Buddhist Luminaries: A Conference on Ecumenism and Tibetan Translation." On that occasion, contributors were able to workshop their translations-in-progress as the basis for a conversation on the art of translation, facilitated by Joshua Schapiro. Integral to the conference was a public panel on "Ecumenism in Tibet" featuring Ringu Tulku, Sarah Harding, Michael Sheehy, and Douglas Duckworth, with Holly Gayley as moderator. Our remarks in the introduction to this anthology synthesize insights from the conference and from the introductory essays that each of the contributors assembled here for publication. For those interested in the translation choices made by our contributors, remarks on translation appear in their introductory essays.

We would like to express our appreciation to the sponsors for the "Translating Buddhist Luminaries" conference. The Center for Asian Studies has been a tremendous support for the study of Tibet and Himalayan regions at CU Boulder, helping to host this conference, to bring guest speakers to campus, and to incubate the interdisciplinary study of the region, which grew into the Tibet Himalaya Initiative in 2015. The Center for Humanities and the Arts at CU Boulder has a longstanding interest in translation and also contributed support to the conference. Beyond the university, the Tsadra Foundation recently opened a Research Center in Boulder, Colorado, that has enhanced the study of Tibetan Buddhism in the region, already well established with the presence of Naropa University and numerous Dharma centers. The Tsadra Foundation made a key contribution through a matching grant and by involving several of its master translators in the conference and this book project, including Sarah Harding, John Canti, and Wulstan Fletcher. Their presence greatly enriched the conversation, bringing decades of experience to bear on perennial questions regarding the process of translation.

From the outside, translation may seem like a transparent act of correlating words in two different languages. But it demands genuine artistry to bridge cultural worlds and capture a foreign literary style. It is heartening that in recent years issues of translation from Tibetan into English have come to the fore and garnered attention in several large-scale conferences gathering together lamas, scholars, and translators. These include conferences hosted by the Light of Berotsana Translation Committee in Boulder in 2008; the Khyentse Foundation and Deer Park Institute in Bir in 2009; Central University of Tibetan Studies and Columbia University in Sarnath in 2011; and the Tsadra Foundation in Keystone, Colorado, in 2014 and at CU Boulder in 2017. Our interest in exploring a literary approach to translating Buddhist works of advice from Tibetan has been inspired by this recent attention and also informed by stimulating presentations and exchanges in the "Religion and the Literary in Tibet" seminar, spearheaded by Kurtis Schaeffer and Andrew Quintman, which was held annually at the American Academy of Religion conference between 2010 and 2014 and has continued elsewhere in periodic gatherings.

We would like to express our appreciation to Ringu Tulku, a leading voice in the "Translating Buddhist Luminaries" conference, for his contribution of the foreword to this book, and to David Kittelstrom of Wisdom Publications, who supported this project from its inception at the conference through the publication of this anthology. His editorial insights and warm encouragement helped enormously to bring it to fruition.

May the translation of Buddhist texts from Tibetan continue to flourish.

Holly Gayley, Boulder
Joshua Schapiro, New York

Introduction

A work that brings together scripture and pith instruction—
know such speech to be the kindness of your guru.[1]

—*Dza Patrul Rinpoché*

Tibetans have routinely recorded the personal instructions of Buddhist masters in works of advice, texts that convey the Dharma intimately and succinctly. One such form is called *shaldam*. Shaldam compositions tend to be pithy and practical exhortations from master to disciple. They urge their audience to integrate Buddhist principles into daily conduct, offer lessons on meditation, and address challenges that arise on the spiritual path. Their seemingly straightforward style often masks profound esoteric teachings—with gems of wisdom folded into colloquial passages of prose and song. Shaldam may also take a self-consciously literary shape as eloquent letters, cautionary verses, and witty narratives to dispense guidance. As Dza Patrul Rinpoché describes in the verse above, shaldam texts embody the benevolence of a Buddhist master in transmitting essential practice advice to disciples.

A Gathering of Brilliant Moons brings together an array of advice from Buddhist luminaries at the core of the nineteenth-century renaissance in eastern Tibet. Luminaries such as Jamgön Kongtrul and Dza Patrul played formative roles in a network of masters and disciples with a keen interest in ecumenism, or *rimé*, and formulated an inclusive approach to the diversity of Tibetan Buddhist philosophical, ritual, and instructional traditions. Their ecumenical impulse extended to their works of advice—inspirational counsel from the esoteric to the profane, from the literary to the colloquial. These texts share an orientation toward practice and by and large eschew polemics. The rimé

---

1. Dza Patrul 2009, 408.

1

masters and their circle of associates have inspired successive generations of tantric practitioners, including many of the Tibetan teachers who brought esoteric forms of Buddhism across the Himalayas in the 1950s. Tibetan Buddhism, as a global phenomenon, owes much of its ecumenical foundation to these religious exemplars.

Ecumenism in the Nineteenth Century

In a landmark essay introducing the 1970 printing of Jamgön Kongtrul's *Treasury of Knowledge*, E. Gene Smith coined the term "nonsectarian movement" to characterize what he identified as an ecumenical impulse among nineteenth-century Buddhist masters in the Degé region of Kham.[2] Their religious projects are now commonly referred to as the "rimé movement."[3] This inclination motivated figures such as Jamgön Kongtrul, Jamyang Khyentsé Wangpo, and their circle of colleagues to seek out teachings and transmissions from diverse lineages of Tibetan Buddhism, and to eventually collect and preserve them in massive collections, such as Kongtrul's Five Great Treasuries.[4] In the essay, Smith traces sectarian and nonsectarian trends throughout Tibetan history, calling special attention to the distinctive features of nineteenth-century ecumenical activity. These features include: first, a proclivity to study with a wide range of teachers in various lineages, with the intention to preserve their texts and transmissions; second, a rejection of ossified polemics and divisive labels, such as sometimes appear in scholastic debate manuals; and third, a return to the study of Indian classics and those original lineages of Mahāyāna and Vajrayāna practice transmitted from India to Tibet.[5]

---

2. This essay has been reprinted in Smith 2001.

3. *Rimé* means "without bias" or "impartial." While the term has a long history of usage in Tibetan literature, over time it came to connote nonsectarianism, insofar as it signaled a rejection of the ongoing contention, both philosophical and political, between Tibetan religious lineages and institutions. Rimé represents an ecumenical attitude in the face of the many differences among Buddhist systems but does not constitute its own school, sect, or denomination.

4. As the coalescence of this inclination, the Five Great Treasuries compiled by Jamgön Kongtrul have a practice orientation: for the most part they consist of instructions and ritual texts anchored in the distinct lineages of Tibetan Buddhism.

5. Eight practice lineages are identified: Nyingma, Kadam, Marpa Kagyü, Shangpa Kagyü, Sakya, Kālacakra, Chöd and Shijé, and Orgyen Nyendrup. Though it forms the ecumenical architecture of his *Treasury of Knowledge* and *Treasury of Precious Instructions* anthologies, the rubric of "eight chariot-like practice lineages" (*drupgyü shingta gyé*) was not invented by Jamgön Kongtrul.

What Smith characterizes as a "movement" might be better understood as a preservation project carried out by a few influential teachers, together with the broader literary circle within which they flourished. The present anthology focuses on works by leading authors from this synergistic network, many of whom served as masters and disciples to one another, including Dudjom Lingpa, Jamgön Kongtrul, Do Khyentsé Yeshé Dorjé, Dza Patrul, Bamda Thupten Gelek Gyatso, Tokden Śākya Śrī, and Ju Mipham. The eclectic and ecumenical impulse that Smith refers to found its expression not only in immense collections of practice-oriented materials but also in original writings. In recent years, the Tsadra Foundation has taken on the project of translating and publishing two of Kongtrul's rimé collections, the *Treasury of Knowledge* (*Sheja Dzö*) and *Treasury of Precious Instructions* (*Damngak Dzö*). But until now the distinct voices of the broader literary circle had yet to be compiled in a single anthology of translations. With this volume, a sampling of their works is at last accessible to the English reader, many appearing in translation for the first time. The short essays that open each chapter touch upon the ways that ecumenism manifests in these works of advice, themselves but a few fruits from the abundant harvest of spiritual eloquence that these authors left for their followers. We draw attention to these figures here to consider how their practice advice—both poetic and urgent, humorous and earnest—reflects a shared set of values, religious orientations, and literary styles.

The very question of sectarianism in the Tibetan milieu demands some clarification. There are many ways to draw distinctions between Tibetan religious identities. Any given practitioner might identify with a lineage of transmission from masters of the past, a monastic institution, an incarnation line, a ritual program, or a philosophical system, to name only a few prominent forms of religious belonging. For this reason, there is also no easy translation for *sect* in Tibetan even though sectarianism and nonsectarianism are recurrent themes throughout Tibetan history. Potential candidates such as *chöluk* (Dharma lineage) and *druptha* (philosophical system) do not imply the same level of institutionality that one finds, for example, in Protestant denominations and sects. One might well suggest that the four major schools of Tibetan Buddhism—Nyingma, Sakya, Kagyü, and Geluk—are comparable to denominations. But as Michael Sheehy argued at an "Ecumenism in Tibet" panel that we organized, the primacy of these four schools, with their officially sanctioned and recognizable hierarchies, are somewhat of a modern invention. The names of the schools have long, culturally significant histories, but their formal contemporary configuration is in part a response to the demands of the Tibetan diaspora. The four major schools have simply not always functioned as they do today. Historically, monasteries were identified with a given school or subschool and connected to a network of branch monasteries. Still, at a single monastery different ritual programs might be followed. Monastic and lay practitioners could and often did study with masters from different schools, even while maintaining a primary affiliation with a single monastery or a single principal teacher (*tsawai lama*).

So what has it meant for Tibetans to adopt a rimé or ecumenical attitude? The contributors to this anthology approach this question in a number of ways. Gedun Rabsal and Nicole Willock cite the Dungkar dictionary's definition of *rimé* as upholding one's own school's theories and practices, yet not looking down on or insulting those of others.[6] From this perspective, rimé entails an active commitment to one particular path to liberation and a firm devotion to the efficacy of one's own lineage, while maintaining open-mindedness toward those paths that one does not pursue. Sarah Harding echoes this interpretation, stating that rimé means committing to "unflinchingly follow one path," while nonetheless recognizing the validity of other approaches. At the ecumenism panel, Ringu Tulku situated the attitude of rimé within the broader Buddhist discourse of skillful means—whereby the Buddha taught multiple vehicles to liberation that, while different from one another, are each suited to the diverse needs and capacities of sentient beings. Each demands firm devotion to its respective transformative techniques in order to be successful, yet does not discount the validity of other techniques and paths per se.

But the nonsectarianism of Jamgön Kongtrul and his associates went beyond mere tolerance for other traditions. It involved an active pluralism that deeply respected the distinctiveness of each lineage of teaching and the heterogeneity of ritual practice.[7] In their preservation and anthologizing efforts, they did not integrate different lineages into a single system; instead, they preserved intact the particularities and integrity of each. As Harding points out, Kongtrul's organizing principle of the eight practice lineages in the *Treasury of Knowledge* and *Treasury of Precious Instructions* was chronological rather than hierarchical. He displayed "all the lineage teachings side by side, equal but separate and distinct."[8] This shows the high value that

---

6. Dungkar Losang Trinlé 2002, 1918.

7. In her work with the Pluralism Project, Diana Eck emphasizes active engagement with diversity as one of the crucial factors separating pluralism from mere tolerance. See www.pluralism.org.

8. Harding 2007, 24.

Kongtrul placed on the distinctiveness of esoteric instructions and ritual systems from diverse lineages, which he treated as skillful means to guide beings along distinct but parallel paths to liberation. One might contrast this ecumenical approach to the eclecticism of Buddhist appropriations today, where traditions from radically different cultures have spread beyond Asia, informing and transforming one another in the process. This contemporary trend is closer to a melting-pot approach, what Jay Garfield describes as the "intra-Buddhist multi-traditional syncretism" that characterizes a number of Buddhist communities in America.[9] By contrast, a pluralistic, rimé approach celebrates the value and necessity of different traditions, but does not blend them together in service of a new synthesis.

Several contributors to this anthology have chosen to reflect on the social and historical significance of rimé in the nineteenth century. John Canti identifies rimé as a Buddhist "renaissance," noting that the work of rimé masters to compile, preserve, and disseminate the transmission of ritual practices and esoteric instructions gave "rise to wide and vigorous lineage(s)." In other words, the preservationist project of Kongtrul and his associates reinvigorated lineages on the verge of extinction and created new mechanisms for their transmission. In the ecumenism panel, Sheehy made the complementary point that Kongtrul employed figures from various lineages such as Jamyang Loter Wangpo and Thupten Gelek Gyatso to recover and consolidate their own traditions, viewing these traditions as living spiritual transmissions that were "endangered species." True to this observation, Kongtrul's catalog to the *Treasury of Precious Instructions* mentions that many of the teachings and transmissions within the eight practice lineages are "extremely rare and nearly going extinct" and that their preservation is necessary "so that the frayed rope of those long lineages would at least not break."[10]

At the ecumenism panel, Douglas Duckworth interpreted rimé within an altogether different context, describing it as a response to Geluk political hegemony in Kham. From this perspective, Kongtrul and Khyentsé's preservation project might be understood as a banding together of minority traditions in eastern Tibet in reaction to the encroaching political power of the Ganden Phodrang government based in Lhasa. One strategy involved explicitly critiquing Geluk religious positions, as Ju Mipham famously did,

---

9. Garfield 2009, 90.

10. Quoted in Harding 2007, 33. This catalog has recently been published in translation by the Tsadra Foundation as *The Catalog of The Treasury of Precious Instructions* (Jamgön Kongtrul 2013).

while adopting certain Geluk forms of religious organization. In the nineteenth century, Nyingma, Kagyü, and Jonang scholars and members of the broader rimé circle, including Khenpo Shenga and Thupten Gelek Gyatso, developed formalized monastic curricula modeled on those used at Geluk monastic colleges. Non-Buddhists also participated in the response, as Geoffrey Barstow brings to our attention in his essay on Bön lama Shardza Tashi Gyaltsen in chapter 4.

Nevertheless, it would be misleading to claim that rimé figures were purely egalitarian and never appealed to hierarchical schemes. As Ringu Tulku mentioned at the ecumenism panel, inclusive yet hierarchical schemes are fundamental organizing strategies in Tibetan Buddhism, exemplified in the arrangement of the three vehicles of Hīnayāna, Mahāyāna, and Vajrayāna. The three vehicles provide a progression in doctrine and practice understood by Tibetans to be both comprehensive and suitable for a gradual path of maturation in view, meditation, and conduct, with the Vajrayāna as the highest and most advanced. One sees a similar approach in the nine-vehicle system of the Nyingma in which Dzokchen, or the Great Perfection, stands at the pinnacle of the path. Doxographic literature in Tibet, which presents the tenet systems of various philosophical schools in ascending order, likewise takes a progressive approach by presenting the tenet systems from lower to higher, thereby creating an inclusive hierarchy that places the author's own system at the apex. Notably, while inclusive and syncretic, this approach has a history of becoming polemical, particularly in texts where an author refutes each tenet system before moving on to the next one.

Rimé masters employed various schemes to create an inclusive hierarchy. For example, Jamgön Kongtrul used the rubric of the *shentong* ("empty of other") philosophical view as one such unifying schema, as Tina Draszczyk's contribution to this anthology in chapter 12 demonstrates. In Kongtrul's formulation, as in important precedents like Tāranātha's writings, shentong embraces all other philosophical developments. It includes its rival *rangtong* (the "empty of self" position) as a provisional truth (*drangdön*) that acts as a building block to the definitive truth (*ngedön*). A more subtle hierarchical integration can be found in works by Do Khyentsé and Dza Patrul in what Holly Gayley describes as "yogic triumphalism" in chapter 6. These authors encourage yogic practice in solitary retreat as a more advanced and essential means to liberation than monastic study, which nonetheless may provide an indispensable foundation. In their writings, tantric practice, and Dzokchen in particular, appears as the pinnacle of the path. Yet, at the same time, the ineffable realization that emerges from Dzokchen practice manifests as an elimination of bias altogether. At the pinnacle of the hierarchy is a form of "awareness" beyond hierarchical and sectarian thinking.

To unpack this point further, Marc-Henri Deroche proposes in chapter 13 a helpful heuristic for organizing the multiple meanings of *rimé*. He uses the term *relative rimé* to describe an attitude of tolerance, which could go further into active pluralism. For example, Dza Patrul's refusal to identify good or bad Dharma lineages in *The Low-Born Sage Speaks* in chapter 2 would be a good representation of relative rimé. In contrast, *absolute rimé* pertains to a mode of meditative practice that achieves a state of "pure awareness" (*rikpa*), often described by these rimé masters as free from bias. To quote Deroche's translation of Kongtrul, "Gain confidence in self-arising, without bias, without grasping, effort, rejection, adoption, or antidote." In *The Call of a Sacred Drum: Advice for Solitary Retreat* in chapter 6, Dza Patrul likewise cautions that one should avoid getting attached to conventional truths, since "Everything has the same taste, whether true or not; / it's nothing but spontaneous chatter, whatever arises." The alternative is to embrace the approach of absolute rimé, "resting in nonthought and non-fixation." For, as Thupten Gelek Gyatso teaches in *Extracting the Essence of Freedoms and Fortunes* in chapter 7, basic awareness is "devoid of partiality" (*chok lhung dralwa*).

The practice orientation of the works of advice that appear in this anthology provides a unique window into Tibetan ecumenism, with their consistent appeal to absolute rimé. Again and again, they return to what lies beyond all bias—ineffable realization—thereby bypassing the long history of debate between schools. At certain potent moments, their authors claim to transcend philosophical tenets and doctrinal exegesis altogether. To invoke a traditional metaphor, their frank exhortations shift attention from the many fingers pointing at the moon to the moon itself. It is no coincidence, then, that an emphasis on absolute rimé is integral to shaldam texts that offer personal advice for practice. As Ringu Tulku suggested at the ecumenism panel, polemical debate rewards sectarianism by orienting debaters toward seeking flaws in their opponent's philosophical position in order to prove the superiority of their own system. In contrast, eso-teric practice instructions encourage nonsectarianism by pointing tantric practitioners toward the nature of mind beyond bias or concept of any kind. To illustrate the difference in these orientations, he recounted a witty Tibetan saying: If two philosophers agree, one is not a philosopher (*tokgewa*); if two realized practitioners disagree, one is not a realized prac-titioner (*drupthop*).

Personal Advice on Practice

The works of rimé masters that appear in this anthology fall under the broad rubric of "personal advice," or shaldam.[11] Etymologically, the Tibetan term *shaldam* suggests pith instructions received directly from the mouth of a master.[12] Works of shaldam convey an aura of intimacy and immediacy, as in an oral transmission from tantric master to disciple. As such they often carry the presumption of a lived encounter with instructions tailored to a specific individual. As Sheehy puts it in his essay, "the term *shaldam* conjures an image of a student sitting so closely to his or her teacher that the warmth from the guru's breath can be felt." Insofar as personal advice is directed at a specific individual, Canti suggests that shaldam recalls the Buddha's discourses in the sūtras, which are prompted by questions from one of his followers. Even when masters are not depicted in the presence of their disciples, they still convey a sense of proximity by providing access to their personal advice.

While shaldam texts retain a quality of spoken advice, they are unmistakably literary. This is the case whether the advice was originally composed in writing or whether it was transcribed and edited from an oral teaching. Shaldam are at once personal advice for a specific disciple and carefully crafted compositions for a broader readership. The audience indicated in these works span from village practitioners to novice monks and from ordinary laity to advanced tantric adepts. Shaldam thus constitute an appealing combination of proximity and accessibility. They provide practical, direct, essential advice for meditation and tantric practice, packaged in a style capable of provoking, at times, strong affective responses.

Shaldam are practical in that they tend to address what the reader needs to do in order to make their life "spiritually fruitful" and ultimately "attain realization," as Canti observes. Theoretical considerations are almost always tied to practical instructions on how to eat, handle challenging situations, relate to a guru, meditate, or behave, broadly speaking. A wonderful example

---

11. Here *shaldam* is used as a broad umbrella term for advice literature. This volume actually includes texts that fit into a range of related forms, including *mengak* (quintessential or esoteric instructions), *michö* (didactic advice on human virtue), *nyingtam* (heart advice), *nyamgur* (songs of experience), and *lapja* (practical advice or counsel). Rather than insist on a particular genre definition that encapsulates all the works that appear in this anthology, we prefer to consider how the rubric of shaldam can help us to see patterns in the stylistic, poetic, and rhetorical ingenuity of these writings.

12. According to Ringu Tulku, the term *dam* (related to *dom*) has the sense of gathering and connotes brief or condensed teachings. *Shal* serves as an honorific for mouth, or face, suggesting a direct encounter.

of the practical nature of shaldam is found in Jikmé Lingpa's advice on how to handle sickness on the path in chapter 8.[13] As Wulstan Fletcher explains, Jikmé Lingpa outlines multiple approaches to dealing with the overwhelming discomfort of illness. Addressing the reader directly, he advises that you can view suffering as the manifestation of bad karma from the past. In that case, enduring sickness purifies your karma by using up the inevitable consequences that were generated in the past by negative actions. Thus sickness is depicted as a "broom that sweeps away your sins and obscurations." Alternatively you can take the experience of illness as an opportunity to familiarize yourself with the nature of your own mind. You do so by searching for "the nature of discomfort." As Jikmé Lingpa asks the reader, "Where does it arise, and stay, and go?" Like Jikmé Lingpa's concrete strategies for dealing with illness, the advice gathered in this anthology is exceedingly practical.

In addition to being practical, the tone of shaldam is often direct and candid. We find plentiful examples of second-person exclamations, which lend a sense of urgency to the communications. "Since this is heart advice, please listen now!" Shangtön Tenpa Gyatso repeatedly urges his students in *A Jeweled Rosary of Advice* in chapter 3. Notice the firm yet supportive entreaty in Thupten Gelek Gyatso's advice to his disciple Tupel in chapter 7: "With great waves of constant devotion . . . don't back down!" Or as Jikmé Lingpa cautions in a letter to the queen of Degé in chapter 5, "During auspicious times such as the full moon, do not wander about doing meaningless things." These second-person exhortations demonstrate the tendency of these authors to demand "reader participation . . . getting one's feet wet and hands dirty," as Duckworth suggests.

Dza Patrul's instructions on meditation exemplify the candidness of shaldam. In this passage from *Clear Elucidation of True Nature* in chapter 10, he addresses the frustrations that meditators might feel when their minds are turbulent with thoughts:

> At some point thoughts might proliferate, and you will get irritated with yourself. You think, "Meditation is just not happening for me." No problem. That is the first meditative experience, "like a waterfall off a steep cliff." The Kagyüpas call it "undivided attention that is distracted by the waves of thought." It is the occasion of the lesser undivided attention. If you bear with that and continue

---

13. Jikmé Lingpa, who lived in the eighteenth century, is included in two chapters as an important precursor to the nineteenth-century figures who are otherwise the focus of the volume.

meditating, sometimes the attention will stay and sometimes be active. It is like a little bird in the water, sometimes slipping in and out of the water, sometimes resting for a bit on a rock.

As this passage illustrates, the candor of shaldam is generally matched with simplicity of form and brevity of delivery. Yet Dza Patrul also makes room for literary flourish—here in the form of an elegant metaphor of a bird dipping in and out of the water, sometimes resting on a rock, to show how attention comes and goes as the mind begins to settle in meditation. Despite the technical nature of his instructions, the tone remains intimate and forthright, as captured in Sarah Harding's lucid translation.

The authors included in this anthology repeatedly remind us that their advice concerns essential points of the utmost importance to Buddhist practice and daily life. As Dudjom Lingpa suggests in *A Song for Chokdrup, the Novice of Abum* in chapter 1, shaldam offers its readers guidance on the most crucial points of practice:

> Experiences,
>   happy or sad, good or bad—whatever may arise,
> not fabricating
>   or changing them, just let them be;
> to recognize
>   but not cling to them, that is the crucial point;
> this
>   is the very pinnacle of all instructions.

Likewise, in *A Beacon to Dispel Darkness* in chapter 11, Ju Mipham also speaks of the "essential point" of practice when making a subtle yet indispensable distinction between forms of awareness that emerge in esoteric meditation. Even though his instructions are geared toward advanced meditators, Mipham asserts that his shaldam is powerful enough to enable "most village practitioners to easily reach the stage of an awareness-holder" without much study or training. This is the potency attributed to quintessential instructions.

While shaldam transmit essential advice directly, they are anything but bland. To the contrary, their literary virtues are abundant. The luminaries included in this anthology betray exceptional prosodic facility, whether in eloquent letters or in folk-song styles employing a variety of rhythms and meter, as in Dudjom Lingpa's song quoted above. Even when using colloquial language, shaldam can be technical and nuanced. And while transmitting essential instructions may be important business, some of the shaldam gathered here are quite playful, even humorous, such as Dza Patrul's *Explanation of Chudrulü* in chapter 2 and Do Khyentsé's *Babble of a Foolish Man* in chapter 6.

Literary Style and Translation

Due to the literary virtues of shaldam, it is both an imperative and a challenge to capture their style and tone in translation. Shaldam create an aura of intimacy and immediacy through a variety of literary devices, including experiential references, emotional tenor, wordplay, earthy examples and metaphors, colloquial expressions, and self-deprecating humor. The art of translation then involves finding English equivalencies for these literary devices and the everyday language in which they are expressed in Tibetan. At their best the works translated in this anthology match pedagogical sophistication with literary simplicity and gracefulness, directly communicating essential practice instructions in ways that are down to earth and experiential—displaying what Canti calls "uncontrived elegance." To capture this uncontrived elegance, the translator is called to craft analogous ways to cajole, inspire, challenge, and edify the reader in English.

How can this be accomplished? Consider a passage from *Words of Advice for Lhawang Tashi* in which Jamgön Kongtrul provokes self-reflection in the reader:

> If you fail to purify your mind,
> you find faults even with a buddha,
> you get angry even with your parents,
> and most of what appears seems hostile.
> In endless waves of hoping, fearing, lusting, hating,
> your human years of useless human life run out.

With stark simplicity, Kongtrul calls on the reader to reflect on the mind's tendency toward anger and the uselessness of such negativity in the short span of a human life. With careful attention to tone and style, Canti's translation uses simple terminology and matches the rhythm of the original in order to convey the predicament of an untrained mind. The passage builds to a crescendo with a string of gerunds to create the literary effect of "endless waves" and then mirrors the Tibetan duplication of "human" in the final line to highlight the folly of squandering a human life, rare and precious in the Buddhist cosmology of six realms. This is just one example of the creative and thoughtful ways that our contributors convey a sense of uncontrived elegance.

This anthology embarks on the worthy experiment of creating translations to match the spirit of shaldam. We have deliberately attempted to stretch the boundaries of how scholars and translators of Tibetan texts conceive of the translation process. The dominant pedagogy of language learning in academic settings requires students to demonstrate their proficiency by replicating every word in a passage in its proper syntactic relationship. While this is an effective way to gauge comprehension, it has encouraged a tendency among academic translations to sacrifice literary style for literalism. Paul Griffiths has called this effect "Buddhist Hybrid English," which in his estimation is "wreaking its havoc upon the English language, creating a dialect comprehensible only to the initiate, written by and for Buddhologists."[14] While his critique is particularly aimed at scholars translating Buddhist texts from Sanskrit into English, we find his call to consider the "literary and aesthetic merit" of texts chosen for translation useful to our enterprise here—namely, to motivate heightened concern for the stylistic features of Tibetan sources.

With this in mind we focused this anthology on inspiring works of advice and asked our contributors to reflect on and experiment with the literary, rather than literal, aspects of translation. On this distinction, Octavio Paz has boldly stated:

> I do not mean to imply that literal translation is impossible; what I am saying is that it is not translation. It is a mechanism, a string of words that helps us read the text in its original language. It is a glossary rather than a translation, which is always a literary activity. Without exception, even when the translator's sole intention is to convey meaning, as in the case of scientific texts, translation implies a transformation of the original. That transformation is not—nor can it be—anything but literary.[15]

According to Paz, a literal rendering of a source is more a mechanism than a translation, whereas translation is by its nature a literary enterprise.[16] A more

---

14. Griffiths 1981, 17. In contrast, full-time translators of Tibetan texts, working at the behest of a lama or as part of a translation committee affiliated with a specific practice tradition, may focus on readability. Nevertheless, they may at times devalue the literary qualities of a text in their emphasis on faithfully reproducing its meaning.

15. Paz 1992, 154.

16. Overall, the notion of a literal rendering is problematic, because it assumes that one can find semantic equivalence for terms and expressions between source and target languages. Even as dictionaries give the impression of semantic equivalence, words that

literal rendering of a primary source may be helpful in certain cases, such as when scholars and translators work with dense philosophical material in Buddhist sources across several languages, thereby assisting in the study and analysis of texts without attempting to make them readable as literature. But we would argue that shaldam texts are not appropriate materials for such an approach. Shaldam deserve readable translations that pay close attention to their literary style, particularly their strategies for conveying advice with intimacy and immediacy—creating the feeling that the reader is indeed receiving oral instructions at the feet of the guru.

How do shaldam create intimacy and immediacy as literary effects? And how can a comparable effect be created in translation? Let us consider these questions in light of a passage from advice by Tokden Śākya Śrī in chapter 9, as translated by Amy Holmes-Tagchungdarpa. Her translation emphasizes Śākya Śrī's repeated use of the imperative to guide his disciple's experience by adding exclamation points (of which there is no equivalent in Tibetan).

> Do not stray into confusion! Do not allow the delusions of the past, present, and future to obstruct your view. Just call out "Phat!" and all of these delusions will dissolve. They will fade away, and when you look for them, there will be only clear space. Do not block this sensation—it will allow you to know the play of all-emptiness.

This passage presents a clear progression, one that follows the experience of a student applying the teacher's instructions. The cadence is short, heightening the sense of immediacy—palpable in both Śākya Śrī's Tibetan and Holmes-Tagchungdarpa's English. A feeling of personal involvement is created through the moment-by-moment pacing and experiential focus of instruction, simulating an oral transmission. In this passage, as is typical of shaldam, literary style and meaning are intertwined, making the translator's sensitivity to questions of style and tone all the more important.

In an effort to capture an aura of intimacy and immediacy, our translators have done well attending to the particular aesthetic effect and rhetorical

---

share a denotation can have quite different connotations and semantic ranges in different languages. In response to this incongruity, Jay Garfield points out that the translator must intervene by fixing a meaning that may be ambiguous or multivalent in the original, while simultaneously losing certain resonances from the source language and adding others from the target language (Garfield 2009, 94). For this reason, translation involves not only a linguistic shift but also a cultural one.

impact of each passage in their source texts. Umberto Eco describes this effort as finding the "functional equivalence" between original and translation, based on identifying the stylistic core of a passage.[17] The idea of functional equivalence is especially important for shaldam, given the rhetorical richness of this type of literature. The stylistic core may involve the emotional tenor or register invoked in the advice, as is the case in *The Faults of Eating Meat* in chapter 4, where Shardza Tashi Gyaltsen describes the painful fate of a yak: "led into the butcher's corral, its limbs are bound, it is turned upside down, and its muzzle is wrapped with cord." In Barstow's translation the rapid pace of this succession has an aesthetic impact, intensifying a sense of dread and revulsion toward the painful realities of slaughter. What a literary translation demands, then, is attention to stylistic devices in the original Tibetan text, recreated in such a way as to deliver a comparable experience for the English reader.

This kind of functional equivalence is perhaps most difficult to capture with regard to humor and wordplay, which can often be lost in translation. For example, Dza Patrul's entire *Explanation of Chudrulü* in chapter 2 is organized around a Tibetan play on words: a false etymology of a colloquial expression that means "nothing." On one level Patrul is clearly joking, while on another level he is quite serious about providing his readers with a complex, esoteric Dharma instruction. Within his playfully serious delivery, he finds time to show off his love of puns, as is the case in a sentence-long riff on different Tibetan words for "wind." The challenge is to make sense of this in English, which sometimes can be done only in commentarial fashion, as Joshua Schapiro discusses in his essay. When the translator gets lucky, a play on the meaning or sound of words manages to come through in translation. For example, in *The Call of a Sacred Drum: Advice for Solitary Retreat* in chapter 6, Dza Patrul engages in a playful repetition of the term "joy" (*gyepa*) in exclaiming: "the adept enjoys the joys of solitude with joyful laughter." This repetition of a single term in different parts of speech marks the beginning of a passage that conveys the delights of solitary retreat, modeled on the author's own experience, thereby creating the feeling of being there alongside him.

Earthy examples and metaphors, rendered in colloquial language, require the translator to match the simplicity of the original and thereby communicate practical instructions with comparable immediacy. In *A Jeweled Rosary of Advice* in chapter 3, Shangtön Tenpa Gyatso exemplifies this tendency, using a host of animal metaphors to criticize immoral and foolish human behavior. Gedun Rabsal and Nicole Willock use everyday language to let the metaphors shine through their translation:

---

17. Eco 2003, 56.

Advising those who don't listen is akin to talking to cattle and
sheep—how senseless!

Like asking a dog to guard raw meat, it is wrong to trust your
wealth to careless people.

Don't be as attached to food as an old dog guarding a dry bone.
Give it to the people!

In other instances everyday metaphors are used to describe otherwise elu-
sive mental states, as with the following examples from Dza Patrul and Ju
Mipham from chapters 10 and 11, translated by Sarah Harding and Douglas
Duckworth, respectively. The first follows a description of the mind settling
in meditation and the second provides an apt image for awareness:

If that is prolonged further in meditation, from time to time
there will be occasional mental activity, but for the most part
there is abiding. For example, it is like an old person who sits
still most of the time.

Awareness is like husked rice separated from the chaff of mentally
conceived experiences.

These metaphors render meditation instructions palpable and practical, and
the spare language of their translation transmits them in an unencumbered
fashion.

The appearance of worldly examples, when conveyed with all their idiosyn-
crasies in translation, can invite the reader into an encounter with a decidedly
different world. In chapter 4, Bön master Shardza Tashi Gyaltsen explains
the karmic consequences of killing insects through an extended example of
picking lice off the body:

As an example, take the killing of a louse. When a louse is feeding
on someone's body, that person knows that the louse is eating them.
This knowledge is the ground element of a complete act. Seeing
the louse on his arm, the killer is motivated by anger. This is the
intention element. He places a fingernail on top of the louse and
begins to press down, applying the means to kill the louse. This is
the application element. Afterward, the bloody louse is removed
from the top of the nail with a cry of triumph, completing the

act of killing. This is the completion element. Killing in this way, motivated by hatred, brings karma that impels one to hell.

Here an everyday example is used to illustrate the phases of a complete karmic act and convey its relevance to daily ethical choices. Yet what might be an everyday occurrence in one setting can seem foreign in translation, since picking lice off one's body will likely be less familiar to contemporary audiences. Barstow's translation, which highlights the idiosyncratic details of the specific example, reminds the reader that Shardza's work of advice is, after all, a translation of a foreign source from quite a different time and place.

Earthy examples and culturally specific metaphors can thus function as strategic opportunities for translators to retain the foreign qualities of a text, especially when a source makes references to Tibetan life or to Indic conventions that had a strong influence on Tibetan literature. Here is a pertinent case from Shangtön Tenpa Gyatso in chapter 3:

> A white moon stained with the form of a rabbit, a beautiful
> flower tainted by a bad scent, wicked companions like two
> dzo yoked together falling off a cliff.
> Bad friends are a source of regret—abandon them!

This passage is strikingly foreign. While Western convention locates a "man in the moon" in the dark and light surfaces of a full moon, due to the tilt of the earth, Indian tradition recognizes a rabbit instead—an image that is retained in Tibetan literature. In this passage, the dark shape of a rabbit on the moon is a metaphor for how bad company can stain one's own character. In the third example above, *dzo* refer to yak-cattle hybrids, which are typically yoked together for hauling loads in Tibetan nomadic areas. Here Shangtön Tenpa Gyatso uses the image of two yoked dzo to illustrate how association with bad company can have disastrous consequences, as when yoked dzo fall off a cliff together. These metaphors simultaneously convey an earthy tone and bring a foreign quality to the translation, connecting the English reader to both the literary and lived worlds of Tibet.

Lawrence Venuti asks translators to make a deliberate effort to foreignize their translation of original sources, rather than domesticate them, thereby using foreign elements to bring the reader closer to the world of a text.[18] In this anthology, foreign elements invite the reader to imagine the nineteenth-century world of eastern Tibet, with its distinctive topography and worldview.

---

18. Venuti 1995, 20, based on the ideas of Friedrich Schleiermacher.

This is a world where tantric adepts share mountain ranges and grasslands with herders tending yak and dzo, as referenced in the Third Dodrupchen's letter to a disciple in chapter 6. A certain degree of domestication is inevitable if one is to render a foreign text intelligible to readers in a different cultural milieu. But it may still be possible to transmit the aroma of foreignness— something akin to Anthony Yu's idea of "preserving foreignness in the very quest for readability."[19] One simple way that our translators have done so is by maintaining Tibetan terms like *dzo* and exclamations like *Kyé ho!* from the Tibetan. More subtle is the challenge of recreating in English literary devices and effects that are quintessentially Tibetan, such as the tendency toward self-deprecation in first-person speech.

Self-deprecation is a common device in Tibetan literature, brilliantly performed in these works of advice. Even as revered luminaries, the authors repeatedly couch their personal advice with disclaimers about their own authority to deliver trustworthy teachings. Dudjom Lingpa's reflexive statements in chapter 1, where he casts himself as a madman, represent this trend well:

> Its worth
>   is small, but if to have this old man's brief advice
> just now
>   seems so important—very well, then, just for you,
> for my part,
>   I shall sing and sing away my crazy song!
>
> Having no way to refuse the request you made,
> I, the foolish and contemptible Dudjom Dorjé
> have responded with this ditty in the form of insane ravings,
> which I hereby give to Chokdrup, the novice of Abum.

Since self-deprecating statements like this are a Tibetan convention, authors can take their tongue-in-cheek statements quite far. For Dudjom Lingpa to call himself "foolish and contemptible" and his advice "insane ravings" makes sense only within a Buddhist framework that renders it taboo for anyone to claim realization directly. Of course, Dudjom Lingpa endears himself to the reader by casting himself as a modest yet gifted spiritual guide; thus his artful humility only strengthens the appeal of his advice. Moreover, the intimacy of oral instructions comes through when he says to Chokdrup, "if to have this old man's brief advice / just now / seems so important—very well, then,

---

19. Yu 2013, 98.

just for you . . ." For the translator to downplay self-deprecating statements out of reverence for the author would spoil the flavor of the passage. Instead, by relishing the distinctiveness of self-effacing humor, the translator has the opportunity to import a foreign element, one that runs against the grain of contemporary conventions in English.

In order to invite the reader into these reflections on literary style and translation, we have asked our contributors to discuss these issues in their introductory essays, alongside brief remarks on the ecumenical dimensions of the work(s) translated. They comment on ambiguous terms and complex connotations, their handling of specific passages, the way that meter is constructed in verse, and questions surrounding authorial voice, linguistic register, and intended audience. In addition, we asked contributors to share any challenges that stood out to them in the translation process as they experimented with ways to capture wordplay, humor, meter, and other distinctive stylistic features of the source texts. In this way, their introductory essays highlight for the reader the literary features of each text as well as the ways in which ecumenism is articulated by these luminaries from nineteenth-century Tibet. For those unfamiliar with the Tibetan language, a glossary of Tibetan terms is available at the back of the anthology, where readers can compare translation choices for a single term.

No translation is ever final. Given the ever-changing nature of language, translations that convey intimacy and immediacy through the colloquialisms of their own day will necessarily become outdated after a generation or two. Nevertheless, we are hopeful that the works included in this volume will be inspirational as advice for practice and become a springboard for an enduring experiment in the literary translation of Tibetan sources.

References

Dungkar Losang Trinlé (Dung dkar Blo bzang 'phrin las), ed. 2002. *Dung dkar Bod rgya Tshig mdzod chen mo.* Beijing: Krung go'i bod rig pa dpe skrun khang.

Dza Patrul Orgyen Jikmé Chökyi Wangpo (Rdza dpal sprul O rgyan 'jigs med chos kyi dbang po). 2009. *Chos dang 'jig rten shes pa'i bstan bcos gdol pa'i drang srong gi gtam thar pa'i them skas.* Collected Works, vol. 1, 391–408. Chengdu: Si khron mi rigs dpe skrun khang.

Eco, Umberto. 2003. *Mouse or Rat? Translation as Negotiation.* London: Orion Publishing Group.

Garfield, Jay L. 2009. "Translation as Transmission and Transformation." In *Trans-Buddhism: Transmission, Translation, Transformation.* Edited by Nalini Bhushan, Jay L. Garfield, Abraham Zablocki, 89–103. Amherst, MA: University of Massachusetts Press.

Griffiths, Paul J. 1981. "Buddhist Hybrid English: Some Notes on Philology and Hermeneutics for Buddhologists." *The Journal of the International Association of Buddhist Studies* 4.2: 17–32.

Harding, Sarah, trans. 2007. *The Treasury of Knowledge: Esoteric Instructions.* Ithaca, NY: Snow Lion Publications.

Jamgön Kongtrul Lodrö Taye. 2013. *The Catalog of The Treasury of Precious Instructions.* Translated by Richard Barron (Chökyi Nyima). New York: Tsadra Foundation.

Paz, Octavio. 1992. "Translation: Literature and Letters." In *Theories of Translation: An Anthology of Essays from Dryden to Derrida.* Edited by Rainer Schulte and John Biguenet, 152–62. Chicago: University of Chicago Press.

Smith, E. Gene. 2001. "'Jam mgon Kong sprul and the Nonsectarian Movement." In *Among Tibetan Texts: History and Literature of the Himalayan Plateau.* Edited by Kurtis Schaeffer, 235–72. Boston: Wisdom Publications.

Venuti, Lawrence. 1995. *The Translator's Invisibility: A History of Translation.* New York: Routledge.

Yu, Anthony C. 1998. "Readability: Religion and the Reception of Translation." *Chinese Literature: Essays, Articles, Reviews* 20: 89–100.

PART I: WORLDLY COUNSEL

1. Facing Your Mind

Jamgön Kongtrul and Dudjom Lingpa
Translated by John Canti

Two Voices, One Message: Don't Look Elsewhere

Individuals at the highest levels of attainment in the Tibetan Buddhist world, whether in past centuries or more recent times, have by no means conformed to a uniform stereotype. Their lifestyles and personalities vary enormously. Indeed, according to Mahāyāna tradition, manifesting in a variety of forms to "train beings according to their needs" is how enlightenment should manifest at the emanational, *nirmāṇakāya* level. The texts I have translated here are by two authors with very different lifestyles. Both were great nineteenth-century masters—masters primarily in the sense of prodigious spiritual accomplishment, but also in the sense of widely recognized literary skill. There, however, many of the obvious similarities end.

Jamgön Kongtrul Lodrö Thayé (1813–99) needs little introduction, for his is the first name that comes to most people's minds at any mention of nineteenth-century ecumenical masters. He is undoubtedly one of the most important figures of the time. Steeped in learning, a lifelong monastic, with an established institutional role and widespread recognition, Kongtrul could hardly be more different than his younger contemporary, the visionary yogin and *tertön* Trakthung Dudjom Lingpa (1835–1904), who had a minimum of formal education, received little by way of teachings and transmissions (at least from human masters), and for much of his life led a materially precarious and peripatetic existence outside any formal affiliations, surrounded by his followers, consorts, and large family.

Descriptions of Kongtrul are so formal and laudatory that it is difficult to unearth details of his personality, but from his own autobiography and other writings, we get the impression of a dignified monk with immense learning worn lightly, great discipline, and a tendency to self-deprecation. He traveled widely but also spent long periods immersing himself in literary projects, performing retreats, and exchanging transmissions. Dudjom Lingpa, we know, was a physically powerful man, direct and uncompromising. A white-robed yogin with a mane of long hair, wearing large earrings, he is said to have had a presence that was both awe-inspiring and terrifying. He spent most of his life in a series of encampments and settlements, moving often but mostly within the confines of Mar, Ser, and Do, three river valleys of Golok in eastern Tibet.

Despite their undoubted differences, however, these two great masters had more in common than appearances might suggest. To start with, Kongtrul, too, was a visionary and a tertön. More important still, the overwhelming concern of both masters was the authentic use and transmission of the very essence of the Buddhist path in all its forms, and the fruit of that concern can be seen in the large cohorts of exceptionally accomplished practitioners that each of them trained, taught, or inspired.

Kongtrul and Jamyang Khyentsé Wangpo, of course, are the masters usually taken to be the origin of the nineteenth-century Buddhist renaissance in eastern Tibet that has become known as the rimé—nonsectarian or ecumenical—movement. Kongtrul had seen for himself that without a change of perspective, Buddhism as practiced in the Tibet of his day was in danger of becoming a series of fossilized systems divided by sectarian bias and divorced from genuine spiritual experience. Worse, sectarian rivalry (often for patronage) had on occasions become a pretext for feuds, open conflict, and even warfare. In his own lifetime Kongtrul had seen at least three such periods of major upheaval. He and other contemporary lamas responded to this state of affairs with an openness and respect for the texts and transmissions of all authentic lineages of Tibetan Buddhism. They made extraordinary efforts to identify practices, texts, traditions, and lineages that were little known or in danger of extinction, to receive and study them, and to ensure their future transmission.

Combating sectarianism and resisting institutional hegemony was a major concern for Kongtrul and Khyentsé, and the impetus they created had far-reaching effects on many other masters of their time and afterward. But the fact that later observers called it the "rimé movement" can give rise to an impression that nonsectarianism was its sole defining characteristic. In fact, "renaissance" seems a better term. The movement was, in essence, a broad-based return to truer Buddhist values. It may have been triggered by the specter of religious bigotry in an extreme and institutionalized form, but it had plenty of positive qualities to promote and not only negative trends to combat and resist.

Indeed, were anti-sectarianism alone taken as the criterion for belonging to this remarkable movement, Dudjom Lingpa would not qualify. He can hardly be described as ecumenical, working as he did entirely within his own revelations, which themselves were firmly based on the system of the Nyingma tantras and the Great Perfection. Geographically, too, while much of Kongtrul and Khyentse's activity was centered on the region of Degé, Dudjom Lingpa, farther east in Golok, was an outlier who had little direct contact with the other masters identified with the phenomenon.[1] Nevertheless, he is often considered to have been part of it.[2] What characterizes most of the masters identified with the rimé movement is that they recognized the dangers of narrow scholasticism, of an overemphasis on institutional concerns, and of spiritual dishonesty in all its forms; in Dudjom Lingpa's case, his whole life was a vigorous rebuttal of those impediments. He may not have been explicitly nonsectarian, but neither was he sectarian: his own tradition was entirely outside any established structure, and he did not promote it above any other. He saw it simply as the path on which his followers could attain enlightenment—and this, according to all accounts, they did in droves. No less than thirteen of his disciples are known to have attained the rainbow-light body (*jalü*), and many more to have reached advanced levels of realization. If giving rise to a wide and vigorous lineage of influential teachers is taken to be the very stuff of which a Buddhist renaissance is made, Dudjom Lingpa should certainly be included. In addition to his own spiritual descendants, he had another resource unavailable to Kongtrul: his eight sons and several grandchildren were all recognized as incarnations of different lineages, and went on to make important contributions to Buddhist culture and practice. His legacy in Golok has proved exceptionally vigorous to the present day.

---

1. Dudjom Lingpa was an outlier not only in a geographic sense but also in terms of his lifestyle and his place in the religious establishment. Recognition by his contemporaries came relatively late in life. Slowly, however, his renown and teachings spread. Dudjom Lingpa's autobiography briefly relates how he spent several months in 1878 in Dzachuka, with his nine-year-old son Dzamling Wangyal (who had been recognized as the reincarnation of Do Khyentsé Yeshé Dorjé), receiving transmissions and teachings from Patrul Rinpoché. Oral tradition also reports that Kongtrul and Jamyang Khyentsé Wangpo approached Dudjom Lingpa with the idea of including his *tersar* in the *Rinchen Terdzö* collection they were compiling, though Dudjom Lingpa politely declined.

2. See, for example, Smith 2001, 250.

Among the writings of masters like these, shaldam is the most person-ally expressive genre. The longer poems translated in this chapter, one from each author, are both in the most classic shaldam format. Addressing a par-ticular individual practitioner, they set out frank advice about what would be the most essential elements in terms of attitudes, practice, and lifestyle for that person to make his or her life—a substantial number of Dudjom Lingpa's shaldam are addressed to women—meaningful and spiritually fruit-ful. Despite being nominally directed to the needs of a specific individual, the fact that they were subsequently preserved and published implies that they were felt likely to be useful to others.

In keeping with their purpose, they are expressed in language close to col-loquial forms and yet at the same time fashioned with considerable literary skill, ranging from the witty to the sublime. Kongtrul's piece here is in plain language but impeccably structured. Dudjom Lingpa's two songs are more original, from a literary point of view. The longer one utilizes concise and elegant phrasing and makes use of a variety of metric rhythms. Kongtrul's focus is on mastering and understanding the mind, but around this central thread he weaves in other essential elements of the path, such as renuncia-tion, reflection on death and impermanence, devotion to a teacher, and the union of emptiness and compassion. Dudjom Lingpa gives more individual-ized advice on lifestyle and livelihood, and then evokes the path and goal in the specific terminology and framework of the Great Perfection. Despite their stylistic differences, both authors answer the same question: in order to attain realization, what does the person being addressed need to do?

Kongtrul's *Words of Advice for Lhawang Tashi*

Kongtrul's voluminous writings cover a vast range of topics and genres yet seem to include relatively few pieces that can be specifically categorized either as shaldam or as spiritual songs (*gur*).[3] The work translated here, *Words of Advice for Lhawang Tashi*, is a shaldam found in his *Treasury of Extensive Teachings* (*Gyachen Kadzö*), which is itself a compilation of those of his writ-ings that did not belong in any of the other themed treasuries.

In the colophon of this poem, Kongtrul refers to himself as "old," so he presumably wrote this advice later in life. The woodblock, unlike those of

---

3. The Paro edition of the *Treasury of Extensive Teachings* (*Gyachen Kadzö*) contains a series of only about twenty short pieces of this kind, while in the equivalent volume in the reorganized and extended Shechen edition, a few further sections of material in the same broad genre have been added.

most of the other texts in the volume, has its own title page and appears to have been originally prepared for independent printing. Otherwise, I have so far been unable to discover anything about the circumstances or date of the piece, or about the identity of the Lhawang Tashi to whom the advice is addressed.

Kongtrul opens with a stanza of obeisance and invocation that includes both Padmasambhava and the Kagyü masters, an unorthodox combination but one certainly coherent with his own eclectic points of reference and personal history. He then launches straight into his theme, the importance of examining, understanding, guarding, and mastering one's own mind.

He sets course for this theme with a wonderfully blunt quote from a short Tengyur text by Atiśa:

When with others, watch your speech,
but when with no one, watch your mind.[4]

To cite an Indian work as his starting point—while a convention common to many genres of Tibetan writing—helps Kongtrul cement the link to an era uncluttered by sectarian bias. Atiśa's terse, frank advice is an important reminder of how far back the shaldam tradition goes. This is also the case when, toward the end of the poem, Kongtrul takes a stanza from the *Way of the Bodhisattva*:

To those who wish to guard their minds,
I press my palms together and implore them:
sustain, with all your efforts,
both mindfulness and vigilance.[5]

Here Śāntideva, in his own innovative way, addresses his readers directly with an exhortation to guard their minds at all costs by maintaining mindfulness and vigilance.[6]

---

4. *Bodhisattvamanevalī*, final verse.

5. Śāntideva, *Bodhicaryāvatāra*, 5:23.

6. In some ways, the shaldam is a return to the original form of the Buddha's teaching. Many sūtras, particularly the shorter ones, record instruction given by the Buddha to a particular audience at a specific time, sometimes in the form of a dialogue. First the abhidharma texts and later the great treatises and their commentaries extracted explicit and implicit meanings from the raw material in the sūtras, and systematized them into a broad framework. The shaldam, in a sense, brings the teachings back to their specificity.

True to these textual foundations, despite occasional references to Mantrayāna notions, the main framework of this piece is built squarely on the general Mahāyāna tradition. Mind, Kongtrul says, is the sole basis of saṃsāra and nirvāṇa, and the difference between buddhahood and suffering is simply a matter of whether the mind is purified. He takes the reader through a sequence of consequences, sadly familiar to any practitioner of meditation, of a Buddhist attempting to practice the path but not paying proper attention to the mind and its nature.

In each case, he says in a key passage, the problem is to have been "led along by a mind you've not made self-sufficient." To make the mind self-sufficient is the first step toward recognizing its nature; it is the confident independence that comes from not expecting gratification, help, or salvation from anywhere else—not out of bravado or resignation, but simply through recognizing that one's own mind is the very basis of all one's experiences.

He continues, giving examples of seeking elsewhere what can be found only in the mind: a quiet place, a teacher, a practice, freedom from distractions, and so forth. Kongtrul reminds us that, similarly, the only way to be rid of enemies is to combat the mind's hostility; that the only way to have all we want is to stop the mind wanting so much; that a positive mind is what leads to higher rebirths; and that understanding mind's nature is what brings liberation. So, too, the only way to put an end to the suffering caused by negative states of mind and the actions to which they lead is to look at the mind's very nature.

Hence the crucial importance of guarding the mind, as the passage from Śāntideva underlines. Now, guarding the mind, in terms of choosing carefully what to do and what not to do, might seem to be unnecessary for someone with a true realization of the ultimate sameness of all phenomena, their single taste as simply the magical display of mind. But for beginners, Kongtrul advises, it is essential to combine a lofty view with actions that are finely considered; here he is abridging a well-known formulation by Padmasambhava, "My view is as high as the sky, but my actions finer than barley flour." Kongtrul follows up this advice by recommending a series of sobering reflections on the impermanent nature of life.

Once again, he returns to the realization of the very nature of the mind. When that realization is maintained, just as it is, everything will be seen as both clarity and emptiness. Evoking the spontaneous compassion that is then engendered toward those who do not have that realization, he identifies emptiness and compassion with ultimate and relative bodhicitta, and he emphasizes their unity as a crucial point of the sūtra and mantra teachings. Rounding off his advice in a final summary, he signs off with the customary self-deprecating colophon.

Kongtrul's language in this piece is simple, as if he did not want his clear message to be attenuated by unfamiliar expressions, or the reader to be distracted by displays of literary prowess. But while the poem is straightforward and without ornamentation, it is also composed with such a sure touch that what he says can hardly be interpreted as mere earnestness. The meter he uses throughout is a regular one of seven syllables (*rabga*), with a standard, alternating stress (in prosodic terms, catalectic trochaic tetrameters, as in William Blake's *The Tyger*). This is the same meter used by the Tibetan translators for the two Tengyur texts from which he quotes—perhaps Kongtrul matches them deliberately, as if to affirm the associations.

As testified by other shaldam in the *Treasury of Extensive Teachings*, Kongtrul was certainly capable of more complex metrical forms. He was also expert in the *kāvya* style of ornate poetics, with its usage of metaphorical language, alliteration, wordplay, and other ornamental forms that he himself described in detail in his chapters on poetics, prosody, and synonymics in book 6 of the *Treasury of Knowledge*. Here, he remains straightforward and sober by choice.

For the translation, I have accordingly tried to keep the language and phrasing simple and to avoid excessive jargon and technical terms. While matching Kongtrul's masterful simplicity would be difficult, my aim was to stay at least in the same register. To tighten the lines of verse into a regular meter would require not only more skill than I have at my disposal, but would also mean introducing artificial "poetic" constructions that would give the translation a more contrived feel than the original. I have nevertheless attempted to keep a regular alternation of stressed and unstressed syllables in order to retain the verse format and make the piece easy to read aloud. I have also, for the most part, kept a line-by-line correspondence with the original so that the English translation can be read alongside the Tibetan text.

Dudjom Lingpa's *Song for Chokdrup, Novice of Abum* and *Untitled Song*

Collectively, the twenty-one volumes of Dudjom Lingpa's writings are usually known as his Treasure Teachings (Terchö), for they consist almost entirely of the treasure texts that he revealed. Even some of his autobiographical texts are considered *terma* or treasure revelations. The texts presented here, however, are from the only section of his writings that are not deemed *terma*, a 240-folio collection of brief shaldam in the form of 132 strikingly original spiritual songs, most of them between one and four folios in length.

The first of the two songs by Dudjom Lingpa translated here is addressed to Chokdrup, a novice of Abum. After briefly invoking Guru Padmasambhava, Dudjom Lingpa reminds his disciple of the unique qualities of a human existence with all of the freedoms and advantages, and exhorts him to make the right choices while he can, evoking the feelings his disciple may have on his deathbed if he fails to take the right path. He stresses the importance of being content with whatever one's material circumstances may be, and of being aware how rare true realization is. When he advises Chokdrup not to ignore his own need for sustenance, Dudjom Lingpa speaks from experience: he himself had to work hard to secure adequate resources for himself and his followers without institutional support, and without compromising either his freedom or his ethical principles. This advice is reinforced by four quatrains that sketch categories of so-called Dharma practitioners whose solutions to the problem of sustenance (doing business with the saṅgha's wealth, performing rituals for money, chasing academic status, and so forth) he must not emulate. Dudjom Lingpa then summarizes what is meant by true meditation practice, true postmeditation practice, and true application of the pith instructions.

Then comes a sudden change of mood. Until now, the first part of the song has been in a meter of eight syllables (*jengak*), each line starting with a stressed syllable followed by three stressed-light pairs (trochees) and a final stressed syllable. But here, heralded by the interjection "Ai!" the song abruptly changes rhythm. It first changes to three lines—outlining the view—that have a nine-syllable (*bṛhatī*) meter of two trochees, a dactyl (stressed-light-light), and a final trochee. This may serve to draw attention to the central, pivotal status of these lines in the song. Then, starting surprisingly with the fourth line of this same stanza, he changes to lines of ten syllables made up of two stressed-light-light-stressed-light sequences (tetrameters of alternating dactyls and trochees). This lilting meter is maintained until the end of the song.

Each stanza is preceded by further, abrupt interjections (such as "Hé hé!" and "Ya ya!"). The instructions continue but now take as their focus inspiring descriptions of the very experiences of realization. They briefly cover the Great Perfection's view, meditation, and practice of *trekchö* (the approach based on primordial purity), the four visions of *thögal* (the yoga of light based on spontaneous presence), and the ultimate fruit. Dudjom Lingpa concludes with a colophon, still part of the song, in which the time-honored tradition of self-deprecation takes the form of his disclaiming his own advice as the ravings of a madman.

The second translation, which has no named addressee, is one of the shortest songs in the collection, a mere eight lines. Its meter is one of regular trochaic tetrameters except for the last line—three trochees followed by three final, stressed syllables. Instead of following one of the customary patterns, such as advice structured on the stages of the path, it starts off with a seemingly straightforward evocation of the pure buddhafields that one might aspire to reach as a result of disciplined practice. The description of this agreeable prospect is maintained for the first five lines of the text. Arriving at the sixth line, however, the reader suddenly realizes that Dudjom Lingpa's first five lines were intended as irony. The true, unsurpassed buddhafield (*okmin*, *Akaniṣṭha*) is the state free of all such projections; it is simply the realization of the view. It is a spontaneously present state, not a destination involving notions of somewhere else to be reached.

Brief though it is, this song is almost a summary of both Kongtrul's poem and Dudjom Lingpa's longer shaldam. Both of the longer pieces stress how important it is not to be taken in by the notion that enlightenment is a state to be found elsewhere, or in another time, when it is actually already present as the nature of mind, "the real thing," right now. And that, indeed, is ultimately what is meant by the term *buddhafield*, just as Kongtrul says in the fifth verse of his poem.

Dudjom Lingpa's style in these songs is poetically expressive and has an uncontrived elegance, even in passages where the terminology is precise and verging on the technical. Remarkably, it is said that he composed his writings in a single-stage process, dictating them to scribes, and often working on several texts in parallel. He would stride around as he spoke or chanted them, loudly. It is perhaps this spontaneous, oral, inspired quality that gives these songs their particular character. The translator's task here is a daunting one, and I cannot claim to have done anything approaching justice to the originals. Their meaning, at least, is not especially obscure, and in these pieces there is little of the play on words, deliberate ambiguity, metaphorical allusion, or any of the other kinds of literary ornamentation with which some of my colleagues in this volume have had to contend.

Dudjom Lingpa's descriptions of the experiential stages of the path draw mostly on general Great Perfection terminology, but he does supplement his descriptions with some characteristic terms of his own. An example is his frequent use of the word *ngoma*, which means "true" or "genuine"—the opposite of false or fake, with the sense of what is really there. It is a useful term, being an everyday word implying the truth, the real thing, and which does not ascribe any ontological status to it. In order to preserve this particularity of his writing, I have tried to be consistent in translating *ngoma* as "the real thing," even when different paraphrases might have produced a better flow. One instance that deserves comment is in Dudjom Lingpa's unique formulation of the view mentioned above:

In the space of the true nature is everything, all of saṃsāra and nirvāṇa,
the real thing without objectivity, interpenetrating,
knowing without a self, present as the guru—
the king of all views; do you recognize it in its own ground?

While the first line sets out what is often called in Great Perfection terms "the ground," the true nature or *dharmatā*, likened here to space, the second line describes the phenomenal world. In the deluded state, this is seen as made up of the objects of the senses; but *ngoma*, "the real thing," is, he says, "without objectivity, interpenetrating" (*yulmé sangthal*)—as described in other Great Perfection texts. His third line, in a word pattern matching the second line, refers to the aspect of awareness: "knowing without a self," followed by "present as the guru," identifying the nature of awareness with the nature of the guru, and perhaps also suggesting that awareness itself becomes the practitioner's mentor and guide.

This, then, is the view—the crucial point—as he chooses to express it here in these three lines. In the fourth line comes his big question to Chokdrup, the "pointing-out": can he recognize that view, not just in theory, not just dualistically "knowing with a self," but as it really is, "in its own ground"?

If the very particular style and flavor of Dudjom Lingpa's language are hard to convey fully in translation, the rhythm and song-like quality of these pieces are far more difficult. Translation of verse from one Western language into another is expected to include some representation of the original meter and verse structure; from Tibetan, this is more challenging. Tibetan, with its detachable particles and coalesced word forms, is easy to compress and expand. English, with its irregularly stressed polysyllables, auxiliaries, and prepositions, is rarely as brief or as rhythmic. I have tried to maintain, at least, the division into lines, as in the Kongtrul shaldam. I have also experimented with the use of layout to do what I cannot do with metric stress.

In the first two thirds of the longer song, using the device of breaking each line near the start, after a word or two, I have attempted to reproduce something of the meter of the Tibetan, which I have described above. In this particular meter, the word chosen as the first of the two initial stressed syllables is often one with a key semantic importance—at least near the beginning of the poem where it is most noticeable. This is a hard act for the author to maintain for long, so its precision tends to fade away as the poem progresses.

To preserve some trace of this structure, I have tried to keep a semantically important word or phrase at the beginning of each line before the interruption of the line break. The result is contrived, and a little obtrusive at first reading, but with familiarity (I hope) becomes less so. As a solution, it remains unsatisfactory and inelegant. But, despite having been tempted to abandon it several times, I have left it in place in the hope that it might stimulate others to seek better methods.

In the final third of the song, I have used italics to mark off the central three-line statement of the view (described and excerpted above), which is made distinct in the original by having a different meter of its own. The characteristic Tibetan interjections I have simply reproduced phonetically; they could have been translated into some approximate equivalents in English (Oh! Hey! Aha! Yeah! Lo!), but this, I think, would have created a slightly comical feel. The lilting meter of the final part of the song proved impossible to reproduce, but its tendency to create a caesura halfway through the line comes through in the translation and has, where syntax allowed, been emphasized with a comma.

Having heard some of Dudjom Lingpa's songs chanted to a traditional melody of eastern Tibet, I cannot help thinking how much richer the experience of hearing them in English might be if they were set to music. I look forward to the day when an appropriate musical genre might evolve, and they could take on a multidimensional texture.

But even in translation—divested, inevitably, of some of their original form—the essence of these striking poems, alive with the wise advice and authentic experience of their very different authors and composed with such brilliance, retains its timeless freshness. Their message can speak to us today much as it must have done to their original recipients.

Acknowledgments

I am most grateful to Pema Wangyal Rinpoché for the reading transmission of the poems, and for clarifying some points of the Dudjom Lingpa songs; to Khenchen Pema Sherab and Khenpo Tenzin Norgye for their careful checking of the various versions of the Tibetan of all three poems; to my colleagues at the "Translating Buddhist Luminaries" conference in Boulder, 2013, for their helpful comments; to Geoff Barstow for kindly reading and commenting on my final draft; to Holly Gayley for her invaluable help and input; and to the Tsadra Foundation, without whose generous support this project in particular, and my translation work in general, would not be possible.

WORDS OF ADVICE FOR LHAWANG TASHI

by Jamgön Kongtrul Lodrö Thayé

> I go for refuge to the Lotus Guru.
> By the blessings of the masters of the instruction lineage,
> may those with faith direct their minds to Dharma,
> and take the path to irreversible freedom.

> Atiśa, Lord of the Land of Snows,
> condensed his advice into these two points:
> "When with others, watch your speech,
> but when with no one, watch your mind."[7]

> The root of wrongdoing is, indeed, the mind,
> and most wrongdoing happens using words;
> so both need guarding, always.

> Saṃsāra and nirvāṇa are but your own mind—
> there's not a speck that comes from somewhere else.
> All joy and sorrow, right and wrong, the noble and the lowly—
> such things are merely notions in the mind.

> If you purify your mind, it's buddhahood,
> the place you are becomes a buddhafield;
> do what you will, it's all within the ultimate nature,
> and all that appears is the detail of wisdom's display.

> If you fail to purify your mind,
> you find faults even with a buddha,
> you get angry even with your parents,
> and most of what appears seems hostile.

---

7. *Bodhisattvamaṇyāvalī*, folio 295.b, line 6.

In endless waves of hoping, fearing, lusting, hating,
your human years of useless human life run out.

Whoever you're with, you don't get on;
wherever you are, you don't feel happy;
whatever you have, it's never enough;
the more you get, the more you need.

As life's apparent dramas take you first this way, then that,
some thought of practicing Dharma may occur to you[8]—
but while you're still about to do it, life will just run out.

When first you feel a fresh determination to be free,
whatever it may take, you're ready for it all;
but then you harden, and can't even give away a needle.

When the devotion you feel is still new,
you think of nothing but the teacher;
but then time passes and you see him with perverted views.

When your faith and inspiration are still new,
on top of one practice you take up yet another;
but as you age they all just fade away.

When first you find a suitable companion,
you treasure his life far more than your own;
but then you lose interest and treat him with aversion.

At root in all these instances is to be led along
by a mind you've not made self-sufficient.
Once capable of mastering your mind:

You need not seek an isolated place elsewhere;
when thoughts are absent, that's an isolated place.

You need not search outside to find a teacher;
mind itself is the enlightened teacher.

---

8. The line in Tibetan has one syllable too many, but this may be how it was composed
rather than a scribal error.

You need not fear you're missing out on some practice;
being free of distraction is the essence of all practice.

You need not purposefully get rid of each distraction;
apply mindfulness and vigilance, and on their own distractions will
    subside.

You need not be afraid of the defilements arising;
for, taken as their very nature, they are wisdoms.

Apart from this momentary mind of yours,
there is no other saṃsāra or nirvāṇa that exists—
so I beg you, be constantly on watch over your mind!

Unless you tame your mind within,
there'll be no end to enemies without.
But if you tame hostility within,
you'll be at peace with all the enemies on earth.

Without contentment in your mind,
acquire what you may—you'll still be like a beggar.
But with renunciation, a person who's content inside
is always rich without possessions.

The propensities of joy arising in your mind
when rightfully engaged in ordinary affairs,
in Dharma practice, or in meritorious deeds
will bring you rebirth in the higher realms;
yet that's impermanent and still saṃsāra,
while if you look at the very nature of that joy,
to see it's empty is the basis of the path to liberation.

In all affairs, religious ones as well as worldly,
your wrongful acts will bring you suffering;
and if you follow after your defiling thoughts—
of anger, hatred, attachment, and the rest—
that's what causes rebirth in the lower realms,
and the sufferings there cannot even be imagined.
So, no matter what defilements and sufferings may arise,

look at their very nature, and they will vanish into emptiness;
apart from that, there is no other wisdom somewhere else.

Never separating from this mind of yours,
it's crucial to constantly guard your mind.
To guard your mind includes all teachings.

As Śāntideva said, on how to guard it,
"To those who wish to guard their minds,
I press my palms together and implore them:
sustain, with all your efforts,
both mindfulness and vigilance."[9]
To put in practice what he says is vital.

Therefore, although whatever may appear to all six senses
is but the magical display of mind itself—and so
to act on things selectively, rejecting and adopting, is deluded,
and best of all is taking as the path their single taste—
for all beginners such a lofty view
should be combined with fine-grained action.

The freedoms and advantages of a human life being hard to find,
reflect repeatedly on death and on impermanence.
Develop strong conviction in the never-failing fruits of your actions.

Each time you see or hear of others dying,
please take it as a sign and teaching for yourself.

Each time you see the summer turning into winter,
remind yourself that everything's impermanent.

Each time you see the bees so busy making honey,
recognize how pointless is your need for wealth.

Each time you see a ruined house or empty market,
recognize your home and household as the same.

---

9. *Bodhicaryāvatāra*, 5:23.

Each time you witness people torn away from those they love,
remind yourself of your own close ones, too.

Each time you see a person facing sudden adverse times,
remind yourself how that may happen to you, too.

Yourself and others, just as in a dream,
have not a speck of true existence.

Without adulterating your mind with fabrications,
maintain its natural state, its very essence:
you'll realize everything, inside or out, is emptiness,
clarity and emptiness together, like the sky,
and that's the ultimate mind of awakening.

Yet beings who do not know that things are so
wander in saṃsāra through the power of dualistic thoughts,
experiencing suffering; so when, toward them all,
a measureless compassion, unfabricated, arises in you by itself,
that's the relative mind of awakening.

Compassion, free of grasping, realizing things are empty;
emptiness, spontaneously manifesting in the rising of compassion—
to unite them is the heart of both the sūtra and the mantra
    teachings;
apply your experience to this fundamental point.

Bring to bear on them, as means for their arising in you,
whatever meritorious actions you can manage;
pray to the Three Jewels
and apply the vital points regarding devotion to your teacher.

Refrain from all wrongdoing to yourself or others,
exhort yourself to all the virtuous action that you can,
and from the Great Vehicle's mind of awakening
and from the purest dedication, never let yourself depart.

At the behest of Devendra, one whose qualities
shine with virtuous intentions like the waxing moon,

a monk called Lodrö Thayé, an old man
with only three ideas,[10] has written this advice.

May your lifespan and attainment of the Dharma reach their furthest
   extent,
and may you spontaneously accomplish the two fulfillments!

Sarvasiddhirastu maṅgalaṃ.

---

10. *Dusumpa* is often explained as sleeping, eating, and defecating, but sometimes (perhaps
out of politeness) the third "idea" is said to be walking around.

Two Songs of Advice

by Traktung Dudjom Lingpa

1. A Song for Chokdrup, the Novice of Abum

Lord,
  sublime embodiment of all present, past, and future buddhas;
Protector,
  sovereign of the hundred families, Lake-Born Lord,
present
  inseparably in the wheel of ultimate reality at my heart, throughout
all three times—
  take care of me, now and always!

Its worth
  is small, but if to have this old man's brief advice
just now
  seems so important—very well, then, just for you,
for my part,
  I shall sing and sing away my crazy song!

The point is,
  now, you have a human life with freedoms and advantages.
The benefits
  it brings you, you should bear in mind and not forget:
to travel
  on the path of freedom—it's your carriage;
to cross
  the ocean of existence—it's your boat;
to gather
  merit that endures—it's your support;
to attain
  supreme and common siddhis—it's your stimulus;
and upward
  on the swift path of great bliss—your escort.

To have
  this life, indeed, must be the fruit of past good deeds.

Here
  is the frontier between saṃsāra and nirvāṇa;
here
  is where you cross or fall back—and that is up to you.
Your life
  till now you've spent on acts with no real meaning;
and now,
  what's left for you to live is like the fading evening sun.
Actions
  that will bring you joy or sorrow, the choice is yours.
For you
  the day you'll die will dawn, and then
the wealth
  of the whole wide world will be of no avail.
Uneasy
  and forlorn, you'll depart for your next life
with none
  of your dear ones, near or far, to protect you.
Do not
  forget that! Quick, apply yourself to Dharma!

A single man
  to feed and clothe, but with the thought of bothering no more,
far off
  to other places you might wander like an errant dog—
but there
  you'll never feel quite satisfied with what you have,
and in the end
  the risk of demons overpowering you is great;
whatever valuables
  you might acquire will just be snatched by others.
This life
  of yours is like a fleeting dream,
it's nothing more—
  so never think that you'll be here forever.
These days,
  among this age's final dregs, reflect:

your life,
   how long it will last is so uncertain;
true fathers,
   the authentic teachers, how rare they are!
The Dharma,
   those accomplishing its view and meditation are so few;
its goal
   is perfectly attained by nobody at all.
Weigh up
   these things—and quick, apply yourself to Dharma.

A lifetime
   won't suffice for all the work you have to do,
your activities
   are many, and you have no time to finish them.
But the careless
   who spend a lifetime living on the saṅgha's wealth—
their tasks
   are never-ending, those restless merchant monks—
such people
   are not for you; stay true to yourself alone.

Shamelessly,
   others break their vows, pretending to be *ngakpas*,
confused
   old uncle-lamas obsessed with having powers,
traders in suffering,
   those aging priests and village exorcists—
such people
   are not for you; stay true to yourself alone.

Fame-craving
   practitioners of *chö* who beat up ghosts,
those creating hells
   of self-destruction, great lamas in appearance,
or seeking greatness
   through vilifying and espousing intellectual tenets—
such people
   are not for you; stay true to yourself alone.

Hoarders of books
  who never study and reflect,
self-infatuated
  lopöns, their status built by other people,
scholars
  babbling so conceitedly but with no hearts—
such people
  are not for you; stay true to yourself alone.

Stay
  in a pleasant grove with all your requisites at hand;
your body,
  leave as it is without fabrication, like a corpse;
your speech,
  leave as it is without fabrication, like a mute's;
your mind,
  leave as it is without fabrication, free of conceptual extremes.
That
  is the very pinnacle of all meditation practice.

While doing
  any task or activity, at any time,
within wisdom,
  primordial, vast, and all-pervading,
to allow
  naturally present gnosis its own freedom—
that
  is the most sublime of all true postmeditation practice.

Experiences,
  happy or sad, good or bad—whatever may arise,
not fabricating
  or changing them, just let them be;
to recognize
  but not cling to them, that is the crucial point;
this
  is the very pinnacle of all instruction.

Your mind's
  long drawn-out plans need cutting short.

Right now
   apply yourself to practicing for death alone.

Ai!
In the space of the true nature is everything, all of saṃsāra and
   nirvāṇa,
the real thing without objectivity, interpenetrating,
knowing without a self, present as the guru—
the king of all views; do you recognize it in its own ground?

Hé hé!
The primordial natural state, once encountered as your very essence,
needs no meditating on or practice; just give it its full freedom.
Buddhahood was always there, and you discover it just where it is;
that lasting state of well-being, here it is for sure!

Ho ho!
Ever-present gnosis is continuous, like a river's flow;
there is nothing you need block or achieve—let go of all activities,
and good or bad, let how you act be uncontrived, the real thing.

Ya ya!
Naturally present primordial radiance, in the wheel of enjoyment,
to the eyes of wisdom, manifests as a spectacle;
the experience increases, matures to reach its culmination,
and the yoga of dharmas' exhaustion unfurls fully in well-being.[11]

Yé yé!
When the yoga of dharmas' exhaustion emerges in the vase body,[12]
in the manifesting of the ever-perfect qualities you find confidence:
here is the real thing, the king of the dharmakāya itself,
and great transference in the radiance of the rainbow-light body is
   certain.

---

11. This stanza makes explicit reference to three of the four visions of *thögal* (*gongphel*, *tsephep*, and *chösé*). See glossary for definitions of these and an explanation of the "wheel of enjoyment" (*longchö kyi khorlo*).

12. *Bumku*, "vase body," is a Great Perfection term referring to the ground's natural radiance while it is still enclosed.

Kyé ho!
Your primordially free nature is nothing other than itself;
yet, by letting that self-arisen gnosis have its own autonomy,
make it the real thing, the experience of unmistaken well-being,
and on the path of omniscience you'll be free—the real thing.

Having no way to refuse the request you made,
I, the foolish and contemptible Dudjom Dorjé,
have responded with this ditty in the form of insane ravings,
which I hereby give to Chokdrup, the novice of Abum.

Virtue! Excellence! Jayantu.

2. Untitled Song

Pleasant, comfortable, pure celestial realms,
if you keep your vows and samayas, are not far away;
soon you'll reach the level of liberation
where, remote from the domain of existence's suffering,
there are cheerful places unsullied by sin, the pure fields—

It's liberation from such ideas that's the true Akaniṣṭha
which, if you realize the view, is the real thing, there by itself;
without needing to depart or arrive, you'll get there just like that.

Written by Dudjom.

Translated Works

Jamgön Kongtrul Lodrö Thayé ('Jam mgon Kong sprul Blo gros mtha' yas). *Lha dbang bkra shis la gnang ba'i zhal gdams.* In Rgya chen bka' mdzod, (i) 1975–76. Palpung (20 volume) edition, vol. 10 (*tha*), 31–38. Paro: Ngodup. (ii) 2002. Expanded (13 volume) edition, vol. 6 (*cha*), 969–75. New Delhi: Shechen. Both editions reproduce the same original xylograph.

Dudjom Lingpa (Bdud 'joms gling pa, Khrag 'thung bdud 'joms rdo rje). *Rje dus gsum rgyal ba'i spyi gzugs sogs a 'bum mchog grub la gnang ba.* In *Sprul pa'i gter chen bdud 'joms gling pa'i zab gter gsang ba'i chos sde* (*gter chos*), (i) 1978. (*Dbu med* edition), vol. 18 (*tsha*), folios 4a–6a. Kalimpong: Dupjung Lama. (ii) 2004. (*Dbu can* edition), vol. 18 (*tsha*), folios 5a–6b (9–12). Thimpu, Bhutan: Lama Kuenzang Wangdue.

———. *Skyid po bde mo dag pa mkha spyod sogs.* In (idem) (i) folio 212a; (ii) folio 189a (377).

Suggested Readings

Barron, Richard, ed. and trans. 2003. *The Autobiography of Jamgön Kongtrul: A Gem of Many Colors.* Ithaca, NY: Snow Lion Publications.

Beyer, Stephan V. 1992. *The Classical Tibetan Language.* Albany: State University of New York Press.

Cabezón, José Ignacio, and Roger R. Jackson, eds. 1996. *Tibetan Literature: Studies in Genre.* Ithaca, NY: Snow Lion Publications.

Dudjom Lingpa, Traktung. 2011. *A Clear Mirror: The Visionary Autobiography of a Tibetan Master.* Translated by Chönyi Drolma. Hong Kong: Rangjung Yeshe Publications.

Gayley, Holly. 2010–11. *The Scions of Dudjom Lingpa* (posted January 21, 2010). *Articulating Lineage in Golok* (posted September 14, 2010). *Who's Who in the Dudjom Lineage?* (posted September 23, 2011). Articles at http://about.tbrc.org /category/research.

Additional References

Atiśa Dīpaṃkaraśrījñāna. *Bodhisattvamaṇyāvalī* (*Byang chub sems dpa'i nor bu'i phreng ba*). (Toh. 3951). Degé Tengyur, vol. 111 (*dbu ma, khi*), folios 294b–296a.

Jamgön Kongtrul. 2012. *The Treasury of Knowledge, Book 6, Parts 1 and 2: Indo-Tibetan Classical Learning and Buddhist Phenomenology.* Translated by Gyurme Dorjé. Boston: Snow Lion Publications.

Śāntideva. *Bodhicaryāvatāra* (*Byang chub sems dpa'i spyod pa la 'jug pa*). (Toh. 3871). Degé Tengyur, vol. 105 (*dbu ma, la*), folios 1a–40a. Translated by the Padmakara Translation Group as *The Way of the Bodhisattva.* Boston: Shambhala Publications, 1997.

Smith, E. Gene. 2001. *Among Tibetan Texts: History and Literature of the Himalayan Plateau.* Boston: Wisdom Publications.

2. Playful Primers on the Path

Dza Patrul Rinpoché

Translated by Joshua Schapiro

Patrul Rinpoché's Wit at Work

This chapter presents two lighthearted sets of religious instructions by the famed nineteenth-century teacher Dza Patrul Orgyen Jikmé Chökyi Wangpo. The works showcase Patrul's compositional prowess, in particular his penchant for creating teachings that are accessible yet profound.[1] In both texts Patrul calls attention to his own virtuosity by framing his teachings as sermons performed in response to an interlocutor's challenge. These performances exemplify Patrul's theatrical style of pedagogy.

The first text is entitled *The Low-Born Sage Speaks: The Ladder to Liberation, a Treatise on Dharmic and Worldly Knowledge*. The text presents itself as a teaching given by a sage living in a retreat cave. When visitors to the cave ask the sage to answer questions about broad Buddhist categories, the sage responds with the verses that constitute the work. One of the visitors presents the following sets of questions and requests, which come across as challenges to the sage's purported knowledge:

Hey! Great sage!
Dharma traditions—what are they?

---

1. The third Dodrupchen incarnation, Jikmé Tenpai Nyima (1865–1926), praised Patrul for his skill in crafting teachings understandable to the average student yet filled with profound meaning. Those writing about Patrul thereafter often repeated this compliment.

Dharma traditions—how do you split them up?
Dharma traditions—which do you cast aside?
Dharma traditions—which do you accept?
The three objects of refuge, the three vows,
the three vehicles: speak to me about these categories.
Explain how to condense each set of three categories into one.
Show me how each one can be sewn up into an essential point.

The sage responds to these queries with a bevy of interlocking verses in a variety of meters. His method is to introduce new vocabulary, define his terms, and relate each defined term to the others. He thereby generates a maze-like network of Buddhist concepts and practices. Yet, miraculously, by the end of each of his two sermons, the sage has succeeded at reducing the entire Buddhist path down to one or two simple practices. The sage's performances function as a primer to Buddhism: introducing his audience to the most essential activities along the Buddhist path and justifying their importance. The sermons are likewise a virtuosic display of teaching competence on the part of the sage.

The composition is an impressive example of Patrul's pedagogical dexterity, particularly the ease with which he addresses multiple levels of audience simultaneously. Its short verses, nursery-rhyme rhythms, and introductory subject matter make the work an ideal introduction to the Buddhist path, appropriate for public audiences. Yet the seeming simplicity of Patrul's stanzas belies a sophisticated architecture that structures the composition at large. Each element that Patrul introduces fits into a larger, intricate plan. And the introductory content—three jewels, three vehicles, three vows—eventually make way for practice instructions that reach to the pinnacle of the Nyingma path—advice on how to reach liberation in every moment by facing the nature of one's own mind.

The second text, *The Explanation of Chudrulü*, is a nine-page-long joke, explicitly so. The editors of Patrul's *Collected Works* label it a humorous discourse (*shegé ki tam*). Some background is necessary for understanding the humor at play. In Patrul's time a story circulated around the region of Kham about a meditation practitioner who was in retreat in a local cave. Whenever his attendant would come to visit him with provisions, the meditator would pester his attendant with questions about what he was missing back home. "What's been happening at the monastery in my absence? What's new in our village? What do you have to tell me?" To each question the young attendant would respond in the same way. "Nothing." But instead of speaking the word *nothing*, the attendant would use a colloquial expression from the

Degé region, slang for "nothing, really," or "nothing at all." The expression in question is *chudrulü*.

Upon hearing this story, Patrul decided to compose a critique of those of his peers who were obsessed with talking (like the meditator in the story). His critique, *The Explanation of Chudrulü*, confronts Buddhist practitioners who are unduly devoted to religious talk, such as composing textual commentaries and engaging in monastic debate. As the text suggests, true practitioners can accomplish their goals without any need for superfluous chatter.

Patrul's critique takes the form of a tongue-in-cheek etymology of the term *chudrulü*. Patrul introduces a group of protagonists—a collection of youth—who explain the meaning of the phrase *chudrulü* to a group of older monks. The youth offer a faux etymology of *chudrulü* (an oral colloquialism with no true spelling), splitting it up into three Tibetan words: *chu*, meaning "water," *dru*, meaning "boat," and *lü*, meaning "body." They explain that water, boats, and bodies all travel to different places but never change, fundamentally. Water may flow from oceans to rivers and lakes, and may be used to drink or to bathe with, but it never fundamentally changes from being water. It always ends up back in the ocean, eventually. Boats may travel across rivers, and bodies may travel in those boats, but neither change during the trip. Bodies and boats just go and return. The youth compare water, boats, and bodies to themselves. The youth may travel to different places to accomplish different tasks, but they never really change. They never learn anything new that is worth reporting to the older monks. The implication is that the older monks should stop asking them to do so.

The youths' analysis of *chudrulü* is highly suggestive and can be read on any number of levels. On the one hand, it is a joke, teasing the scholars (the elder monks in the story) for their constant thirst for new teachings and obsession with formal commentary. On another level, it defends creative and informal teachings, exemplified by the etymology of *chudrulü*. This explanation of *chudrulü* is itself a demonstration of the skill of "confident eloquence," one of the four oratory proficiencies that bodhisattvas possess, to which Patrul alludes in the opening lines of *The Explanation of Chudrulü*.[2] Finally, one might even read the youths' teaching as a subtle allegory about the nature of Buddhist practice, or perhaps the nature of the human mind.[3]

Just like *The Low-Born Sage Speaks*, *The Explanation of Chudrulü* frames itself as a performance. The elder monks challenge the youth to give them an

---

2. Confident eloquence (*popa*) is one of the four "thorough, perfect knowledges" (*so so yangdak par rikpa*).

3. For a discussion of such possibilities, see Schapiro 2011.

explanation of the phrase *chudrulü*, in response to which the youth deliver their dazzling deconstruction of the term. The youth eventually give credit for the *chudrulü* teaching to Patrul himself and subsequently list his many qualities as a superior teacher. Ultimately, *The Explanation of Chudrulü* proves Patrul to be capable of delivering a brilliant discourse about even the silliest topic. As the text boasts, Patrul's intelligence "can never be used up," even when he is teaching about "nothing"!

The two texts translated below well capture some of the most striking facets of Patrul's reputed personality. On the one hand, he was self-effacing, as when he compares himself in *The Low-Born Sage Speaks* to an outcast (or low-born, *dölpa*) hermit who only pretends to be "disciplined," when in fact he has no internal mastery over himself. There are any number of stories about Patrul hiding his identity, eschewing the royal treatment that might otherwise befit a teacher of his fame and stature. On the other hand, Patrul was a talented showman whose writings go out of their way to highlight their very status as eloquent speech. One might say that Patrul's writings call attention to themselves in ways that Patrul the human being often avoided doing. The two texts that appear here are a case in point, showcasing Patrul's deft manipulation of Buddhist categories in *The Low-Born Sage Speaks* and highlighting his creativity in *The Explanation of Chudrulü*.

The two works also support Patrul's reputation for giving teachings that are accessible yet profound. Patrul delivers short, digestible bits of teaching—compact, orderly, and playful. But these bits add up to wholes greater than their parts—multivalent, provocative, and speaking to a far-reaching Nyingma view of innate liberation. So, for example, *The Low-Born Sage Speaks* effectively reduces the entire path of awakening to a few simple practices. Yet these simple practices, such as "looking at your own mind" (*rangi sem la tawa*), have the power to lead practitioners to a realization about the nature of all things that appear in the world. *The Explanation of Chudrulü* is, on one level, an accessible joke, a way to tease scholastic monks that everyone can enjoy. On another level, it can be read as a cryptic allegory about how our minds are capable of interacting with the world yet remain eternally pure—unchanging in their emptiness. Both works are easy to understand, on the one hand, and densely packed with meaning on the other. For these reasons they are ideal representatives of witty Tibetan advice writing (*shaldam*).

Translating Patrul's Works

The most interesting features of these two works are the very aspects that make them challenging to translate. They contain numerous puns and are humorous in ways not easily communicable in translation. They also utilize verse, compact in expression yet highly concentrated with significance. Communicating the semantic sense of these verses while simultaneously capturing their elliptical, choppy style is a challenge. So too is giving the reader a taste for the rhythm of the verses and their shifting meter. A few examples will hopefully suffice to introduce the kinds of puns, lively wordplay, and humor that appear in *The Low-Born Sage Speaks* and *The Explanation of Chudrulü*.

The following stanza uses double meanings in order to show how the guru's instructions capture the intent of all three baskets of the Buddha's teachings (a traditional way to organize the authoritative utterances of the historical Buddha and his close followers).

> It principally trains your afflictive emotions.
> It gathers in brief only the most essential point of the entire Dharma.
> It demonstrates the way of being of suchness.
> The speech of the guru is the three baskets of Dharma.

The first line incorporates the phrase "trains" (*dulwa*), referring both to training one's emotions as well as to one basket of the Buddha's teachings: *dulwa* (better known as Vinaya, in Sanskrit). The second line uses the phrase "in brief" (*do*) to stand in for a second basket: *dodé* (Sūtra). Finally, the third line includes the verbal phrase "demonstrates" (*ngöndu tön*) using the verbal modifier *ngön*, alluding to the third basket of *ngönchö* (Abhidharma). Patrul thereby incorporates the names of all three baskets into his description of the qualities of a guru's speech.

The Explanation of Chudrulü also contains punning and creatively multivalent turns of phrase. To cite one example, the youth brag that Patrul is capable of masterfully interpreting the meaning of words without needing to quote from scripture in order to lend authority to his interpretations.

> The complete Kangyur and Tengyur are well known, like the wind.
> But knowledge is that which corrects scripture.
> It is well known to society's many scholars
> that there is no need for scriptural quotations over and above
> knowledge.

These lines appeal to a pun on Tibetan terms for the wind. The youth state that knowledge, which Patrul has in spades, is "that which corrects scripture." This short phrase actually contains two puns on "the wind," referenced in the prior sentence. The Tibetan term for "correct" or "edit" (*dakjé*), which literally means "that which makes pure," is a figurative term for "wind." (It is likewise a figurative term for "water"—the subject of one third of *The Explanation of Chudrulü*.) The Tibetan term for "scripture" (*lung*) is also a homonym for "wind." So the youth declare that if the Buddhist scriptures (the Kangyur and Tengyur) are like the wind, so too is knowledge. Knowledge is, on the semantic level of the sentence, "that which corrects scripture." Knowledge is also "the wind," insofar as the phrase *corrects scripture* contains a double pun on "wind."

From one perspective, the entirety of *The Explanation of Chudrulü* is a grand play on words. The text opens by praising Mañjuśrī, crediting him with possessing the four thorough and perfect knowledges that all bodhisattvas achieve along the path to liberation—four ways of categorizing their capacity to teach the Buddha's way to others.

> Reverence to you, Gentle Protector, sun of the heart
> who possesses the thorough and perfect knowledges
> of phenomena and their meaning, confident eloquence, and the
>   etymology of words.
> Reverence to you.

I would suggest thinking of the youth's explanation of *chudrulü* as a humorous exemplification of these bodhisattva skills, invoked here in the introductory verse. The verse also suggests a larger play on words at work in the composition. The fourth perfect knowledge is usually understood to mean that advanced bodhisattvas know how to speak about all phenomena using human or nonhuman languages. The literal meaning of this term, *ngepai tsik*, is the knowledge of the "etymology of words." Patrul humorously captures the flexibility in the meaning of this fourth knowledge. He has his text's surprise bodhisattvas—the youth—show their understanding of all human language (including Degé dialect) by quite literally offering an etymology of *chudrulü*. Funny as it may sound, their capacity to spin a creative interpretation of the constituent syllables of *chu-dru-lü* is, in the broader scheme of the text, a demonstration of their bodhisattva skills.

Patrul and Rimé

While Patrul had relationships with Jamyang Khyentsé Wangpo and Chokgyur Lingpa, two of the most celebrated masters associated with rimé in nineteenth-century Kham, he did not participate in the collection of visionary cycles and spiritual instructions that seemingly define the era. His primary institutional affiliations were all Nyingma, including Dzokchen, Gemang, Yarlung Pemakö, and Dzagyal monasteries. With that said, Patrul's biographers go out of their way to emphasize his ecumenical attitude. They note that he respected Longchenpa, Sakya Paṇḍita, and Tsongkhapa as equals, and that he had students from a variety of lineages and taught the *Bodhicaryāvatāra* using commentaries best suited to his specific audiences (a Sakya commentary for a Sakya audience, a Geluk commentary for a Geluk audience).

The two works that follow may offer some insight into the complexity of the issue of ecumenism in nineteenth-century Kham. *The Low-Born Sage Speaks* offers a playful take on the pettiness of sectarian competition, thereby displaying an ecumenical attitude toward all Buddhist lineages. The text opens with a visitor asking the sage to explain the differences between Dharma lineages (*chöluk*), wishing to know which ones are better and which worse. The sage artfully dodges the question by answering with reference to the entirety of the Buddha's teaching (*chö*) and tradition of practice (*luk*). While the questioner seemingly seeks a sectarian response, the sage treats it as an opportunity to speak about the practices that undergird all Buddhist teachings and practice, such as devotion to the guru and training one's mind through the discipline of mindfulness.

Patrul's refusal to play favorites among Tibetan Buddhist lineages calls to mind a hilarious story documented for posterity by E. Gene Smith.[4] Like the sage of our text, Patrul was practicing in a retreat cave when visitors arrived to ask him questions. They tried to ascertain Patrul's lineage affiliation through various means, finally asking for his secret name—the name that Patrul would have received when he took tantric vows. Their hope was that this name would reveal his lineage affiliation. Much to their shock, Patrul exposed himself, playing on the Tibetan word for "secret name" (*sangtsen*), which colloquially means "penis." This story speaks to Patrul's enjoyment of puns and wordplay. Such playfulness is in ample supply in his texts that appear in this volume.

A nonsectarian approach does not mean an uncritical acceptance of all Buddhists, however. *The Explanation of Chudrulü*, while also filled with punning and witty manipulation of language, shows a slightly different side of Patrul. It overtly criticizes an excessively scholastic approach to Buddhist training, one exemplified by the old men in the text. They are so singularly obsessed with the formal standards of textual commentary and monastic debate that they are blinded to the brilliance of the *chudrulü* teaching that

---

4. Smith 2001, 246. Sarah Harding also mentions this popular story in her contribution to this book.

they have just witnessed. The text is quite clear that these conservative monks are missing out on other expressions of the Buddha's teachings: teachings that are accessible to everyone, such as the six-syllable mantra (*oṃ maṇi padme hūṃ*).

One could read the text as a sectarian joke about Geluk monastic scholars, who are famous for emphasizing scholastic study and monastic debate above meditation and retreat practice. Still, since the Geluk lineage is never named in *The Explanation of Chudrulü*, one could just as well interpret Patrul's critique as directed at monks from all different lineages. The nineteenth century did find a variety of lineages in Kham, including the Nyingma, developing scholastic curricula for their monks. Patrul himself composed influential and technical scriptural commentaries and served for a time as the abbot of Dzogchen Monastery's Śrī Siṃha monastic college. Surely, Patrul did value the activities of composition, exposition, and debate. The humor of *The Explanation of Chudrulü* makes more sense as a playful teasing than an outright rejection. Even when making a joke, it seems, Patrul could be both accessible and cryptic, straightforward and nuanced, simple and profound.

Acknowledgments

Sincere thanks to Tulku Thondup, Lobsang Shastri, Ringu Tulku, Janet Gyatso, Marc-Henri Deroche, Jann Ronis, Kalsang Gurung, Douglas Duckworth, and the participants in the Translating Buddhist Luminaries conference, all of whom helped me immeasurably with these texts.

The Low-Born Sage Speaks: The Ladder to Liberation, a Treatise on Dharmic and Worldly Knowledge

by Dza Patrul Rinpoché

Homage to Avalokiteśvara

> The Terrifying one—known as *Time*
> forms food out of the threefold world
> vanquishing time itself: the sweet-voiced savior
> whose Residence Resounds with Sound.[5]

> There stays the low-born sage
> whose name is known as *Śrī*,
> wild, yet feigning discipline
> ablaze, presenting himself at peace.

> He has no good acts to offer
> but he has good speech to speak.
> So everyone comes to ask him questions
> and to them he counsels properly.

> Someone asks him:

> Hey! Great sage!
> *Dharma traditions*—what are they?
> *Dharma traditions*—how do you split them up?

---

5. The opening verses refer to the cave where Patrul composed this work, called Mañjughoṣa's Skeleton with Clenched Fangs Palace (Jampaiyang Kengrü Chewa Tsikpai Phodrang) in the colophon. Another name for this cave is embedded in the first verse, which finds Patrul playing on the word *dra*, a homonym meaning both "sound" and "enemy." This cave is where Patrul wrote his famous *Words of My Perfect Teacher*. In that text he calls his retreat shelter The Palace of the Terrifying One Lord Over Time and Enemies (Jikjé Düdrai Wangpoi Phodrang). See Dza Patrul 2009c, 560. For the English translation, see Patrul 2008, 374.

Dharma traditions—which do you cast aside?
Dharma traditions—which do you accept?

He says:

Dharma is everything to be known.
Tradition is the defining characteristic of that.
Dharma is the things to be taken and forsaken.
Tradition is the practice of that.

When you split up the Dharma—what is to be known—
you get two: the cycle of rebirth and liberation.
When you split up the Dharma—things to be taken and forsaken—
you get two: virtue and wrongdoing.

The first two are really suffering
　　—pacifying or not pacifying it.
The latter two are really suffering
　　—producing or not producing it.

Of those, the cycle of rebirth is what you should cast aside.
But if you don't cast aside the cause of the cycle—wrongdoing—
you can't cast aside the cycle.
So first cast aside wrongdoing.

Liberation from suffering is what you should accept.
But if you don't practice its cause—virtue—
you can't accept liberation from suffering.
So first accept virtue.

Even though you should cast aside the cycle of rebirth,
if you don't adhere to Dharma within the cycle
you can't enter the path of liberation from suffering.
So first it is crucial to know the nature of the cycle.

There are two great paths in this cycle of rebirth.
They are the straight and the crooked.
By the straight path you become a god or a human being.
By the crooked path, the bad rebirths.

In this realm here, if many people act straight
the divine realm above will fill right up.
In this realm here, if many people act crooked
the bad rebirths below will greatly increase.

The straight is what's known as the Dharma tradition of humans.
To act exceedingly straight, that is the Dharma tradition of gods.
The crooked is the Dharma tradition of degenerate actions.
The exceedingly crooked is the Dharma tradition of hell.

The straight—what is that?
It's having completely cast aside deceitfulness,
having aligned your mouth with your purpose,
having aligned the outside with the inside.

Your mouth is the talk that you speak. Your purpose is putting that
    talk into practice.
The outside is your body and your speech. The inside is your mind.

As for purpose:
For the crooked, since the mouth is straight though the inside is
    crooked, the outside seems straight. So the crooked is hidden by
    the straight. That is the Dharma tradition of degenerates.

Casting aside deceitfulness of the mind—
this alone is straight action.
It is the supreme Dharma tradition of humans.
All human Dharma is captured in this point.

The mental activity of desire is the crooked.
Minimizing desire is the straight.
If you cast aside the goal of accomplishing your desires
that is the Dharma tradition of gods.

All degenerate beings
with their crooked bodies act as frauds
with their crooked talk speak with deception
with their crooked minds conjure plans of seduction,
this encapsulates all undesirable behavior.

By these acts, you won't achieve your desires.
To these beings, gods and sages react with scorn.
For these beings, a bad rebirth does not far follow.

The exceedingly crooked act to hurt others.
They hide their true intentions and have deceitful minds.
Having rejected all paths of virtuous activity,
they will burn in the blazing fires of hell below the earth.

For this reason, you should cast these aside and accept the Dharma
    of the cycle of rebirth.
Knowing these instructions, you should stick to straight behavior.
A person who does so will obtain true liberation from suffering.
The cause of that liberation is the Conqueror's supreme teaching.

The Conqueror's teaching has two parts: scripture and realization.
Scripture is the Dharma that is explained.
Realization is practicing the meaning of that Dharma.
These two are equivalent to the three baskets of scripture and the
    three trainings, respectively.

The precious Vinaya, Sūtra, and Abhidharma
are the Sage's three baskets of scripture.
They are the Dharma of scripture—the Dharma that's explained.
Their words and meaning should be heard and reflected upon.

The precious conduct, concentration, and wisdom
are the Conqueror's sons' three trainings.
They are the Dharma of realization—the Dharma that's practiced.
These three should be put into practice and cultivated.

Even if you don't know
the entirety of the Sage's three baskets of scripture,
if you know the meaning of one word—
even that constitutes the teaching of scripture.

Even though it's difficult to complete
the entirety of the Conqueror's sons' three trainings,
if you arouse one virtuous mental moment—
even that constitutes the teaching of realization.

So if you desire to acquire the Conqueror's teaching,
don't look for the teaching outside, practice it inside.
If you internalize your practice, the teaching trains your mind.
If your mind is trained, that's liberation from suffering.

In this way, casting aside and accepting the cycle of rebirth and
     liberation
is just taking and forsaking virtue and wrongdoing. Still, now,
for the purpose of distilling the essential point of how to put this
     into practice,
listen and practice according to this explanation of how to cast away
     and take up
virtue and wrongdoing:

Virtue is a thought.
Wrongdoing is also a thought.
Knowing for sure that virtue and wrongdoing don't exist outside,
look for virtue and wrongdoing in your mind.

If your mind is virtuous, your body and speech are also virtuous.
If your mind does wrong, your body and speech also do wrong.
Therefore, the root of all Dharma is the mind, so it is said.

As the Supreme Sage said about the method for training the mind:
     "At all times, look at your own mind.
     At every moment, look at your own mind.
     In moments of nondistraction, look at your own mind.
     At every instant, look at your own mind.
     In times when many people are gathered and at times when you
          are alone,
     in these times, do it like this."

After you make such a virtuous vow,
establish mindful attention. Exhaustively,
at all times, look this way at your own mind.

When eating, and lying down, and going, and walking, and sitting,
in all paths of action, with mindful attention, watch your mind.
Dismissing both purposelessness and the desire to achieve something,
with awareness, at every moment, look this way at your own mind.

These very thoughts: they are absent of all extremes.
Thoughts left uninhibited, not cast aside: grab them with the hook
of mindfulness.
Neither casting aside nor accepting them: let thoughts be liberated
by themselves.
In moments of nondistraction, look this way at your own mind.

Moreover, since beginners have many distractions,
it's right for you to hold tight when mindfully looking at the mind.
Even so, when your own mind becomes distracted and mistaken: you
should investigate that!
At every instant, look this way at your own mind.

If you cultivate looking at the mind,
you'll come to know the mind's secret essential point.
If you come to know the mind's secret essential point,
you'll know the suchness of all things.
The very nature of all things
is this very same nature of the mind.

The way it is can't be expressed.
When you engage in analysis, knowledge becomes distant.
But if there is nothing to analyze, what do you realize?
Realizing and analyzing are merely conventions.
Beyond conventions is the ultimate meaning.
Knowing that is what's called liberation from suffering.

Hey friends! Look at your own minds.
Virtue, wrongdoing, the cycle of rebirth, liberation: they are all in
your own mind,
where there's no physical or verbal action at all.
Training your own mind is the Buddha's teaching.

Again, someone asks:

The three objects of refuge, the three vows,
the three vehicles: speak to me about these categories.
Explain how to condense each set of three categories into one.
Show me how each one can be sewn up into an essential point.

He says:

He who is not mistaken is the teacher.
The good path that is unmistaken is what he teaches.
He leads beings out of the depths of the cycle of rebirth.
The teacher is the refuge that is the Buddha.

That which does not deceive is the teaching.
If you practice in accordance with the teaching, you will not be
    deceived.
The source of protection that leads beings along the correct path—
that is the refuge that is the true Dharma.

Those who are not separated are practitioners.
The meaning of the teachings is what you shouldn't be separated
    from.
If you stick to it, you will become like the practitioners.
Such leaders are the refuge that is the Saṅgha.

The teacher is the Buddha and the source of protection is the true
    Dharma.
The leaders are the great Saṅgha. Liberation is the refuge you aspire to.
Whoever cleaves to them, at all times and moments, is never
    deceived.
I assert the perfect three objects of refuge to be like that.

The cycle of rebirth is a house of suffering.
For that reason, suffering is never not produced.
The state of mind that is certain in its desire to be liberated from
    that suffering
is the vow of individual liberation.

All beings in the three realms are your father and mother.
There is no one who has not cared for you with kindness at some
    time.
The state of mind that desires that they all attain buddhahood
is the bodhisattva vow.

The world and its inhabitants are a pure realm.
They never appear as impure.

Knowing the phenomenal world to be a *cakra-maṇḍala*
is the secret mantra vow.

Renunciation is the individual liberation vow. Benefitting others is
    the bodhisattva vow.
Pure vision is the secret mantra vow. Vowing not to harm others,
not to focus on one's own needs, and not to project qualities onto
    things—
I assert the three perfect vows to be like that.

Seeing the cycle of rebirth as a pit of fire.
Principally adhering to one's own needs.
Striving for the goal of liberation.
This is known as the Lesser Vehicle.

Seeing all beings as one's loving parents.
Principally adhering to the needs of others.
Striving for the goal of omniscience for all.
This is called the Great Vehicle.

Seeing the cycle of rebirth and liberation as equal.
Accomplishing one's own and others' needs equally.
Achieving spontaneous realization.
This is the Unsurpassed Vehicle.

Holding supreme one's own needs, others' needs, or the needs of
    both.
Acting with a small, middling, or great and powerful mental
    intention.
Fearing the cycle of rebirth, not fearing it, or being devoid of fear
    altogether.
I assert these practices to be the three perfect vehicles.

The three objects of refuge are encapsulated by the lord guru.
The three vows are encapsulated by abandoning thoughts.
The three vehicles are encapsulated by training your own mind.
All of them are encapsulated by realizing the suchness of things.

The supreme true guru: he is the essence of the three supreme jewels.
If you pacify your mind's thoughts: that completes the three vows.

If you train your mind with Dharma: that's the essential point of the
three vehicles, no other.
If you realize the suchness of your mind: you'll pacify thoughts, train
your mindstream, and mix your mind with your guru's.

It doesn't differentiate in the expanse of *dharmakāya*.
It enters into the union of the generation and completion stages as
sambhogakāya.
It conceives of beings with the compassion of the *nirmāṇakāya*.
The mind of the guru is Buddha.

It principally trains your afflictive emotions.
It gathers in brief only the most essential point of the entire Dharma.
It demonstrates the way of being of suchness.
The speech of the guru is the three baskets of Dharma.

It pacifies and trains with the method of *śrāvakas*.
It acts for the benefit of others with the method of bodhisattvas.
It is like a village of *ḍākas* and *ḍākinīs*.
The guru's body is the assembly (Saṅgha) of the three vehicles.

His mind: Buddha. Speech: true Dharma. Body: Saṅgha.
So the singular guru encapsulates all of the supreme jewels.
Knowing that, always follow him, envisioning him on the crown of
your head, never separated.
Like medicine, this brings you all blessings of the three objects of refuge.

The self is *brahman*, blissful, permanent.
Believing such improper views—
that is the root of all faults.
Abandon this thinking: that's individual liberation.

Seeing oneself as important
but not so others—
that is considering only oneself.
Abandoning this thinking: that's bodhicitta.

Becoming attached to ordinary appearances,
becoming attached to sublime deities—
that is projecting qualities onto things.

Abandoning this thinking is the mantra vow.

Not believing in what is false, not considering one's own needs only,
not projecting qualities onto things, not considering anything at all—
in such a state free of thoughts, purify all three vows at once and
    enter them.
Like rivers running into the great ocean, there is no inherent
    difference between them.

Not wanting to remain in the three realms,
eliminating grasping and craving,
training, primarily, the desiring mind—
this is the Lesser Vehicle.

Growing fond of beings out of compassion—
this is the mental attitude of great love.
Training, primarily, the mind of anger—
this is what's known as the Great Vehicle.

Unifying wisdom and skillful means, the generation-stage and
    completion-stage practices,
using the meditative concentration of great equanimity,
training, primarily, the delusionary mind—
this is the Unsurpassed Vehicle itself.

If you know there is no self, who gets attached? If self and other are equal,
    who do you hate?
When there is no self and other, things that appear separate to your
    mind are nondual in the expanse beyond the mind.
When experience becomes like this, that's what's called taming the mind.
    All phenomena come under your control.
For that reason, training the mind is no different than
    the three vehicles gathered together.

If you properly realize the suchness of mind,
you know the three objects of refuge to be one's own mind.
Your mind becomes mixed with the supreme guru's mind.
So it is condensed into that.

If you properly realize the suchness of mind,

thinking subsides just as it arises.
Thinking arises continually as wisdom.
So it is condensed into that.

If you properly realize the suchness of mind,
mental appearances and mind come under your control.
In the expanse of suchness, the cognizer is tamed.
So it is condensed into that.

In the expanse of suchness, the guru's mind is not different from
    your very own mind.
If you can rest there, all thinking subsides,
    and the three false poisons are properly tamed.
When you realize the refuse and remedy as one taste,
    you'll love all beings with compassion.
Realizing suchness, all things are subsumed, like the world in the
    empty expanse of space.

Insofar as all the buddhas
in dharmakāya's expanse are the same,
so too are all the gurus
in nirmāṇakāya's expanse just the same.

All gurus are buddhas.
The enlightened mind is inseparable from dharmakāya.
All buddhas are gurus.
Those fit for training appear as disciples.

Under the influence of how things are, the single moon
appears differently, over and over, greater or smaller.
Under the influence of the needs of disciples, the single guru
arrives over and over in manifold guises.

Under the influence of water bowls, the single moon
appears at one moment as many moons.[6]
Under the influence of many beings' minds, the single guru

---

6. The single moon appears, separately, in each water bowl as a reflection.

appears at the same time as many gurus.

Under the influence or absence of clouds, the single moon's
light rays appear variously, dim or bright.
Under the influence of thoughts, the single guru
appears variously as bad or good, faulty or virtuous.

Under the influence of your karma, the single moon
appears to each person, bringing cold weather or drought.
Under the influence of your desire, the single guru
appears as an object of faith or false views.

Under the influence of day and night, the single moon
appears to rise or set.
Under the influence of different beings' needs, the single guru
appears to leave or stay.

The body of all gurus is one.
Your root guru is genuinely enlightened.
He shows your own mind to be dharmakāya.
His kindness is greater than that of all buddhas.

The bodies of all gurus of the three lineages share the same essence.
All the many different gurus are undifferentiable.
Their actions are not distinct—they neither move nor rest.
Whatever they do is kindness. Realizing this is the root teaching.

One who acts according to others' needs is a guru.
One who accomplishes only his own needs is not.
One who teaches the three vehicles is a guru.
If he teaches what's not Dharma, he's not.

One who trains the minds of his students is a guru.
If he doesn't train minds, he's not.
If he applies himself to virtue, he is a guru.
If he does not apply himself to virtue, he's not.

One who benefits whomever he encounters is a guru.
One who doesn't benefit others is not.
One who possesses a compassionate mind is a guru.

If he's without compassion, he's not.

Those that are called guru,
while they may have different qualities and manifestations,
their dharmakāya is equal, their enlightened activity is equal,
and their aspiration and benefit to beings is equal.

One who teaches Dharma to meet the needs of others,
    who trains his students' mindstreams,
who introduces whomever he meets to the path of true virtue,
at whose root is the compassionate mind;
he is a guru. All who are like that are equal.

Depending on a guru and serving a guru,
these are the condensation of the 84,000 entryways to the Dharma.
The single, final, essential point of those entryways is devotion:
the singular, sufficient, pure remedy.

It unlocks the door to all Dharma.
It clears the obstacles to all practice.
It brings out the benefits of all oral instructions.
It is devotion, and should be known as such.

It is offering a request to the guru's completely compassionate mind
and it becomes a vessel for all blessings.
It gathers the quintessence of all meditative accomplishments.
It is devotion—the singular, sufficient, pure remedy.

It can't be conquered by any demons.
It can't be stopped by obstacles.
It cleanses itself of all defiling stains.
It is devotion, and should be known as such.

It prevents the birth of false desires.
At the time of death there's no pain of life suddenly cut short.
It pacifies the false appearances of the *bardo*.
It is devotion, and should be known as such.

In this life, the true ones adhere to it.
At the moment of death, it arises as your guru's visage.
In the next life it'll send you to a pure realm.
It is devotion, and should be known as such.

It's inseparable from the objects of refuge gathered together.
It brings quickly whatever one wants.
It ultimately accomplishes both one's own needs and others'.
It is devotion, and should be known as such.

It raises thoughts to the status of virtuous mental states.
It grows in the context of realizing the stages and the paths.
It ultimately causes your mind to mix with the guru's.
It is devotion, and should be known as such.

Guru devotion is just this:
if you accomplished it by invariably relying on the guru,
whether you offered reverence or not,
whether you made supplication prayers or not,
it clears away the obstacles to receiving the blessings that are
    gathered together in the essential oral instructions.
It clears away all of the false appearances of birth, death, and the *bardo*,
    and thereby brings bliss.
It accomplishes whatever one desires, and finally leads you to achieve
    buddhahood.
It is devotion. It is the single essential point of thousands of oral
    instructions.

The method of depending on the guru is devotion.
    It is not offering reverence.
The method of practicing for the guru is devotion.
    It is not offering supplication prayers.
Where there is devotion, anything that you've done becomes a
    blessing.
Where there is no devotion, anything that you've done will be
    without benefit.

The three vows and the three vehicles,
while different in name, have a single meaning.
Abandoning thinking and subduing one's mindstream

are different in name, but have a single meaning.
Therefore, all are condensed into one.
By means of the guru's advice, subdue one's own mindstream.
These are one hundred waters below a single bridge.
Six are condensed into one, as are nine condensed into one.[7]

What's called "the mindstream" is thinking.
There is no mindstream that doesn't consist of thinking.
Training thoughts is the doorway to the Dharma.
84,000 teachings are thus condensed into one.

In this way, whatever appears in the cycle of rebirth
is merely imputed by the process of thought.
In this way, so too even liberation from suffering
is merely imputed by the process of thought.

Thus virtue and wrongdoing are thoughts.
What is path and what is not are thoughts.
Self and selflessness are merely thoughts.

All doxographic views are thoughts.
So training the process of thought
is the essential point of all the earlier and later teachings.[8]
What was taught earlier is taught again now.
Because of its great meaning, I will repeat it and explain.

If you ask, "How do you train thoughts?"
First, differentiate and train thoughts.
In the middle, look at and train thoughts.
In the end, establish and train thoughts.

---

7. The six (three vows and three vehicles) are condensed into the one practice of subduing one's mindstream. Likewise, the nine (three vows, three vehicles, and three objects of refuge that amount to the guru) are condensed into the one practice of subduing one's mindstream.

8. This may well be a reference to the earlier spreading (*nga dar*) and the later spreading (*chi dar*) of the Dharma to Tibet. But it also likely refers to Patrul's own teaching in this text—his response to the first (earlier) questions and his response to the second (later) question.

First, divide thoughts into white and black.
Increase white and eliminate black.
Faith, bodhicitta, and wisdom are white.
Desire, anger, and delusion are black.
The three whites are on the side of liberation.
As one they are virtue: temporary or profound.
The three black ones are on the side of wrongdoing.
As one they are misdeeds: temporary or profound.

Faith gathers together all roots of virtue.
Bodhicitta is the ground of the Great Bodhisattva Vehicle in its
    entirety.
Wisdom is the root of the path to liberation in its entirety.
Therefore, these three should be generated.

Desire grasps at all worldly existence.
Anger generates all suffering.
Delusion is both ground and fruit of desire and anger.
Therefore, these three should be cast aside.

Confidence in the true Dharma is faith.
Wishing to meet others' needs and have them reach buddhahood is
    bodhicitta.
Realizing that all things are not real is the supreme wisdom.
These three purify the three poisons and clear away the two
    obscurations.

In the middle, look at and train thoughts.
Grasp them freely with mindfulness, without sending them away.
Later, when they transform, do not let them escape,
    but sustain them with attentiveness.
At the moment of recognizing them, look at their nature.

By merely having looked, you will recognize them as empty.
Entering into analysis of them is not needed.
Free of movement and without substance, they are empty of essence.
The nature of this emptiness is self-radiant clarity.

If you know this empty nature of mind,
you know the empty nature of all things.

Analyzing various objects is unnecessary.
If you cut the root, the branches dry up.

Because this mind of yours is the ground of all things,
the emptiness of mind is the emptiness of all things.
The mental state immediately after having seen this is itself empty.
There is no leisure time for extensive analysis of it.

In the end, meet the face of mind.
It is inexpressible, unimaginable.
It is not an object perceived. It's without a fixed point of reference.
It is what's called "luminous clarity."

If you realize the meaning of being free from "being this,"
the experience emerges of being without a reference point.
Realization or nonrealization: who is it who knows them?
Search for where "what is to be realized" and "that which realizes" are.

At that point, it's not necessary to cast aside thoughts.
Cunning is not necessary, nor is control.
You don't forge a path, nor is liberation necessary.
It puts itself in its own place, and is liberated on its own.

At the time of appearing it is empty, at the time of being empty it
    appears.
Appearance and emptiness undifferentiated are self-radiant clarity.
The compassionate energy of clarity is not at all restricted.

The nature of wisdom—self-liberated subject and object—
and of stainless mind is radiant clarity.
The nature of suchness—nondual subject and object—is bodhicitta.

Seeing this innate, great, bliss truth
is the fruit of the path of devotion to your guru.
Of all methods for training thoughts
mindfulness is the root one, just that.

First, deliberate attention. In the middle, mindfulness of the expanse.
In the end, absence of mindfulness, which is a state of radiant clarity.

Through mindfulness you cast aside all wrongdoing.
Through mindfulness you bring all virtue together.
Through mindfulness you train your own mind.
Mindfulness is the root of all Dharma.

When you are in the midst of many people, rely on mindfulness.
When you are alone, too, rely on mindfulness.
At all times, rely on mindfulness.
When you have a single nondistracted moment, rely on mindfulness.

Devotion is the nose-rope entrusted into the hand of the guru.
Mindfulness is a stake that prevents wavering, planted into the ground.
Using various methods, train your own mind.
Such a person, supreme, rides the Great Vehicle.

A work that makes divisions is a scripture.
One that assembles the essential point is a pith instruction.
One that brings together scripture and pith instruction—
know such speech to be the kindness of your guru.

May whatever virtue that comes from delivering this teaching
coalesce in the mind of the one who requested it.
Until the state of perfect omniscience,
may it continually be so!

Thus composed the great scholar of Kham, known as Śubhaṃśrī, in Mañjughoṣa's Skeleton with Clenched Fangs Palace.

The Explanation of Chudrulü

by Dza Patrul Rinpoché

The explanation of *chudrulü*:

> Reverence to you, Gentle Protector, sun of the heart
> who possesses the thorough and perfect knowledges
> of phenomena and their meaning, confident eloquence, and the
>   etymology of words.
> Reverence to you.

Here, it will be explained:

At one time, some old people were resting, in relaxation, when some young people passed by, heading off in a different direction to do some errands. Having headed off, and eventually having completed whatever they had to do, they came back.

So the old men asked them,

> Young men who should live for many years hence, what have you heard, what have you understood, what do you have to explain to us?

The youth said in response,

> Oh respected elders of many years, we haven't heard anything, understood anything, and we have nothing to explain to you at all. *Chudrulü.*

The old men said,

> Youngsters, we understood some of what you just said. But some we did not understand.

> Namely, with regard to the word *heard*, we asked you if you had heard, via your ear canals, any conversation from the various places where

you traveled. To that question, you said you did not. That much we understood.

With regard to the word *understood*, we asked whether you had attained certainty with respect to something new on the basis of hearing or seeing someone doing something—such that you could think to yourselves "that's the way it is." To that question, you said there was no such thing. That much we also understood.

However, when you youth said *chudrulü*, we did not understand. What is that? Please explain what that is.

The youth said,

While you comprehend well the meaning of the word *heard* and the meaning of the word *understood*, we will elucidate the meaning of *chudrulü* by giving examples.

The old men said,

Youngsters, what is an example of *chudrulü*? Explain how its meaning works.

The youth said,

We'll give you three meanings of *chudrulü* and also three metaphorical examples.

Chu [water] is as follows:

Water comes from the Great Ocean for the purpose of eliminating stains and eliminating the thirst of the world. It goes from place to place. Finally, it flows and spills back into the Great Ocean, which is the resting place for all water.[9] Still, that water has had nothing at all added to or taken away from it. Nor is the water ever sullied or stained. Just as it is when it leaves the Great Ocean, so it is when it returns to the Great Ocean, once again. And yet, on its way about the world, different people drink it, bathe with it, channel it, and so on. So it seems.

---

9. This is a traditional Tibetan conception of the path of rivers: from the ocean, to the ocean.

In the very same way, we youth leave our homes for various purposes. We go from place to place, meet different people in these places, talk about things, enjoy ourselves, and so on. Still, there is nothing new to understand that we had not heard, understood, or known before we left. Our leaving is just like the example of water.

That's the first metaphorical example and its meaning.

Dru [boats], furthermore, is as follows:

For the purpose of transporting people, boats go from one side of the river to the other and then come back again. They go and return continually. Sometimes boats transport merchants, sometimes other guests: women, monks, gurus, brahmans, thieves, butchers, and so on. But after they come back again, however they were before they left, they are still that way. They aren't filled with anything new, nor have they been depleted of anything. They don't do anything different for good passengers or bad. Still, while boats exist in the exact same way as they did before their trip, afterward they must go again, repeatedly, from the near side to the far side, and from the far side to the near side.

In the very same way, we leave our homes and go to other people's homes and then later come back to our own homes. Thus we continually go out from our own homes, return, and so on. During that time, sometimes we meet and see men, sometimes women, and sometimes children. Still, we never hear anything or understand anything new from them that we had not heard or understood previously. In this example, just like boats, we repeatedly, again and again, must go out from and return to our homes.

That's the second metaphorical example and its meaning.

Lü [body] is as follows:

For the purpose of crossing over rivers, people's bodies enter boats and emerge again out of boats. Upon entering a boat, a person does not accomplish or gain anything at all. Nothing at all is left over or remains[10] of that person in the boat. The boat is just as it was before. The person is also just as he was before he entered, or after he emerged from, the boat. Still, it is not the

---

10. Here Patrul puns on the verb "to remain" (*lüpa*), which has the same root as the word for "body" (*lü*).

case that no purpose is accomplished at all when a person enters a boat to cross a river.

Just like in this example, we also go out from our own homes, enter others' homes, and emerge again. Still, there is absolutely nothing new for us to explain that we had not heard or understood prior. But it is not the case that we do not take care of our own business while out. Therefore, it is like the example of bodies entering boats.

That's the third metaphorical example and its meaning.

Furthermore, water is the base, boats enter water, and bodies subsequently enter boats. Boats rest on water and bodies rest in boats. For that reason, we presented the three examples of *chu*, *dru*, and *lü* in that order—according to the order of support and thing supported.

Also, for the purpose of performing ritual ceremonies, or for the purpose of offering virtuous kindness toward people from different places who have become sick or who have died, we commonly attend gatherings of the monastic community. There, we recite mantras, chant, meditate, and so on. Sometimes we also leave our homes for some minor personal business.

We will therefore set forth three sets of metaphorical examples for you, in order, in relation to these activities.

Going out for the purpose of ritual ceremonies sponsored by a patron is connected with the example of water. Water eliminates stains, eliminates the thirst of beings, and accomplishes various benefits. It keeps people alive. And in the end, it enters the Great Ocean.

In the same way, in our activities, we eliminate the stain of illness. And we activate the power of medicines and so on that wipe out any harm caused by demons, harm that is comparable to the thorn-like pain of thirst. We bring about various benefits and keep the sick alive for a long time. At the end of all that work, by offering a final dedication prayer, we cause the merit of our virtuous activity to flow into the ocean of omniscience. In this way these pursuits of ours are connected to the example of water.

Because we transfer the consciousness of dead people to a new resting place, our job of keeping the dead company is connected to the example of boats.

Sometimes guests, who are on the near side of a river, wish to go to the far side. Because the great river cuts off the path to that far side, however, they are not able to cross by their own power. For those like us, who rely on the great boat of the noble community and the true Dharma, it is easy to transfer the *bardo* consciousness—which is just like a person stuck in the middle of a river—and set it down on the dry land of liberation. Therefore our work of transferring the consciousness of the recently deceased is just like the example of a boat.

Going out for the purpose of small, provisional business is connected to the example of bodies. You do not enter a boat, you know, for the good of the river. Nor do you enter a boat for the good of the boat. Nor for anyone else, for that matter. To the contrary, you only put your body into a boat for your own sake, or maybe . . . also for the sake of the hat and clothing that you're wearing.

In the same way, when we go out to take care of some small, provisional, personal business, we only go out for the purpose of accomplishing our own small needs . . . and the needs of our friends, like you guys, who depend on us. So, going out for no other business than our own is like the example of bodies.

In terms of these three examples, we do have our own business of whatever kind to be done. But there are absolutely no other things beyond that business to be heard, to be understood, or to be explained. So, beyond whatever business we go out to take care of for ourselves, there is absolutely nothing to be heard, to be understood, or to be explained. Thus we present you with the three *chudrulü* metaphorical examples and their meanings.

> If you were to try to write down the meaning of *chudrulü*
> you could use up all of the paper that you could find at the store
> and all of the ink that a scholar possesses,
> but you would never deplete our intelligence.
> Nor would you use up the meaning of *chudrulü*.

The old men answered:

> *Oṃ maṇi padme hūṃ.*
> To you, the compassionate, who always looks
> with an eye toward the six realms of beings,

those who are always generating suffering,
reverent homage to you, our protector.

Some composers of tantric commentaries
correctly affix meaningless grammatical particles and ornamental
    words
to the true root words of the tantra.
Your treatment of *chudrulü* violates this approach.

In terms of looking for evidence that you composed
your commentary in accord with the tantra,
the *chudrulü* explanation does not use the support
of any scriptural testimony, such as explanatory tantras and
    treatises.

Having arranged confusing words in a way that is easy to follow,
your composition is just a heap of meaningless commentaries.

Upon analysis, there are also some contradictions,
like your commentary and root words being disconnected.
And no one has subjected your commentary to monastic debate.
Please elaborate with an additional explanation.

The youth responded to this:

Since engaging in explanation, debate, and composition
is, in general, indispensable for leaders of monasteries,
you too have composed this polemical critique.
And although you have done so,
the explanation of *chudrulü*
is nonetheless well known to scholars at superior monasteries.

The composer, named Gewai Pal,[11]
is one whose intelligence gained from meditation is entirely lucid.

---

11. Gewai Pal is an inversion of Patrul's own name: Palgé. Palgi Gewa, a few lines below, is another reference to Patrul's name.

Like the example of a butter flame inside of a vase,
he has the power to decide the moment of his own death.[12]

It is not possible that he would be without confidence,
knowing as he does that he can never be trampled in debate.
Nor is it possible that he would ever speak nonsense.
The composer of the commentary, Palgi Gewa,
has the understanding gained from opening hundreds of texts
and the confident eloquence from publicly speaking hundreds of
    words.

If he were to be the defendant in a debate, he would propose a firm
    thesis,
as he has the intelligence to prove his assertion.
If he were the opponent, he would engage in sharp debate
as he has the knowledge to destroy another's assertions.

His intellect, just like a burning bonfire,
can use anything for fuel.
He is an elder of excellent intelligence.
He is a master of one thousand disciples.
He is the embodiment of many scholars.
And a metaphorical teaching that comes from him is extremely
    difficult to challenge.

The six-syllable *mani* is said to be the essence of the Dharma.
As for its spreading, it has spread throughout Tibet.
As for its fame, even old women know it.
As for being recited, even beggars recite it.
As for being written, even children know how to write it.
But for those who compose scholarly treatises,
the *mani* has no value for them.

That root word in three syllables, *chudrulü*,
has in the past been transmitted from ear to ear.

---

12. The butter-fueled flame is protected by the vase. No one can put it out. Rather, it
burns out slowly, on its own. Patrul likewise is not subject to disturbance by others. He
has the capacity to control his own fate.

But—not including the one who made the commentary upon it—
it is said that it has never been rendered into metaphorical
    examples.

With regard to your point that the explanation
does not add grammatical endings to the "root text,"
the explanation itself is the teaching that matters.
It does not establish the meaning of something beyond itself.

In regards to your assertion about the root tantra,
we asserted in various contexts
the relationship of the commentary to the three—*chu, dru, lü.*
If you claim the contrary, it will be difficult to prove.
Because of the relationship explained, the explanation is "a
    connection."[13]

The complete Kangyur and Tengyur are well known, like the
    wind.
But knowledge is that which corrects scripture.
It is well known to society's many scholars
that there is no need for scriptural quotations over and above
    knowledge.
Even if there were a need for such quotations,
he, Gewai Pal, would be able to provide them.

With respect to the arrangement of words that are easy to follow,
while there is a general system for how to make commentaries on the
    Kangyur and Tengyur,
some transmit practice to be their method instead.
Some in the tradition of the Nyingma and Bön
have this approach, while other groups of people do not.

---

13. The youth are punning on the Tibetan word for *tantra* (*gyü*). The word *gyü*,
while generally referring to *mantrayāna* root texts (*tantras*) upon which scholars write
commentaries, also has the meaning of "a connection." While the youths' explanation
of *chudrulü* is, of course, not at all like a commentary on a root tantra, it is in fact a
demonstration of a "connection," namely their capacity to make connections between the
syllables and their eloquent interpretations.

Furthermore, if there are many contradictions
to be shown, who will show them?
If there are no contradictions, holding a debate would be foolish.

May it be auspicious! May it be auspicious! May it be auspicious!

Translated Works

Dza Patrul Orgyen Jikmé Chökyi Wangpo (Rdza dpal sprul O rgyan 'jigs med chos kyi dbang po). 2009a. *Chos dang 'jig rten shes pa'i bstan bcos gdol pa'i drang srong gi gtam thar pa'i them skas.* Collected Works, vol. 1, 391–408. Chengdu: Si khron mi rigs dpe skrun khang.
———. 2009b. *Chu gru lus kyi rnam bshad.* Collected Works, vol. 1, 489–98.

Suggested Readings

Dilgo Khyentse. 1992. *The Heart Treasure of the Enlightened Ones.* Translated by Padmakara Translation Group. Boston: Shambhala Publications.
Khenpo Ngawang Pelzang. 2004. *A Guide to the Words of My Perfect Teacher.* Translated by Padmakara Translation Group. Boston: Shambhala Publications.
Low, James, trans. 1998. *Simply Being: Texts in the Dzogchen Tradition.* London: Vajra Press.
Patrul Rinpoche. 1998. *The Words of My Perfect Teacher.* Translated by Padmakara Translation Group. Boston: Shambhala Publications.
Reynolds, John Myrdhin, ed. 1996. *The Golden Letters: The Three Statements of Garab Dorjé.* Ithaca, NY: Snow Lion Publications.
Thondup, Tulku. 1997. *Enlightened Living: Teachings of Tibetan Buddhist Masters.* Edited by Harold Talbott. Hong Kong: Rangjung Yeshe Publications.

Additional References

Dodrupchen Jikmé Tenpai Nyima (Rdo grub chen 'Jigs med bstan pa'i nyi ma). 2003. *Mtshungs bral rgyal ba'i myu gu o rgyan 'jigs med chos kyi dbang po'i rtogs brjod phyogs tsam gleng ba bdud rtsi'i zil thigs.* Collected Works, vol. 5, 451–81. Chengdu: Si khron mi rigs dpe skrun khang.
Dza Patrul Orgyen Jikmé Chökyi Wangpo. 2009c. *Rdzogs pa chen po klong chen snying tig gi sngon 'dro'i khrid yig kun bzang bla ma'i zhal lung.* Collected Works, vol. 7, 1–561.
Schapiro, Joshua. 2011. "Nothing to Teach: Patrul's Peculiar Preaching on Water, Boats, and Bodies." *Revue d'Études Tibétaines* 22: 243–77.
Smith, E. Gene. 2001. *Among Tibetan Texts.* Edited by Kurtis R. Schaeffer. Boston: Wisdom Publications.

3. Dictums for Developing Virtue

Shangtön Tenpa Gyatso
Translated by Gedun Rabsal and Nicole Willock

Expressing Human Virtues

This chapter presents the didactic aphorisms found in Shangtön Tenpa Gyatso's *Jeweled Rosary of Advice*, a work belonging to the literary genre of *michö*, meaning "human virtue." The michö label often appears paired with the term *lhachö*, which refers to behavior conducive to positive future lives or to Buddhist practice broadly speaking. In contrast, michö instructions generally focus on human activities concerning this current life.[1] The colophon to *A Jeweled Rosary of Advice* identifies Shangtön's work as a commentary to *A Rosary of Essential Human Virtues*, composed centuries earlier by Dromtön Gyalwai Jungné (1004/5–64).[2] Fitting to the michö genre, both Dromtön and Shangtön's works provide playful proverbs that address the nature of our mortal existence.

By translating Shangtön's lively text, we hope to correct the misperception that all Geluk monastic scholars of the late nineteenth century were biased toward their own teachings and practices. In fact, many were not.

---

1. R.A. Stein, in his seminal introduction to Tibetan civilization, views a connection between ancient Tibetan ethics and the later development of michö as a literary genre of didactic aphorisms. He argues that michö maxims "bear the stamp of Chinese ethical and Buddhist religious ideas. But . . . retain a purely Tibetan flavor." See Stein 1972, 259.

2. Shangtön 2004, 286. Dromtön's Tibetan text is entitled *Michö Nekyi Trengwa*.

The Geluk polymath Shangtön Tenpa Gyatso (1825–97) was of the latter group. Shangtön was "someone who clearly upheld his own sect's theories and practices (*drubta*) and yet did not oppose, look down upon, or insult other sects," thus personifying this contemporary definition of *rimé*.[3]

Relative to other Buddhist luminaries that appear in this anthology, Shangtön is little known in the West, so a few words on his life and legacy may be helpful. Born into a family of humble means, Shangtön eventually joined the ranks of prominent Geluk monastic literati while also becoming an accomplished severance (*chö*) practitioner. Shangtön was born in the village of Khotsé, one of the spiritual communities surrounding the large monastic complex of Labrang Tashikhyil in Amdo.[4] At age seven, he took his initiate vows and received the name Könchok Thapkhé—a name that would stay with him long after his death, most commonly in the form Akhu Thapkhé ("Monk Thapkhé"). At age thirteen, he took up study at Labrang Tashikhyil, where he quickly excelled. He received an elite education in Buddhist dialectics from the foremost nineteenth-century luminaries of Labrang, but he never studied at any of the "three great seats of learning" in Lhasa (Drepung, Sera, and Ganden). His choice reflected a growing trend among accomplished Geluk scholars to study exclusively in Amdo, a pattern that continued into the twentieth century, as exemplified by some of His Holiness the Fourteenth Dalai Lama's teachers.[5] At age twenty-one, Shangtön took full monastic vows and eventually earned the scholastic degrees of *rabjampa* and *kachuwa*. His colleagues repeatedly recognized Shangtön for his erudition, appointing him as tutor to important incarnate lamas and Geluk hierarchs. While Shangtön joined the ranks of the elite Geluk literati in Amdo, he also remained a devout and open-minded practitioner. For example, he received severance instructions at age sixty-five from a female practitioner named Gungru Khandroma. He later authored her biography, making public his reverence for her.

Shangtön had ambivalent feelings about his elite status. Toward the end of his life, he was asked to pass on numerous transmissions to high-positioned lamas. By most accounts this would be considered an honor. Yet Shangtön reportedly stated, "I am not any better off for giving teachings to these high-ranking lamas. In fact, it is somewhat annoying and uncomfortable. Neverthe-

---

3. This definition of *rimé* appears in Dungkar Losang Trinlé 2002, 1918.

4. Nietupski 2011, 60.

5. Jikmé Damchö Gyatso (1898–1946) was exclusively schooled in Amdo, for example. His Holiness the Dalai Lama's teachings on *drang-ngé* (provisional and definitive teachings) are based on Jikmé Damchö Gyatso's writings.

less, I could never turn down such requests. Besides, transmitting teachings is important work."[6]

Shangtön's contributions to Tibetan literary form are well represented by *A Jeweled Rosary of Advice*. The text follows the formal features of its literary predecessor, Dromtön's *Rosary of Essential Human Virtues*, in both style and content. Shangtön closely emulates Dromtön's *Rosary* by using a nine-syllable meter and directly citing Dromtön's words of advice. Yet Shangtön plays with the conventions of the michö genre, freely expressing his own voice and establishing new discursive terrain on which later Tibetan writers would build. For instance, he engages the long-deceased author in debate by presenting counterarguments to Dromtön's original statements. While Dromtön originally advises, "Whatever you do, getting along with others is fundamental to human virtues," Shangtön counters, "While getting along with others is fundamental, mimicking everything you see is brainless."

The colophon states that the intended audience of the text is one of Shangtön's attendants by the name of Thayé Gyatso, who had requested teachings from his master. He is likely the "son" or "disciple" addressed in the text. But Shangtön's style and language indicate that his writing is intended not only for elite monastics. Shangtön's succinct and straightforward style emphasizing human virtues is fitting to the michö genre. Note the forthright tone and colloquial language in pithy phrases such as "Don't make promises to just anybody; shame comes from not keeping them. Be practical!"

A Jeweled Rosary of Advice imparts advice to a wide spectrum of people: from drunkards to *geshés*, from merchants to *ngakpas*, from servants to aristocrats, from murderers to those who give life (mothers and fathers). This further supports the contention that the text is meant to address the lives of all sorts of people, not just an elite group of scholars. A broad audience would be capable of embracing many of his ideas, such as the imperative of being honest with oneself:

No one else can throw you into heaven by your hands.
No one else can throw you into hell by your feet.
Happiness and suffering lie in your own hands.
Don't deceive yourself—that is essential!

Other phrases of direct speech such as "listen now!" and the use of colloquialisms, particularly in the Amdo dialect (e.g., *kyakshor*, "cowardly"), also point to a wide-ranging intended audience.

---

6. Losang Tsultrim Gyatso 2004, 116.

Shangtön's penchant for playfulness has had a tremendous influence on Tibetan scholars, particularly his technique of engaging the dead in debate. While traveling to Gönlung Monastery, Shangtön traversed the town of Yadzi (in today's Hualong County of Qinghai Province) and condemned it as a hell realm in the following verse:

This road I take from Labrang to the north is as arduous as the
narrow *bardo* pass.
The arid plain devoid of water and grass with many barbarian towns
en route.
Like *torma*, mountains red of blood and flesh, with people as poor as
hungry ghosts.
I think this is a hell realm, when I recall my birthplace Tseshung and
its fields of herbs.[7]

The twentieth-century monastic scholar the Sixth Tseten Zhabdrung Jikmé Rikpai Lodrö (1910–85) was born in Yadzi a decade after Shangtön's death and naturally disagreed with Shangtön's hellish characterization of his birthplace. Drawing upon Shangtön's technique of playing with the words of a deceased master, the Sixth Tseten Zhabdrung here emulates the meter of Shangtön's verse but offers a counterargument. Yadzi is now an unequivocally positive place, comparable to Jālandhara, which for this group of Tibetan scholars was considered the site of the Fourth Buddhist Council (ca. 150 CE):

The mountains, appearing devoid of green pasture,
resemble to me a relative of Jālandhara,
a natural coral in color, without applying paint,
radiating inner heat of *tummo*: a sacred site.[8]

Just as Shangtön debates with the long-deceased Dromtön Gyalwai Jungné in *A Jeweled Rosary of Advice*, here Tseten Zhabdrung takes on Shangtön.

Shangtön's words of advice continue to be used in new and innovative ways by contemporary Tibetan artists and intellectuals. Notice, for example, the ubiquity of the famous maxim from *A Jeweled Rosary of Advice*, "While knowing many languages is praiseworthy, forgetting your mother tongue is shameful." Shangtön's judgment has taken on new shades of meaning in

---

7. Tseten Zhabdrung 1987, 503.
8. Tseten Zhabdrung 1987, 503; cf. Willock 2011, 121–23.

the sociopolitical context of modern Tibetan culture. Numerous Tibetan-language blogs feature the maxim.[9] A recent short film even organizes its narrative around the aphorism. The story concerns a young Tibetan girl living in an anonymous Chinese city who has forgotten her cultural roots. The final frames consist of the maxim only—it occupies the screen for one full minute, as if the filmmaker is arguing with the lead character for not adhering to Shangtön's advice.[10]

Our complete translation of *A Jeweled Rosary of Advice* is the first attempt to translate any of Shangtön's works for an English-language readership. The text is predominantly clear-cut and not overly difficult to render into English. But we have not attempted to recreate the nine-syllable meter of Shangtön's verse. Instead, we translated the aphorisms into pithy statements fitting to the English language. Line and paragraph breaks follow the grammatical shifts in the Tibetan, with a line space indicating a shift in topic or sentiment. The most difficult aspect of the translation concerns Shangtön's heavy use of colloquialisms. Although one of the translators is a native of Amdo, we still felt the need to consult another native speaker about select terms. We therefore wish to thank Geshe Lobten for his contributions.

---

9. Although Tibetan-language blogs frequently appear and disappear on the web, the following posts emphasize the issue of Tibetan language preservation by drawing upon Shangtön's saying: http://www.ihearttibet.org/music-from-tibet/30-alphabets, http://blog .amdotibet.cn/pengmao/archives/93014.aspx, http://blog.amdotibet.cn/group/5/default .aspx (all accessed August 29, 2013).

10. The short film could be found at http://www.bodrigs.com/entertainment/video/ 2012-03-23/44.html as of August 2013.

A Jeweled Rosary of Advice

by Shangtön Tenpa Gyatso

Homage to the Guru! As a disciple of a holy lama, a great spiritual master, I have heard many teachings and thus became an eloquent speaker. As I have spent time among people of diverse ethnicities, I am very worldly. So, my dear disciple, I have something to tell you, and it is this:

> While getting along with others is fundamental, mimicking everything you see is brainless.
> While knowing many languages is praiseworthy, forgetting your mother tongue is shameful.
> While acting in accordance with customs is virtuous, breaking the laws of the Buddhadharma is rotten-hearted.
> While feverishly working for the benefit of others carries merit, bringing suffering upon yourself causes your downfall.
> While not insulting others is smart, not differentiating between good and bad is foolish.
> While not having attachments to wealth is beneficial, being overly cautious is cowardly; and you lose two by grasping at one—what a waste!
> While upholding the public good is constructive, being overly careful is unfortunate.
> You may accrue bounteous fortune, but showing it off in public calls a *gongdré*[11] spirit.
> You may uphold superior standards for everyone, but excessive arrogance causes disaster for yourself and others.
> You may be a *geshé*, but insulting others excessively invites enemies.
>
> While kindly fostering subordinates is agreeable, playing favorites drives disputes.

---

11. By showing off one's wealth, one tempts others to take it away. A *gongdré* is a type of spirit known for destroying wealth.

While being respected as head of the assembly is proper, not
differentiating among ranks destroys customs.
Although it's necessary to pay respects to those equal in rank, being
excessively pompous makes you a monkey.[12]
While teaching the Dharma to everyone is beneficial, done with
excessive frequency, it becomes a beggar's mantra.
Although necessary to explicate matters to your examiners, by talking
too much, you can end up with your head cut off.
Although not concerning yourself with fees for teaching is vital, if
gold has no value, then it becomes dirt and stone.
While hiding profound tantric teachings is appropriate, if too
secretive, the instructions will rot from within.

Ah—these are coarse words of counsel! Nonetheless, since this is
heart advice, please listen now!
Without clairvoyance, finding confidence in friendship is challenging.
If you don't trust anyone, you are like a ghost.
If you trust everyone, you will be ruined.
So the art of friendship is found through your enemies—this is
profound!

Even to your dear friends and beloved children, don't reveal heart
advice prematurely; hide it for a while!
In times of rapturous joy or in moments of anger lie the dangers of
expressing whatever is on your mind!
Therefore practice mindfulness first and hold utterances in your
throat—this is virtuosity!

Even if you keep horrific misconduct secret, shame will accompany
eventual revelations.
For that reason, with every action of body and speech, don't perform
misconduct—this is wisdom!

Chiseling away at your faults is appropriate.
For others to follow your example is appropriate.
For you to follow the example of others is even more appropriate.
Therefore analyzing and thinking sensibly is essential!

---

12. Makes you a "copycat."

A nasty person speaks about others behind their backs.
Knowingly being dishonest is cruel.
However, it is rare to acknowledge one's own misconduct, and it is
    more comfortable to ignore others' misdeeds.

Explaining excellence to trustworthy people is unnecessary.
Giving them delicacies and fineries is also pointless.
In times of need, whatever good or bad ensues, caring for the needy
    with love and honesty—this is magnificent!

Since this is heart advice, please listen now!

Ethnicities are as different as uneven horsehairs.
Thoughts are as dissimilar as bolts of colorful Nepali cloth.
It follows that without scrutinizing first, giving heart advice too soon
    is erroneous.

Impulsiveness and friendliness get mixed up.
Cruelty and compassion are easily confused.
What starts out good can later become bad.
Therefore trusting without discernment is misguided!

Placing trust in the actions of improper people—those who drink,
    sing, play dice, and gamble, or those who mimic everything they
    hear and see, or do whatever is on their mind—is mistaken!
Like asking a dog to guard raw meat, it is wrong to trust your wealth
    to careless people.
It is wrong to take as students unfaithful people who insult teachers
    while folding their hands in devotion.
Taking an uncompassionate person who trades teachings for wealth
    as a teacher is misguided!
Ignorant of your kindness despite all efforts—taking these shameless
    people as your friends is stupid!

Advising those who don't listen is akin to talking to cattle and
    sheep—how senseless!
Seeking counsel from the ignorant who have no regard for past or
    future is dumb!
If you don't avoid misdeeds, especially when you recognize the action
    as wrong, then consider yourself crazy!

Since this is heart advice, please listen now!

Three nights after killing your father, you forget about it.
When given some money, you behead your mother.
When necessary, you deceive your lama.
When desired, you even sell your child.

Vile people in evil times are like the sun between the clouds.[13]
Whether near or far, if you entrust others with your tasks without
    knowing them for at least a year, then you will quickly experience
    remorse.
You are responsible for your own horrific misconduct.
When the wind carries a negative reputation, nothing holds it back.

Although mobs cause disorder and mayhem, one person is
    "disgraceful" when caught with his pants down.
Confessing openly too often causes you to lose a sense of self, but
    making admissions skillfully is wise.
A saying goes "ghosts surround superstitious people"; so if you
    welcome doubts, demons will be happy.
Knowing the method of transforming obstacles into assets makes it
    hard, even for Māra, to conquer you.[14]

Don't be as attached to food as an old dog guarding a dry bone.
Give it to the people!

Don't be as miserly with money as a pitiful hungry ghost guarding
    its treasure.
Spend it on the Dharma!

Don't show as many faces as the sun between summer clouds.
Welcome others with a smile!

Don't make as many rips and tears with your friends and enemies as
    hilltop prayer flags fluttering in the wind.
Cultivate balance!

---

13. The sun between the clouds implies that a person's character and mood are changeable,
one minute a sunny disposition and the next gloomy or mean.

14. Māra is the Indian deity who attempted to seduce Siddhartha Gautama before he
achieved enlightenment.

Don't be too quick in declaring your retinue as this year's profit but next year's loss. Look at their hearts!

Don't be too quick to look down upon people; bad people can be turned toward good.
So, foster them wisely!

Don't make promises to just anybody; shame comes from not keeping them.
Be practical!

Don't place blame on everything; no need to worry excessively.
Be proud!

Since this is heart advice, please listen now!

A foul mouth has a sickle for a tongue, gesturing to the enemy troops like a venomous snake producing poisonous breath.
Restrain that tongue!

A busy bee takes up whatever comes to mind, a messenger beckoning all kinds of trouble and regret, like sandpaper that scours both mind and body.
Don't do so much: relax!

A busy mind thinks too much, an instigator of trouble incapable of sticking to a single goal—agitated by day, sleepless by night.
Halt overthinking completely!

A bad character can't bear much of anything, suffering this life in both body and mind, like a broom sweeping away any virtuous karma for the next life.
Be good-natured and open-minded!

If the mind inside you does not rise up as your enemy, it will be difficult for any outside force to conquer you.

To distrust for no reason is the work of Māra, causing you to stray.
Superstitions are devastating demons—abandon them!

When a serpent coils around a sandalwood tree of good
    characteristics, no one goes near it.
Roguish companions are like thorns around a beautiful flower and
    become a source of gossip—abandon them!
A white moon stained with the form of a rabbit,[15] a beautiful flower
    tainted by a bad scent, wicked companions like two dzo[16] yoked
    together falling off a cliff.
Bad friends are a source of regret—abandon them!

A wicked relative is like a bottomless vessel.[17]
A bad place is like a wheel of suffering—abandon these!

Saying, "Yes, I know; I can," makes you a slave with no pay, a fetter
    of human virtue—abandon this!

Since this is heart advice, please listen now!

Having too much love or hate sparks a wild grass fire.
In dark times, evil forces flutter in the wind.
Like demons, hate and love harm Dharma practitioners.
So wherever you go, please restrain your passions!

By remaining humble, you arrive at a high position.
So whatever you do, take a modest approach!

Nowadays people make friendships so quickly.
Take stock of your friendships after a few years and months pass!

Bending and bowing does not make one a religious practitioner.
Be wary of nonbelievers pretending to be religious!

Speaking mellifluously does not make one kindhearted.
Be cautious of smooth-talkers with cruel hearts!

---

15. In Tibetan and Chinese folklore, the markings on the moon are considered to take
the form of a rabbit, similar to the notion of the "man in the moon." Shangtön's verse
implies that the moon, beautiful and round when full, is spoiled by the rabbit's form the
way a beautiful flower is spoiled by a bad scent.

16. A dzo is a hybrid, the offspring of a yak and a cow.

17. Comparing a wicked relative to a bottomless vessel implies that the blood relation is
impossible to satisfy no matter what you say or do.

If someone looks into your misdeeds and speaks openly to you, this is a sign of goodwill. Keep your own anger in check!

Be cautious of tricks and deception, and don't trust those who say, "Yes, I can; I know."

Be cautious of those of equal rank who disrespectfully demand, "You come here! You stay there!"

If someone gives fineries and expensive gifts, he is not necessarily being generous.
Be on the lookout for future payback!

Even if poor people cry for help, their cry is not necessarily genuine.
Be cautious of *gongpo* spirits reaching out their hands to you![18]

Don't be envious of those up high—humbly show respect!
Don't insult those below—nurture with patience!
Don't argue over rank with those equal to you—be friendly with equanimity!

Although you will not see the effects immediately, positive circumstances are the result of pure and virtuous deeds.
Although malevolent forces untamed will soar high, the law of karma is inevitable, so evil will eventually fall.

No one else can throw you into heaven by your hands.
No one else can throw you into hell by your feet.
Happiness and suffering lie in your own hands.
Don't deceive yourself—that is essential!

Those sitting in a high position face the danger of falling low.
Those occupying a lower position have the opportunity to rise up.
Those who don't understand the limits of happiness always find suffering in the end.
If you put a lid on boiling milk, it will flow over.
Even if you fall, happiness will come if you are good; after the moon wanes, it waxes.

---

18. *Gongpo* is a synonym for the *gongdré* spirit, who takes away worldly wealth.

While everyone understands advice as spoken, implementing what is necessary is as rare as stars during the day!

Tricksters can deceive others;
heroes have no fear of others.
Clever people understand meaning upon analysis.
Lucid speakers amaze upon speaking.
Selfish people strive for their own personal needs.
But such people should not be called "wise."

You may be able to deceive others with tricks, but one day the payback will circle back to you!
A hero has no fear, but having no hesitation is like a moth jumping into a flame!
When you're analyzing other people's actions, you're very clever, but it is rare for a butter lamp to illuminate its base.[19]

Wise people are conscientious in their pursuits,
knowing how to discriminate between good and bad.
A lama speaks for the benefit of others—oh, how exceptional!
A child listens to this—oh, how unusual!
Many seek words of advice, but how uncommon to study them!
Many speak about the holy Dharma, but how rare to practice it!
There is no benefit in mere speech alone.
The true benefit lies in its long-term analysis!

My disciple, you have treated me properly since your youth; so please take this old man's advice to heart! In the future, you won't hear it like this; and even if you do, you'll find it hard to know if it is heart advice or not! So wherever you go, near or far, please take this advice to heart, my son!

---

19. The butter lamp is a metaphor for oneself. The implication is that it is exceedingly difficult for people to clearly analyze their own behavior.

Translated Work

Shangtön Tenpa Gyatso (Zhang ston Bstan pa rgya mtsho). 2004. *Bslab bya nor bu'i phreng ba.* Collected Works, vol. 4. Lanzhou: Mi rigs dpe skrun khang, 279–87.

Suggested Readings

Losang Chödrak (Blo bzang chos grags) and Sonam Tsemo (Bsod nams rtse mo), eds. 1988. *Golden Essays by Tibetan Scholars. Gangs ljongs mkhas dbang rim byon gyi rtsom yig gser gyi sbram bu.* Qinghai: Mtsho sngon mi rigs dpe skrun khang.

Nietupski, Paul Kocot. 2011. *Labrang Monastery: A Tibetan Buddhist Community on the Inner Asian Borderlands, 1709–1958.* Lanham, MD: Lexington Books.

Additional References

Dungkar Losang Trinlé (Dung dkar Blo bzang 'phrin las), ed. 2002. *Dung dkar Bod rgya Tshig mdzod chen mo.* Beijing: Krung go'i bod rig pa dpe skrun khang.

Losang Tsultrim Gyatso (Blo bzang tshul khrims rgya mtsho). 2004. *Bka' drin mtshungs med zhang ston rdo rje 'chang bstan pa rgya mtsho dpal bzang po'i zhal snga nas kyi rnam par thar ba gzur gnas mkhas pa'i gtsug nor zhes bya ba.* In Collected Works of Shangtön Tenpa Gyatso, vol. 1. Lanzhou: Mi rigs dpe skrun khang.

Stein, R.A. 1972. *Tibetan Civilization.* Stanford, CA: Stanford University Press.

Tseten Zhabdrung (Tshe tan zhabs drung Jigs med rigs pa'i blo gros). 1987. *Mnyam med shākya'i dbang bo'i rjes zhugs pa'jigs med rigs pa'i blo gros rang gi byung ba brjod pa bden gtam rna ba'i bdud rtsi.* Collected Works, vol. 1. Xining: Qinghai Nationality Publishing House.

Willock, Nicole. 2011. *A Tibetan Buddhist Polymath in Modern China.* PhD Diss., Indiana University.

4. Bold Judgments on Eating Meat

Shardza Tashi Gyaltsen
Translated by Geoffrey Barstow

A Necessary Evil

Meat has long been a staple of the Tibetan diet. Both the high-altitude environment and cultural predispositions have made the adoption of a vegetarian diet difficult for Tibetans. At the same time, Tibetan religious beliefs enshrine compassion toward all beings as the highest motivation. Drawing on these beliefs, some religious leaders have argued that despite the difficulties of maintaining a vegetarian diet, meat should be abandoned. *The Faults of Eating Meat* contains one such argument.

The text's author, Shardza Tashi Gyaltsen, was a member of the Bön religion and is the only figure represented in this volume to belong to this tradition. Bön adherents view themselves as practitioners of Tibet's native religion, in contrast to Buddhism's Indian origins. Over the centuries Bön has come to resemble Buddhism in many ways, but it has nevertheless always maintained a separate identity.

Shardza was born in 1859 in the eastern Tibetan region of Kham. He took full ordination at age thirty, and quickly developed a reputation for adhering strictly to the Vinaya (*dulwa*), or monastic code. Over the course of his life, Shardza wrote numerous philosophical works, often with a focus on the view and practice of Dzokchen. By the time of his death in 1935, he had become the most influential Bön scholar and practitioner of his time.[1]

---

1. Gorvine 2006, 240–370.

Shardza and Vegetarianism

Shardza was not the first Tibetan religious leader to argue against meat. His predecessors each approached the issue from a distinct perspective. Among Buddhists, Dölpopa (1292–1361) emphasized the incompatibility of meat with the various vows taken by monks.[2] Centuries later Jikmé Lingpa (1730–98) praised vegetarianism effusively but refrained from actually mandating such a diet among his students.[3] Shabkar (1781–1851), in contrast, presented a no-holds-barred criticism of all types of meat eating, using vivid descriptions of animal suffering to bring his message home.[4] On the Bön side, Nyamé Sherab Gyaltsen (1356–1415), the founder of Menri Monastery, argued forcefully that Bön monks must not eat meat.[5] These are only a few of the many Tibetan religious leaders who have spoken out against the consumption of meat.

Shardza's text is therefore not unique in its critique of eating meat. *The Faults of Eating Meat* is unusual, however, for its attempt to balance ethical concern for the suffering of animals with an awareness of the difficulties of a vegetarian diet. Shardza opens with a strong denunciation of eating meat. He equates meat eaters with demons, insisting, "Those who eat meat have not even a trace of compassion or kindness." As a result, those who eat meat can expect to be reborn in hell, where they will have to pay the karmic debts they have incurred. Following this strong denunciation, Shardza abruptly changes course, arguing that one *must* eat meat. Echoing the Tibetan medical tradition, Shardza claims that without meat the body will weaken and become ill.[6] Avoiding meat is therefore "throwing away one's body." This in turn jeopardizes one's ability to practice the Dharma and bring benefit to other beings. In this context vegetarianism is not a virtue.

Shardza's readers are thus left with a conflict: eating meat leads to birth in hell, but it is also necessary in order to practice religion. The solution is to eat only "suitable" meat, which he defines as meat that is "free of having been seen, heard, or suspected." Shardza thus invokes the rule of threefold purity (*namsum dakpai sha*), found in both Buddhist and Bön versions of the Vinaya. This rule states that a monk may eat meat as long as he has not

2. Mochizuki 2009.

3. Barstow 2013a.

4. Shabkar 2004.

5. Nyamé Sherab Gyaltsen, 49.

6. Tibetan doctors in Amdo and Kham have reported to me that being vegetarian leads to "wind" (*lung*) disorders and a general weakening of the body.

seen it killed specifically for him, has not heard that it was killed specifically for him, or does not suspect that it was killed specifically for him.

In practice this means that not only are monks not allowed to slaughter animals themselves, but they are also not allowed to ask someone else to do it for them. Neither are monks allowed to accept meat from a patron if they believe that the patron specifically killed the animal in order to offer its meat to them. Should a monk perform a ritual in a patron's home, he should not, according to the rule of threefold purity, accept any meat that the patron slaughtered for his visit.

Shardza provides a solution that fulfills the standard of threefold purity: meat from animals that have died naturally. While most Tibetans will not eat the meat of animals that have died of old age or of illness, they will gladly consume animals that have died in lightning strikes, wolf attacks, or other accidents. In these cases, the consumer can legitimately claim to have had no involvement in the death of the animal. Such meat is thereby free of defilement. Shardza himself adhered to such a diet from the moment of his ordination at age thirty, refusing the meat of any animal that had been slaughtered.[7]

In the end, *The Faults of Eating Meat* acknowledges both the ethical concerns that surround eating meat as well as the practical difficulties of maintaining a vegetarian diet, and tries to find a middle path. It is unreservedly critical of those who wantonly eat meat, but it is also disapproving of those who insist on strict vegetarianism. As such, it occupies an important position within the corpus of Tibetan writings on vegetarianism.

The Rimé Movement

While vegetarianism has never been common among Tibetans, it has experienced several periods of relative prosperity. One such period occurred in late nineteenth- and early twentieth-century Kham. Biographical and historical sources suggest that the various forms of vegetarian diet were more popular at this time than at any other point in Tibetan history.[8]

Interestingly, vegetarianism flourished most widely among members of the Nyingma, Kagyü, and Sakya schools, precisely the same communities most deeply involved in the rimé movement. Just as the Geluk school was at the periphery of the rimé movement, there is strikingly little evidence of vegetarianism among Geluk practitioners of this period. While I can only assume

---

7. Dratön Kalzang Tenpai Gyaltsen 2011, 91.

8. Barstow 2017, 35–40.

that some Gelukpas adopted such a diet during this time, they did not leave many records behind to prove it.

As *The Faults of Eating Meat* makes clear, Shardza was an active participant in the vegetarian movement in Kham. While the text makes no explicit mention of sectarianism or sectarian identity, Shardza was also deeply concerned with the problem of sectarianism. As during many other points in Tibetan history, Bönpos in nineteenth- and twentieth-century Kham were frequently denigrated, and sometimes even physically assaulted, by their Buddhist counterparts. Shardza himself experienced an extreme form of anti-Bön violence, witnessing the destruction of the Bön-affiliated Tengchen Monastery at the hands of monks from a local Geluk monastery in 1902.[9]

Despite this experience, Shardza maintained friendships with Buddhist lamas from all traditions. For example, Shardza's biography, the *Pleasure Garden of Wish-Fulfilling Trees*, recalls conversations that he had with many eminent Buddhists. It also contains letters from some of them, praising their erudition and religious attainment. Shardza's biographers call attention to the respect that he earned from Buddhist figures and explicitly celebrate his nonsectarian ideals.[10]

Style and Audience

Like other works in this volume, *The Faults of Eating Meat* is written in a lively, colloquial style. Shardza does not mince words or waste time with complicated, scholastic exegesis. He presents his text in language calculated to appeal to his readers' emotions. Meat is described as nauseating, and meat eaters are compared to fearsome demons. Not all Tibetan texts opposed to meat discuss the issue with such vivid terminology.

Shardza also eschews standard scholastic metaphors in favor of examples drawn from Tibetans' daily experiences, such as references to killing a louse and a yak. His audience can no doubt sympathize with a person intent on crushing a louse, or with a farmer who desires to sell his yaks for money. By choosing everyday examples, Shardza asks his readers to consider difficult ethical choices. Such issues, he insists, are not abstract topics to be debated but rules of conduct to be implemented in one's actual life.

This rhetorical approach stands in sharp contrast to Shardza's other major treatment of meat eating, which appears in his *Differentiating the Three Vows*.[11] In this work, Shardza employs a legalistic writing style to show that

9. Gorvine 2006, 175.

10. Gorvine 2006, 187–200.

11. Shardza Tashi Gyaltsen 2011b, 168.

meat is incompatible with the three types of vows taken by monks. He uses little of the evocative language and everyday examples found in *The Faults of Eating Meat*. Given its subject matter, *Differentiating the Three Vows* is clearly intended for a monastic audience. The less formal language in *The Faults of Eating Meat*, on the other hand, suggests that it may have been intended for a more popular audience. Shardza's lack of concern with the specifics of Vinaya requirements, combined with the colloquial nature of his rhetoric, suggests that *The Faults of Eating Meat* targets a fairly wide audience.

At the same time, the text was requested by three of Shardza's most prominent disciples. Shardza repeatedly cites both canonical and extra-canonical Bön literature, suggesting that he assumes that his readers would be familiar with these works. These factors indicate that while Shardza may have been targeting an audience beyond the monastery, he still wanted to speak to an educated audience. He includes enough scriptural citations to appeal to an educated, monastic audience, but he also writes in a way that will be intelligible to a literate layperson.

Notes on the Translation

The Faults of Eating Meat rarely resorts to esoteric or otherwise difficult language. Individual passages are sometimes convoluted, but the meaning is usually clear. This made the process of translation relatively straightforward. When translation questions did emerge, they usually pertained to how best to capture Shardza's tone. For instance, Shardza asks how people who eat meat could possibly be called followers of the Buddha. In translating this passage, I struggled to balance a desire to communicate Shardza's sarcastic tone with adherence to the actual words and structure that he uses.

Shardza opens and closes his work in verse. While the opening verses were not especially problematic, the closing verses proved far more difficult. The first and third of the three closing verses are written in standard nine-syllable lines, but the second verse carries an unusual poetic device: the final syllable of each line is repeated as the first syllable of the line that follows. I tried, repeatedly, to craft an English verse that mirrored this strategy, but the results were never satisfactory.

Perhaps the most interesting translation question this text provoked, however, was how to render the terms *deshek* (*bde gshegs*) and *sangyé* (*sangs rgyas*). Usually rendered as *sugata* and *buddha*, respectively, these terms are both proper titles for the Buddha. This poses little issue except for the fact that this is a Bön text, not a Buddhist one. As such, invocations of the Buddha seem slightly out of place. Some colleagues who read early drafts of this translation suggested that I use alternate terminology, perhaps specifying that Shardza was referring to Tönpa Shenrab, the founder of Bön. Shardza, however, does not make this attribution clear. He might be referring to Tönpa Shenrab, or he might be invoking the Buddha known to Buddhists. After consulting with several Bön monks and scholars, I have elected to translate these terms as I found them. This will preserve the ambiguity present in the original text and perhaps give readers something to consider when reflecting on the place of Bön in the rimé activities of nineteenth-century Kham.

THE FAULTS OF EATING MEAT[12]

by Shardza Tashi Gyaltsen

> Possessing twofold purity,
> your body is that of a sugata, your speech the vast and profound
> realization of Bön.
> Possessing twofold knowledge and liberation,
> your mind is that of a bodhisattva. Lord, you unite the three
> jewels into one.
> Possessing twofold wisdom and compassion,
> gracious guru, you are a glorious wish-fulfilling jewel.
> Possessing twofold devotion,
> I continually praise you with fierce longing. Care for me with
> compassion!

A sūtra says, "The activity of the teachings is compassion. Use compassion to guard beings!"

Compassion is the essence of all the Buddha's teachings. Become completely absorbed with this, so that you guard beings with great compassion, steadfast and immeasurable. Motivate yourself with the aim of establishing all beings in both temporary and ultimate happiness! With this as your intention, perform positive actions of body and speech. Exert yourself in this to the best of your ability, as everything is contained in this.

One who practices in this way is renowned as a follower of the Buddha. Some other people, however, act only out of desire for their own benefit, bringing harm to other beings. Such people might call themselves "followers of the Buddha," but is it really acceptable to call them this?

If someone is motivated by desire to eat the flesh of beings, then butchers will seize animals such as yaks or sheep and sever their minds from their bodies. How can those who consume meat and blood as food be followers of the Buddha? Such people pridefully consider themselves to be benefitting beings and protecting the weak, but their actions contradict the precepts! Meat is nothing but the cause of amassing terrifying sins.

---

12. This text is untitled. I have adapted this title from the work's colophon, where Shardza reports that he has "described the faults of religious people eating meat."

It would be impossible to eat meat if beings were not killed. As it says in a sūtra, "This food called 'meat' comes from the killing of animals." As for the karmic results of that killing, a scripture says, "Among the ten kinds of nonvirtue, killing is the worst." Killing, therefore, has the worst karma of the nonvirtuous sins. Even if you kill just one being, you will have to repay this karmic debt with your life five hundred times. Moreover, killing a being is especially severe if the four elements of a complete action are present. Looking at the specific issue of meat, we see that it is derived from killing. Therefore it contains all four elements and produces the karma of a complete act of killing.

Further, the severity of the intention determines which lower realm one is born in. Acting through hatred leads to hell, desire leads to the realm of hungry ghosts, and ignorance leads to birth in the animal realm.

As an example, take the killing of a louse. When a louse is feeding on someone's body, that person knows that the louse is eating them. This knowledge is the ground element of a complete act (*shi yenlak*). Seeing the louse on his arm, the killer is motivated by anger. This is the intention element (*sampai yenlak*). He places a fingernail on top of the louse and begins to press down, applying the means to kill the louse. This is the application element (*jorwai yenlak*). Afterward, the bloody louse is removed from the top of the nail with a cry of triumph, completing the act of killing. This is the completion element (*thartuk gi yenlak*). Killing in this way, motivated by hatred, brings karma that impels one to hell. The karma of anger will ripen like a burning flame, and you will be born in a hot or a cold hell. This is explained in the sūtras.

As another example, take the killing of a yak. First, one thinks, "If I kill this yak, there will be lots of meat." This is the ground element, the knowledge that the object to be killed is a yak. Then, thinking, "Those yaks are a herd of wealth," either you or someone else strings a rope around the animal's neck.[13] This is the intention element, the thought to kill the yak. Continuing from this, the yak is led into the butcher's corral, its limbs are bound, it is turned upside down, and its muzzle is wrapped with cord.[14] This is the application element, when the actual killing is done. Then the yak's breath is cut off and its mind is severed from its body. When its eyes bulge and its life force has

---

13. For many Tibetans, wealth is measured by the number of yaks in one's herd. In order to make use of this wealth, however, it must first be converted into currency or other more portable forms of wealth. This is usually done by either killing the animal or selling it for slaughter.

14. Sheep and yak are often suffocated by binding a cord around their muzzle. The meat produced by this method, still rich with blood, is said to be particularly tasty.

been completely destroyed, this is the completion element. Killing in this way, motivated by desire, brings the karma that impels one to the realm of hungry ghosts (*yidak*). The karma of desire will ripen like boiling water, and you will wander through the realm of hungry ghosts, always hungry and thirsty. This is explained in the sūtras.

Moreover, some non-Buddhists believe killing is a virtue that will benefit them after death, so they slaughter animals. This is certainly ignorance, and the sūtras explain it to be the cause for being impelled into a birth as a draft animal.

Eating meat is motivated by desire, so it is a cause of birth as a hungry ghost. At the same time, however, it also definitely impels one toward hell. The *Stainless*[15] says, "Meat is a sinful transgression. Through it you will be born in the hell of being boiled and burned, where many worms will claim their karmic debts."[16] Therefore meat—this food that harms beings—is a very heavy fault.

Speaking generally, this thing called "meat" arises from a father's semen and a mother's blood, so it is made from unclean substances. The *Compendium of the Vinaya*[17] says, "The causes and conditions of meat are the white and red conjugal substances of both a father and mother. If you saw this with your eyes, you would tremble with fear. How pitiful it would be to take it in your hands! Just smelling it brings on nausea. Once it is tasted by the tongue, how can it be kept down?"

Similarly, since all the beings of the three worlds have all been our father and mother, there is not a shred of difference between our parents and our food. The *Stainless* says, "Of all the beings of the six realms, not one has not been your father or mother. There is no difference between the flesh of one's kind parents and whatever meat one desires to eat."

Those who eat meat have not even a trace of compassion or kindness. As Jetsun Jangpa says, "Meat eaters have no compassion." Meat eaters are no different than demons who eat their own flesh. A sūtra says, "All who eat meat are demons whose karma is to eat the flesh of their own body. They have no shame about nonvirtuous activity and cannot be distinguished from the sons of demons."

Those who enjoy the flesh and blood taken from other beings cannot stand it if a thorn pierces their own body. Asking such people to be the refuge and

---

15. *Do Drimé Siji.* The most extensive biography of Tönpa Shenrab, the founder of Bön.

16. When one being harms another, the former is said to be in the latter's debt. At some future time, the harmer will become the harmed, and the victim will claim his karmic debt.

17. *Dulwa Kunlé Tü.* A commentary on the Vinaya by Metön Sherab Öser (1058–1132).

protector of beings is no different from thinking of a flesh-eating demon as an object of offerings (*chöné*). The *Nail Hole*[18] says, "If even a single thorn pierces our body, it is completely unbearable. Some say that we need to eat the meat of many slaughtered beings. Whoever says this is a demon."

By killing a single being for meat, the lives of innumerable tiny beings are damaged.[19] Therefore the karmic retribution for the sin of eating meat is immeasurable. The *Vinaya Transmission*[20] says, "For each animal that is killed, innumerable tiny beings die." Through eating meat one will become more vital, but it also causes one's suffering and negative emotions to increase. The *Stainless* says, "Therefore, when one engages with meat and blood, the roots of the five poisons are present." The same text also says, "Meat gives rise to the causes of all five poisons, so all evil will arise from that meat."

In the future, the karmic consequences of eating meat will ripen in one's own flesh and blood. The *Sutra Separating Causes and Effects* says, "Karmic debts incurred in the past pursue you now. Karmic debts incurred today will pursue you in the future." It is certain that consuming the meat and blood of beings out of desire will result in being flung to the lower realms. For this reason, it is important to abandon meat forever.

At the same time, however, the Buddha is the extraordinary support for practice, and this free and favored human life is difficult to obtain.[21] Eating meat supports long life, making it necessary for obtaining the supreme objective. If you do not eat it, your bodily strength will be feeble, you will not be able to perform virtue, and your life force will be weak, as if you had a wind (*lung*) disorder.[22] If you do not rely on a skillful method like this, you are throwing away your body. It is said to be a fault similar to tearing down the four supporting pillars in a temple. It is important to nourish your body with suitable meat and other foods so that you can practice virtue.

If you ask "What meat is suitable?" the answer is: when you buy it, the meat must be free of having been seen, heard, or suspected.[23] This also applies

---

18. *Do Sermik*. Middle-length biography of Tönpa Shenrab.

19. Though the scientific concept of bacteria was unknown in Tibet, there was an understanding that very tiny beings lived in and depended upon larger creatures.

20. *Dulgyü*. The Bön canon contains a series of six texts under the heading *Dulwa Gyüdruk*. This quote is likely from one of them. See Martin, Nagano, and Kværne 2003, 189–203.

21. A human birth is said to be rare and the only opportunity to fully practice the Buddha's teachings.

22. A wind disorder is a common ailment in the Tibetan medical tradition, generally characterized by physical weakness and instability.

23. According to the Vinaya, meat may be eaten if the consumer has not seen that the meat was killed specifically for him, has not heard that the meat was killed specifically

to meat purchased for you by others. For example, meat from animals that have died naturally is suitable. The Vinaya says, "Abandon your desire for meat and, for the sake of nourishing the body, eat meat that has died naturally at the end of its time or that was purchased in the market."

A ho!

The precious Bön is the three trainings of the Lord's teachings.
In order to benefit beings, I have composed in accordance
with the great vehicle of the renunciant bodhisattvas
who skillfully bring beings to definitive goodness and the fulfillment
    of all desires.

I have clarified this according to the tradition
of the texts spoken by Mé,[24] who collected the best teachings
that aligned with the precepts of the hundred supreme protectors
renowned in the three worlds as the protectors of gods and men.

Having brought all beings to certainty in this way,
their minds have been tamed by gentle thoughts
without causing harm to each other.
May all be liberated into the space of equality.

Here I have briefly explained the faults of religious people eating meat. Following requests by the Supreme Incarnation Yungdrung, Namkha Öser—a pure monk of Gongyel Monastery, and Yungdrung Tri Ö—the meditator of Nyakrong, this was written in an isolated mountain range by the mad vagabond of the rocks with the name Manga Wershi.[25] May it be virtuous!

---

for him, and does not suspect that the meat was killed specifically for him. Such meat is said to have "threefold purity."

24. According to scholars at Shardza Ritrö, this refers to Yorpo Mepal (1134–69).

25. Achard identifies Manga Wershi as the Shangshung version of Shardza's proper name, Tashi Gyaltsen (Achard 2008, xxix). Shangshung is a kingdom in western Tibet conquered by the Tibetan empire in the eighth century. Bön adherents trace their origins to this civilization, preserving its language for use in special contexts.

Translated Work

Shardza Tashi Gyaltsen (Shar rdza Bskra shis rgyal mtshan). 2011a. Untitled. Collected Works, vol. 15, 148–54. Chengdu: Si khron mi rigs dpe skrun khang.

Suggested Readings

Barstow, Geoffrey. 2017. *Food of Sinful Demons: Meat, Vegetarianism, and the Limits of Buddhism in Tibet.* New York: Columbia University Press.

Gorvine, William M. 2006. *The Life of a Bönpo Luminary: Sainthood, Partisanship and Literary Representation in a 20th Century Tibetan Biography.* PhD Diss., University of Virginia.

Karmay, Samten, ed. and trans. 1972. *The Treasury of Good Sayings: A Tibetan History of Bon.* Oxford: Oxford University Press.

Shabkar. 2004. *Food of Bodhisattvas: Buddhist Teachings on Abstaining from Meat.* Translated by Padmakara Translation Group. Boston: Shambhala Publications.

Additional References

Achard, Jean-Luc. 2008. *Enlightened Rainbows: The Life and Works of Shardza Tashi Gyaltsen.* Leiden: Brill.

Dratön Kalzang Tenpai Gyaltsen (Dbra ston Skal bzang bstan pa'i rgyal mtshan). 2011. *Rje btsun bla ma dam pa nges pa don gyi gyung drung 'chad dbang dpal shar rdza pa chen po bkra shis rgyal mtsan dpal bzang po'i rnam thar pa ngo mtshar nor.* In Collected Works of Shardza Tashi Gyaltsen, vol. 1, 1–437. Chengdu: Si khron mi rigs dpe skrun khang.

Martin, Dan, Yasuhiko Nagano, and Per Kværne. 2003. *A Catalogue of the Bon Kanjur.* Osaka: National Museum of Ethnology.

Mochizuki, Kaie. 2009. "On the Scriptures Introducing the Prohibition of Meat and Alcohol by Dol Po Pa." In *Acta Tibetica et Buddhica* 2, edited by Kaie Mochizuki, 25–64. Minobu: Department of Tibetan Studies, Faculty of Buddhism, Minobusan University.

Nyamé Sherab Gyaltsen (Mnyam med Shes rab rgyal mtshan). *'Dul ba mdor bsdus kyi 'grel pa.* Typset edition of unknown publication, courtesy of a private collection in Beijing.

Shardza Tashi Gyaltsen (Shar rdza Bskra shis rgyal mtshan). 2011b. *Sdom gsum rnam par 'byed pa'i gzhung don gsal bar byed pa'i 'grel pa legs bshad 'phrul gyi lde mig ces bya ba.* Collected Works, vol. 14, 51–400. Chengdu: Si khron mi rigs dpe skrun khang.

5. A Letter to the Queen

Jikmé Lingpa and Getsé Mahāpaṇḍita
Translated by Jann Ronis

Powerful Woman, Potent Illusions

Tsewang Lhamo (d. 1812) was the queen of the eastern Tibetan kingdom of Degé for over fifteen years at the turn of the nineteenth century. She was born in the late 1760s into an aristocratic family in Degé and married the Degé crown prince Sawang Sangpo in 1786.[1] The young couple had one son and one daughter who survived infancy (they also lost two children). In 1788, when the royals were in their early twenties, Tsewang Lhamo and Sawang Sangpo traveled to Central Tibet to present themselves to the Dalai Lama's government and to the ruling family of Sakya. Along the way, the youthful couple visited Jikmé Lingpa. Thus began a long and pivotal relationship between the lama and Tsewang Lhamo, largely conducted through letters such as the one translated here. Tsewang Lhamo became a stalwart patron of Jikmé Lingpa and through her bold acts of generosity transformed Degé into the heartland of the Longchen Nyingthik tradition. Through this patronage Tsewang Lhamo rivaled the Dharma kings of prior generations and made a signal contribution toward the propagation of Jikmé Lingpa's

---

1. Sawang Sangpo's father was a monk for the first half of his life. Because of a shortage of heirs to the throne, he was forced to marry. He entered into a marriage of state with a relative of the Seventh Dalai Lama. The king died while Sawang Sangpo was still a child, and the boy's aunt, Yangchen Drölma, a nun, served as Sawang Sangpo's regent for more than ten years.

treasures, which have been the mainstream of the Nyingma ever since. The present work is a letter of advice from Jikmé Lingpa to Tsewang Lhamo and was composed for her shortly after their meeting in Central Tibet. Although it is one of his many minor masterpieces, it is virtually unknown in Tibetan and scholarly circles; this is the first published translation and discussion of it.

The year before Tsewang Lhamo and her husband's meeting with Jikmé Lingpa, the couple sent an advance party to request that he travel to Degé to serve as the royal chaplain. At the time he was the most brilliant Nyingma lama in Tibet and was renowned in Kham, though he had never traveled to the region. Jikmé Lingpa declined the invitation to visit but did agree to provide religious services to Degé. Instead of gracing the king with his bodily presence, he composed a long epistle to the king comprising seventy-one verses and entrusted the king's advance party to deliver it. The royal couple's visit with Jikmé Lingpa is well known to students of Tibetan culture through Janet Gyatso's studies of Jikmé Lingpa's autobiographies. One of her works is a translation of a passage from his outer autobiography detailing the first few days of their visit. Following convention, Jikmé Lingpa's description of his royal patrons is initially quite ambivalent about the king and queen. He thinks they are sincere enough but acknowledges that the logistics of their visit is a disruption to his favored activities of meditation and composition, and that they made onerous demands on the local peasants. However, as the chronicle of their visit progresses, the language changes. There is an especially rich episode from the pilgrimage made by Jikmé Lingpa and the king to Samyé. Upon an elaborate offering ceremony in front of the central Padmasambhava statue at Samyé, Jikmé Lingpa offers a benediction in which he likens the Degé king to Trisong Detsen (reign 756–800), who invited Padmasambhava to Tibet, and likens himself to Padmasambhava.

This *Letter to the Queen* was composed within days of their departure. It comprises sixteen verses and includes an autocommentary that offers prose elaborations of each of the verses. In this work Jikmé Lingpa calls Tsewang Lhamo an emanation of Ngangtsul Jangchup Gyalmo, wife of Mutik Tsenpo, himself the son of Trisong Detsen. The authorship statement at the conclusion of *A Letter to the Queen* reads, "The Dzokchen practitioner Rangjung Dorjé (a.k.a. Jikmé Lingpa) completed these instructions for Ngangtsul Jangchup Gyalmo, the excellent queen of Degé." In 1790 Tsewang Lhamo was widowed when the king died after years of illness. She thereupon became the head of state and ruled Degé until her son ascended the throne toward the end of the first decade of the nineteenth century. Her reign was momentous.

After Sawang Sangpo's death, Tsewang Lhamo emerged as the foremost benefactor of the Nyingma tradition of her generation. Though priest and patroness never met again, she continued her patronage of Jikmé Lingpa and his community throughout her reign. Jikmé Lingpa stayed in regular contact with her and her son, and he sent his chief disciple—the first Dodrupchen lama Jikmé Trinlé Öser (1745–1821)—to Degé for many long stays to help with Nyingma projects. Tsewang Lhamo had broad editorial control over the renowned Degé printing house and saw to it that all of Jikmé Lingpa's writings were published there. While he was alive, she printed his major work, the *Treasury of Precious Qualities*, and after his death Dodrupchen oversaw the publication of the collected works of Jikmé Lingpa in nine volumes. Under orders from Jikmé Lingpa, Tsewang Lhamo also sponsored the publication of the Degé edition of the *Collected Tantras of the Ancients*, the only xylograph edition of the canon of Nyingma scriptures. Additionally, she supported the founding of new Nyingma monasteries in Degé and built a large statue of Padmasambhava at the state temple, adorning it with precious stones and metals extracted from her heirloom jewelry.

Root Text and Autocommentary

The ornamental title of the work is *The Treasury of Advice for Excellent Beings*, which indicates that it is intended to be a depository of Dharma instructions for the spiritually advanced, such as Tsewang Lhamo. The work spans all three vehicles—Hīnayāna, Mahāyāna, and Vajrayāna—and the Great Perfection. Much of the work's sixteen verses are devoted to the architecture of the path and to delineating the three vehicles. Verses 2 through 7 address topics in the Hīnayāna (which Jikmé Lingpa refers to as the "code of individual liberation"), such as the precious human rebirth, renunciation, and upholding a layperson's vows. Verses 8 and 9 introduce Mahāyāna topics, such as the mind of enlightenment, and allude to skillful means. The remaining verses are devoted to the Vajrayāna and the Great Perfection, with topics including the higher initiations, practice with a sexual consort, the two stages of tantric practice, and the nature of mind.

Because *The Treasury of Advice for Excellent Beings* lays out a general presentation of the three vehicles, it is light on concrete advice. Nevertheless, the root text and autocommentary address Tsewang Lhamo personally and intimately, making this an unmistakable work of spiritual counsel. From beginning to end it speaks directly to the recipient's multiple subject positions: her status as a layperson, monarch, and woman. Thus, for example, the sections about Hīnayāna and Vajrayāna both predominantly focus on nonmonastic practices, such as occasional fasting and consort practice. On multiple occasions the text addresses Tsewang Lhamo's status as a royal ("even though you live in a palace . . ."). There is even an encouraging account of the enlightenment of the king Bimbisāra that is meant to serve as an exemplary precedent. But Jikmé Lingpa's approach to Tsewang Lhamo's gender is particularly noteworthy. The Mahāyāna and Vajrayāna sections go remarkably far in valorizing her as a woman. The Mahāyāna section references a previous life of the Buddha in which he was a woman who used gender-specific skillful means to benefit beings. It concludes with the second-person command, "In similar ways should you show benevolence for your subjects." The Vajrayāna section contains several evocative passages that counter the standard misogyny of the exoteric scriptures by deifying the female anatomy and asserting the indispensability of women to tantric rituals and attainment.

The root text consists of verses in quatrains with nine-syllable lines, and shares much in common with versified classics in the Tengyur. Luis Gomez, a leading scholar of Śāntideva, has the following to say about the language of the *Way of the Bodhisattva* (*Bodhisattvacaryāvatāra*): "The text is allusive, relying on echoes and indirect references; it abounds in literary conceits that may strike the modern reader as mixed metaphors or obscure puns that combine imagery and scholastic jargon."[2] Jikmé Lingpa's *Letter to the Queen* is highly allusive, and it can be argued that its most sophisticated literary quality is the network of scriptural allusions that crisscross the work. For instance, verse 11 cites a passage in the *Renunciation Sūtra* (*Abhiniṣkramaṇa Sūtra*) about the qualities of the wife of a universal monarch. This was a masterful choice of *locus classicus* about queens because a completely different passage in this same sūtra—which Jikmé Lingpa does not cite explicitly—echoes through several of the later verses. In other words, while Jikmé Lingpa cites the *Renunciation Sūtra* for its canonical description of the qualities of the ideal queen, *allusively* he calls upon the sūtra's equally canonical presentation of the Buddha's mother Mahāmāyā to bolster verses in *A Letter to the Queen* about illusion (*māyā*) and about the so-called mother of all buddhas. Likewise, "mixed metaphors or obscure puns that combine imagery and scholastic jargon" are on full display in Jikmé Lingpa's text. Verse 4 is about the four noble truths and perfectly illustrates this trait. It compares the relationship of suffering and its causes to artwork and its creator. True causes are likened to an artist and true sufferings to the images created by said artist. It is a striking image that perhaps owes more to Yogācāra philosophy than to standard expositions of the four noble truths.

Another literary element of *A Letter to the Queen* is its suffusion with several leitmotifs that create both a high degree of internal coherence and

---

2. Gómez 1999, 274.

make possible multiple levels of meaning, such as exoteric and esoteric. To cite an example, the theme of illusion (*gyuma, māyā*) is central to many verses in the Mahāyāna and Vajrayāna sections. *The Princeton Dictionary of Buddhism*'s definition for *māyā* is entirely negative: "deceit, deception, trickery, fraudulence."[3] While the Sanskrit *māyā* (and Tibetan *gyuma*) does mean these things, it can also connote illusion in a less unequivocally negative sense. In fact, many Mahāyāna sūtras and Buddhist tantras give *māyā* a positive valence.

In this epistle, Jikmé Lingpa skillfully exploits a wide range of meanings of the term for "illusion." The word *gyuma/māyā* is first used in verse 9: "Bodhisattva Drowé Palmo conjured illusions when she danced and by means of them carried out loving actions for sentient beings." In one of his many lives as a bodhisattva, Buddha took birth as the beautiful daughter of a dance instructor. Her name was Drowé Palmo, and she dedicated herself to liberating men with strong desire and lust. Her method for benefitting these afflicted beings was to adorn her body with beautiful jewelry and dance seductively in large crowds of men. Once she had their undivided attention, she would sing arresting songs about the impermanence of youthful beauty. We can understand Drowé Palmo's illusion as a purposeful dressing up in order to seduce and ultimately benefit her audience—in no way a mere fraudulence. Verse 12, which comes in the Vajrayāna section, uses the term *māyā* twice to make the point that ḍākinīs and consorts are "queens of illusion" (*gyumai palmo*), meaning that they are embodiments of illusion. The image of a ḍākinī as a "queen of illusion" is repeated again in verse 13. Certain verses employ the theme of *māyā* in a manner that not only is allusive but requires a high degree of learning to understand. Needless to say, as a translator, I must confess I am not positive that I have unlocked all such highly arcane allusions.

Jikmé Lingpa's epistles to the members of the Degé royal family were included in his Miscellaneous Writings and published as part of his collected works. The Miscellaneous Writings contains at least one other letter to the queen and correspondence with the crown prince as well. Although these works have long been accessible to interested readers in possession of his Miscellaneous Writings, they were clearly not intended for a general readership. One may wonder, even, whether Jikmé Lingpa intended for Tsewang Lhamo to read and study this epistle. I think that at a minimum he hoped that she would become familiar with the content of the text. As mentioned above, this work is addressed not to women or monarchs at large but to Tsewang Lhamo herself. A valid and open question, however, concerns her literacy.

---

3. Buswell and Lopez 2014, 535.

We have no positive evidence of her ability to read Buddhist writings such as Jikmé Lingpa's *Letter to the Queen*, but we should assume she was moderately well educated. She grew up among the ruling classes during a time of cultural efflorescence in a broader culture that had no a priori restrictions on women's education. At the least, it is highly likely Tsewang Lhamo was able to recite liturgies and prayers from the page. Furthermore, her demanding occupation as head of state would have also necessitated some degree of literacy. Considering her interest in Dharma, it is not unreasonable to assume that she eventually learned to read Buddhist treatises such as Jikmé Lingpa's epistle to her.

The autocommentary is written in standard scholastic prose. The comments address the broader significance of each verse but do not unpack each and every word—though on many occasions they are crucial for understanding the language of the root text. In all Tibetan versions of this work, the autocommentary begins after the last verse of the root text. Here I have braided them together in my translation for ease of understanding. *The Treasury of Advice for Excellent Beings* was difficult to translate. The original letter is in verse, but it would have been nearly impossible to translate it into English stanzas composed of lines of more or less equal length. One reason is that the units of meaning within each stanza do not easily map onto the individual lines.

With that said, the biggest obstacle to achieving a versified translation is the Delphic quality of Jikmé Lingpa's writing. Without interpolation of (sometimes lengthy) phrases, the translation would have been incoherent. These interpolations more often than not turned the translation of individual units of meaning into full sentences, resulting in a prose rendition of the text. Because the interpolations make up a sizable percentage of the overall translation, confining them to parentheses would mar the text. I therefore folded the interpolations into the flow of the translation.

As Jikmé's Lingpa's *Letter to the Queen* is a minor work, the lamas I consulted on the text could be helpful only up to a point in their explanations of the knottiest passages. Absent a living oral explanatory tradition of the text, they were often reticent to speak decisively about the correct interpretation of the phrasings and allusions that vexed me. Fortunately, I was able to take counsel from a commentary by Getsé Mahāpaṇḍita (1761–1829), Tsewang Lhamo's most trusted chaplain in Degé and a student of Jikmé Lingpa. His autobiography is one of the best contemporary sources for Tsewang Lhamo's life, recording many of her acts of devotion, and mentions several political and military episodes in which she was involved.

Getsé's commentary unravels the verses of *A Letter to the Queen* through scholastic prose that makes explicit its complex doctrinal framework. It was often indispensable to unpacking a verse. It saved me from publishing several howlers that appeared in my first drafts, and on occasion it gave me reassurance that certain of my own intuitions were correct. I followed Jikmé Lingpa's autocommentary and Getsé's commentary whenever it provided clarification or needed information, but there were many occasions when I was left to my own interpretive wits. This may give the translation a certain "illusion-like" quality, but such is the nature of reality.

A Letter to the Queen: The Treasury of Advice for Excellent Beings

Homage to Tārā!

1. Hearing the name of he who appeared out of the stamen of a lotus soon after Buddha passed away in Kuśinagarī enhances the value of the ears of all who hear it—concretely, not figuratively. May he grant his blessings!

The precious master Padmasambhava came to this world by magically appearing in a lotus soon after the Buddha passed away in Kuśinagarī. The ear of one who has heard the name of the precious master is different from one who has not, the value of the former being equal to beryl. This is not a poetic flourish or falsehood.

2. Although mired in the ocean of saṃsāra, you rejected a life lacking leisure. Having reached the jeweled island of leisure and fortune, you enjoy the seven qualities of the higher realms. How wonderful!

Despite living in saṃsāra, you have acquired a physical form replete with all eighteen leisures and endowments as described in the Abhidharma commentaries, including being devoid of the eight leisureless states and in possession of the seven qualities of the higher states, such as the long-life gods.

3. At present the lasso of the five degenerations fetters the Victor's teachings, fount of jewels. Nevertheless, while residing in the royal palace, it is still possible to generate the attitude of renunciation, the genuine seed of the code of individual liberation.

These days the Victor's teachings are widespread but fledgling. Consequently this age is fettered by the five degenerations, such as the degeneration of views. Nevertheless, even though you live in the royal palace, it is still possible to generate the spirit of renunciation toward saṃsāra. In fact, the essence of the code of individual liberation is the generation of, or presence of, renunciation in the mindstream.

> 4. The *sources* are likened to an artist and the *sufferings* likened to the images created by him or her. Seeing clearly the incontrovertibility of cause and effect, one cultivates the *paths* and attains the *cessations*. This is the teaching of the Buddha.

Regarding the four noble truths: the *sources* are the mental afflictions and the *sufferings* are their results. Practicing the *paths*—abandoning sin and accomplishing virtue due to conviction in the aforementioned system of causality—is the method leading to the *cessation* of further rebirths. This is the Vinaya's true tenet.

> 5. As we are now in the early stages of the period of the vestigial signs of the Dharma, ordained renunciants weaken, flout, break, and irrevocably nullify their vows. Nevertheless, it is still possible to uphold the eight occasional vows and maintain at least one permanent vow while living as a householder.

The present time is fast approaching the period of the vestigial signs of the Dharma, and hence even ordained renunciants violate the training. They commit the triad of weakening, flouting, and breaking individual vows and commit the major transgressions in which all of one's vows are irrevocably nullified. Nevertheless, these days householders are able to (1) undertake the occasional vows, including the practice of fasting, as explained in the Abhidharma's treatment of the eight vows on the full moon, new moon, and eighth lunar day, and (2) permanently maintain a single vow, thereby abandoning one of the nonvirtues, such as killing or lying.

> 6. For this reason, during auspicious times such as the full moon, do not wander about doing meaningless things. Rather, adhere to the paths leading to the higher states and liberation—namely, the eight occasional vows: the four root vows and abstention from intoxicants, wearing garlands, high beds, and meals after noon.

Do not be idle on auspicious days such as the full and new moons. Observe the eight occasional vows, the infallible cause for obtaining rebirth in the higher realms.

7. Having upheld the aforementioned ethical codes, king Bimbisāra of yore attained arhatship while living in his palace. Success is not foreordained, but by all means exert yourself in following his example.

Apropos of householders, reflect on the fact that when the Buddha was alive, king Bimbisāra undertook the aforementioned ethical codes and thereby achieved arhatship while leading the life of a layman.

8. More important still is the sun-like Mahāyāna, which is conveyed by the horse-drawn chariot of the mind of enlightenment. The Mahāyāna canon's locus of training is not the body but the mind. Therefore govern your great land[4] by means of the sunlight of the two types of the mind of enlightenment, aspirational and engaged.

More important still is the Mahāyāna, whose practice is predicated on the mind of enlightenment. Furthermore, the Mahāyāna vows do not concern the regulation of observable behavior such as that of body and speech, as occurs in the Śrāvaka Vehicle. Rather, they are predicated on the good heart, which is mental. Therefore govern your vast land solely by means of the aspirational and engaged minds of enlightenment.

9. The śrāvaka's elephant cannot bear the same burdens as the horse-drawn chariots of altruism and great compassion. Bodhisattva Drowé Palmo conjured illusions when she danced and by means of them carried out loving actions for sentient beings. In similar ways should you show benevolence for your subjects.

Altruistic actions motivated by the mind of enlightenment as such are not prescribed by the śrāvaka canon. By means of an analogy to elephants and horses, one can illustrate the relative sizes of the spiritual burdens of their respective adherents. The *Hundred Birth Stories of Buddha* narrates the episode of the bodhisattva's birth as the female dancer Drowé Palmo, who benefitted beings through dancing. Neither are you hindered by a lowly female birth; like Drowé Palmo, you should affectionately protect your subjects.

---

4. "Govern your great land" (*sa chenpo kyong*) is a pun on the title for the rulers of Degé, called "rulers of the earth" (*sakyong*).

10. The *Inquiry of Ugra the Householder Sūtra* discourses on the sixty faults entailed in the setback of birth as a woman.[5] But actually these faults do not inhere within women's essential goodness. Rather, women embody a crucial connection to enlightenment because they possess the channels of the five Buddha lineages.

The *Inquiry of Ugra the Householder Sūtra* discourses about the sixty-plus faults of women. Contrary to this, the secret mantra texts proclaim that women embody a crucial connection to enlightenment because of being endowed with channels of the five Buddha lineages. Therefore the aforementioned faults are not found within women's intrinsically good nature. Women's inferior bodies are not an impediment to the practice of the Mahāyāna Dharma.

11. Regarding the ḍākinīs from the pure lands, the *Abhiniṣkramaṇa Sūtra's* eulogistic discourse on the seven royal treasures states that the ideal queen is devoid of the five opposing forces and possesses the eight positive qualities.[6] How amazing!

Ḍākinīs from the pure lands sometimes appear in the world as the precious queen of a *cakravartin*. The *Sūtra of Definitive Emergence's* explanation of the seven attributes of kingship affirms that the precious queen is free of the five faults common to women and is endowed with eight positive qualities. Indeed, these traits are innate within you.

12. The ḍākinī embodies a method faster than ordinary methods. The mantra piṭaka extols her as the true nature of all illusions, the queen of bewildering illusions, the excellent treasury of the wisdom of bliss-emptiness. All this redounds to you alone.

---

5. The faults are actually about wives and not women in general. See Nattier 2003 for a translation of this section of the sūtra in which over ninety faults of wives are enumerated. Nattier's analysis reveals that this long tirade is found only in the later editions of the text, such as the Tibetan translation, and is not found in the much earlier Chinese translation or Prakrit fragments.

6. The commentary by Getsé Mahāpaṇḍita cites the section of this sūtra enumerating the qualities of a woman that a bodhisattva dwelling in Tuṣita heaven would choose to be his portal into the world for his final birth and attainment of nirvāṇa.

13. The so-called innate joy, from among the sixteen joys, is a dependently arisen phenomenon that issues forth from the third initiation's queen of illusion, who embodies the knowledge mantras of Prajñāpāramitā. You are that mistress of wisdom.

14. You are by nature the supreme queen of wisdom, but this primordially produced trait must be activated by conditions— namely, the ambrosial rain of the ripening initiations and liberating instructions. Now that you have been instructed, apply yourself to the two stages.

The explanation of the preceding three verses is as follows: The Vajrayāna canon is distinguished by a skillful means that is superior to ordinary skillful means—namely, the queen of wisdom. When one does not rely upon her dexterity with illusions, the third initiation is not bestowed. Because you alone are the very embodiment of her, now that you have been instructed in the nexus of practices that brings into being the abandonments and realizations—namely, the ripening instructions and the liberating guidance—apply yourself to the two stages, the paths of generation and completion.

15. The Mother of All Buddhas is called "the expanse of reality," and its nature is the faculty of mindfulness. Nirvāṇa arises from this mindfulness alone, and uncontrived mindfulness is the Great Completion.

The modus operandi of the Great Completion is to be introduced to the nature of mind and subsequently cultivate mindfulness.

16. If you acquaint yourself with the truth of that and attain mental isolation—even while living in the royal palace—you will become intimate with the one taste of all phenomena within the primordial field. I pray that the auspicious connections for such arise. May there be virtue for you!

If you habituate yourself to mindfulness, then even amid the tumult of the royal palace you will be able to sequester your mind, and through knowing how to take distracting thoughts onto the path, seeing the mode of abiding will be effortless. I pray and make benedictions that you will behold the original face of the primordial Buddha.

Colophon

The Dzokchen practitioner Rangjung Dorjé (a.k.a. Jikmé Lingpa) completed these instructions for Ngangtsul Jangchup Gyalmo, the excellent queen of Degé, kingdom of the Earth Protectors (*sakyong*).

Translated Work

Jikmé Lingpa Khyentsé Öser ('Jigs med gling pa Mkhyen brtse 'od zer). 1991. "Btsun mo la spring ba'i gtam." *Gtam gyi tshogs thag pa'i rgya mtsho*, 160–65. Lhasa: Bod ljongs bod yig dpe rnying dpe skrun khang.

Suggested Readings

Gyatso, Janet. 1998. *Apparitions of the Self: The Secret Autobiographies of a Tibetan Visionary—A Translation and Study of Jigme Lingpa's "Dancing Moon in the Water" and Ḍākki's "Grand Secret-Talk."* Princeton, NJ: Princeton University Press.

Longchen Yeshe Dorje and Jigme Lingpa. 2010. *Treasury of Precious Qualities: Book One.* Translated by Padmakara Translation Group. Boston: Shambhala Publications.

———. 2013. *Treasury of Precious Qualities: Book Two.* Translated by the Padmakara Translation Group. Boston: Shambhala Publications.

Paul, Diana Y. 1985. *Women in Buddhism: Images of the Feminine in the Mahāyāna Tradition.* Berkeley: University of California Press.

Ronis, Jann. 2011. "Powerful Women in the History of Degé: Reassessing the Eventful Reign of the Dowager Queen Tsewang Lhamo (d. 1812)." *Revue d'Etudes Tibétaines* 21: 61–81.

Van Schaik, Sam. 2004. *Approaching the Great Perfection: Simultaneous and Gradual Approaches to Dzogchen Practice in Jigme Lingpa's Longchen Nyingtig.* Boston: Wisdom Publications.

Westerhoff, Jan. 2010. *Twelve Examples of Illusion.* Oxford, New York: Oxford University Press.

Additional References

Abhiniṣkramaṇa Sūtra (*Mngon par 'byung ba'i mdo*). Toh 301.

Buswell, Robert E., and Donald S. Lopez. 2014. *The Princeton Dictionary of Buddhism.* Princeton: Princeton University Press.

Gómez, Luis O. 1999. "The Way of the Translators: Three Recent Translations of Śāntideva's *Bodhicaryāvatāra.*" *Buddhist Literature* 1: 262–354.

Gyurmé Tsewang Chokdrup ('Gyur med tshe dbang mchog grub). 2001. "Btsun mo la springs pa'i gtam gyi 'grel pa." Collected Works, vol. 1, 221–36. Khreng tu'u: Dmangs khrod dpe dkon sdud sgrig khang.

Longchen Yeshe Dorje and Nāgārjuna. 2005. *Nagarjuna's Letter to a Friend: With Commentary by Kangyur Rinpoche.* Translated by the Padmakara Translation Group. Ithaca, NY: Snow Lion Publications.

Nattier, Jan. 2003. *A Few Good Men: The Bodhisattva Path according to "The Inquiry of Ugra" (Ugraparipṛcchā).* Honolulu: University of Hawai'i.

Part II: Meditation Advice

6. Advice for Solitary Retreat

Do Khyentsé, Dza Patrul Rinpoché, and the Third Dodrupchen
Translated by Holly Gayley

Satire and Nonsectarianism

Solitary retreat is heralded by Dza Patrul Rinpoché as the site where the path to liberation is near at hand. By removing oneself from the distractions and commotion of everyday life, he avows, negative emotions naturally subside and the mind is more easily tamed. In retreat the sights and sounds of the natural world—the song of birds, the gurgling of a creek, and the clear expanse of the sky—provide a serene setting for practice, inspiring renunciation, diligence, and insight. This chapter introduces and translates three works of advice for solitary retreat composed by great masters of the Longchen Nyingthik lineage in eastern Tibet, who served as teachers and disciples to one another.[1] These works by Do Khyentsé Yeshé Dorjé, Patrul Rinpoché, and the Third Dodrupchen, Jikmé Tenpai Nyima, are poignant in their pith instructions and lively in their literary style, often using satire to convey their message. Yet despite the similarity in subject matter, each work has a distinctive style and emphasis.

---

1. Do Khyentsé Yeshé Dorjé was a teacher to Patrul Rinpoché, who served as a teacher to the Third Dodrupchen, Jikmé Tenpai Nyima. For brief biographies of these figures, see Tulku Thondup 1996. Do Khyentsé and Patrul Rinpoché were also known respectively as the mind and speech emanation of Jikmé Lingpa, who revealed the Longchen Nyingthik, a widely practiced set of esoteric Nyingma teachings.

The first work of advice, by Do Khyentsé Yeshé Dorjé (1800–66), presents detailed instructions on the creation stage (*kyerim*) and completion stage (*dzokrim*) of tantric practice through an imaginary encounter between an old *ngakpa*, or tantric practitioner, and a young *gelong*, or monk, who is preparing to enter solitary retreat. This work, *The Babble of a Foolish Man: Notes on Creation and Completion to Clarify the True Nature*, is a purposefully humorous and colloquial dialogue, far from a highbrow presentation on the topic. As the colophon specifies, his instructions are condensed into "an amusing discourse, using the colloquial expressions of villagers." While the old ngakpa's instructions on creation and completion are thorough and meant to be taken at face value, his encounter with the young gelong can also be read allegorically as an assertion of nonsectarianism in Nyingma terms. What makes this work so appealing is how Do Khyentsé's humor is woven into his comprehensive survey of the Buddhist path and his detailed instructions on tantric visualization, making his teachings both approachable and profound.

The second work, by Patrul Rinpoché (1808–87), is a witty and extensive verse text of advice, *The Call of a Sacred Drum: Advice for Solitary Retreat*. His stated purpose in composing the work is to inspire enthusiasm for solitary retreat. Akin to the "call of a sacred drum," his advice summons the reader away from mundane preoccupations toward a dedicated period of solitude and meditation. Patrul Rinpoché offers a thorough appraisal of worldly concerns, eloquent praises of solitude, potent instructions on esoteric practice, and a satirical critique of scholasticism and sectarian bias. Employing the Dzokchen rhetoric of resting at ease without contrivance, Patrul Rinpoché points to the absurdity of spending too much energy on analyzing and debating the tenets of philosophical schools, given the conditional nature of all suppositions. His final verses build to a crescendo where he questions all sectarian orientation, philosophical views, and even the veracity of language itself in the face of ineffable realization.

The last work, by the Third Dodrupchen, Jikmé Tenpai Nyima (1865–1926), is shorter than the other two. It consists of a letter that the Third Dodrupchen composed for a monastic disciple about to embark on solitary retreat. The letter appears as the first entry in a section of his collected works dedicated to advice, *A Heap of Deliciously Sweet Honey: Heartfelt Words of Counsel*. Overall, the literary style of his letter is more formal and erudite than the other two works translated in this chapter. As with his predecessors, the Third Dodrupchen places solitary retreat unequivocally higher on the hierarchy of religious pursuits than scholastic study of the monastic curriculum. Yet he also warns that if one has not taken the "four thoughts that turn the mind" (*lodok namshi*) to heart, one may be too carefree in approaching the demanding requirements of retreat practice. In that case one's practice will be no more efficacious than if one were a herder reclining on the mountain-side—relaxing while looking out over the grassland and tending yak.

As Nyingma masters and spokespeople for the yogic tradition, Do Khyen-tsé, Patrul Rinpoché, and the Third Dodrupchen echo one another in identi-fying the pursuit of scholasticism and philosophical debate for its own sake as a distraction, at best, and a breeding ground for pride and sectarian strife, at worst. As a result, these masters valorize lineage transmission over tex-tual authority as the preferred source for practicing with the proper view. A hierarchy of values emerges within these works, one that seeks to harmonize monastic scholasticism with tantric meditation techniques by arranging them in a graded order, in terms of their place on the path and their ultimate value in the pursuit of liberation. This sets the stage for what I call *yogic triumpha-lism*, in which Nyingma techniques of transmission and practice offer unique access to the culmination of the Buddhist path. Not coincidentally, they also provide an essential means of entry into the ultimate form of nonsectarian-ism: freedom from the bias of thought and duality altogether.

Let me now introduce each of these works in more detail by discussing their literary styles, the content of their instructions, and their approaches to nonsectarianism.

The Babble of a Foolish Man

The iconoclast Do Khyentsé blends satire and nonsectarianism in this ani-mated text of advice about the essentials of tantric practice, framed as a dia-logue between a young gelong and an old ngakpa near a retreat hermitage. While the bulk of *The Babble of a Foolish Man* consists of a detailed descrip-tion of the creation and completion stages, its frame story traces the con-version of the gelong, initially condescending in his queries, into a devoted disciple of the old ngakpa. In setting the scene, Do Khyentsé names the site "Appearance Grasped as Reality," suggesting that the encounter between the gelong and the ngakpa is allegorical in nature.[2] As this name suggests, the interplay between the appearance and nature of things is a theme through-out the work. The two figures' interaction ultimately subverts the human tendency—here exemplified in the monk—to prejudge others based on

---

2. A later reference places the dialogue in Repkong, where a thriving ngakpa community still exists today, though Do Khyentsé himself was a native of Golok and taught extensively throughout Kham.

sectarian identity. It does so by relegating identity markers to the sphere of mere appearance. In contrast, the ultimate nature of reality is revealed through the perspicacious advice of the old ngakpa who, despite his self-effacing remarks, proves capable of leading the young gelong to liberation. The interplay between appearance and nature also appears in criticisms of the facade of religiosity among monastic and yogic communities alike and in the final passage praising the old ngakpa as a hidden buddha.

The rhetoric of nonsectarianism is fully evident in the opening lines of the encounter. The young gelong asks:

> You, old ngakpa, in this land of Tibet, there are a lot of disputes between schools over the early and late diffusions of the Dharma and the old and new tantras. Do you know the reason why? Which tradition do you belong to?

The old ngakpa agrees on this point—"These days in Tibet, there are too many disputes among the schools"—and offers a schema to harmonize sectarian vantage points:

> If you want to know what this old ngakpa thinks, all those can be subsumed into three great traditions. What are these three? The ground is the Great Seal, the path is the Great Middle Way, and the fruition is the Great Perfection.

This threefold classification offers a preview of the yogic triumphalism of the work as a whole. It harmonizes the systems of sūtra and tantra, specifically Madhyamaka, or the Middle Way, and Mahāmudrā, or the Great Seal. Yet it proposes a schema whereby Dzokchen, or the Great Perfection, the specialty of the Nyingma, is the fruition and pinnacle of the path.

From there the text covers a wide swath of topics—from a terse historical overview of the distinction between the early and later diffusions of Buddhism in Tibet to a detailed discussion of the facets of creation and completion practice. Along the way, Do Khyentsé covers many key topics in tantric practice: the three vows, the four great streams of transmission, the three samādhis, the seven aspects of creation-stage practice, and the two main aspects of completion-stage practice. It is a pithy yet comprehensive survey of the tantric path. Indeed, it reads like a handbook for ngakpas who have little formal education, presented in brief and simple form, perhaps intended to be accompanied by oral explanation (as are so many Tibetan exegeses). According to the colophon, Do Khyentsé wrote the text in response to requests from his young ngakpa disciples. So in actuality the work may be less about educating monastics in tantric techniques or converting the reader to a Nyingma sensibility and more about the Nyingmapas performing their own preeminence to themselves. This is accomplished within the work through the dramatic conversion of the gelong.

Allegorically, I would suggest that the young gelong stands for scholastic monasticism at large and, by extension, the Sarma or "new schools" that emerged out of the later diffusion of Buddhism in Tibet from the eleventh century forward. With that said, the gelong's sectarian affiliation is never explicitly stated. The old ngakpa represents an esoteric, nonmonastic milieu, explicitly Nyingma or "old school," which is based on the early diffusion and translations of Buddhist texts during the seventh to ninth centuries. In the opening lines of the text, Do Khyentsé refers to the old ngakpa as "a lineage holder of seeing whatever arises as self-liberated and taking sensual enjoyments as the path." Through this characterization, he wishes to assure the reader of his character's enlightened status. By contrast, in a humilific stance common to the first-person voice in Tibetan literature, the old ngakpa provides a disclaimer before proceeding with his instructions:

> From the time of my ancestors, my family has belonged to the Nyingma school, based on the early translations. Even though I myself don't know anything about these schools, I follow the tantric teachings passed down by my father.

From the outset of the work, the arrogant young gelong and humble old ngakpa are positioned as foils, allegorically standing for the "new" and "old" schools of Tibetan Buddhism. The text positions the characters at the opposite poles of a series of dichotomies: monastic versus yogic, exoteric versus esoteric, and scholastic in prioritizing textual study versus devotional in relying on oral transmission. In their dialogue the gelong acts as the questioner, with his transformation from an arrogant skeptic to a devoted disciple providing the dramatic arc of the work. The respondent is the old ngakpa, thereby positioned in the role of the teacher. The ngakpa is tacitly Do Khyentsé himself, an iconoclastic lama who operated outside of the monastic fold, thinly fictionalized in the encounter.[3]

---

3. It is possible that *The Babble of a Foolish Man* as the title of the work refers to Do Khyentsé himself or the old ngakpa, given his self-deprecating comments. I translate *luntam* as the "babble of a foolish man" according to the preference of Ringu Tulku, with whom I first translated this work at approximately the same time that Rosemarie Fuchs completed her translation of the same text. Her translation is embedded within Ringu Tulku's commentary in *Daring Steps toward Fearlessness* (Ringu Tulku 2005).

How does Do Khyentsé employ the literary techniques of allegory and satire to engage in a critique of sectarianism? Two passages exemplify Do Khyentsé's use of satire. In both examples, the two main characters engage in self-ridicule regarding their respective vocations. In the first case, the old ngakpa reproaches tantric practitioners for self-deception. The passage satirizes the rote performance of ritual in which devotees are said to "prostrate until their foreheads are swollen with lumps" and "fumble their rosaries until their fingernails become cracked" without understanding even the refuge vow. These tantric practitioners perform the *gaṇacakra* feast improperly, without prescribed meat and liquor, and refuse to wear the ngakpa garb of white and red robes. According to the old ngakpa, they thereby fail to understand the dictates of the vows that they have undertaken, tantric or otherwise. On top of that they engage in self-deception, imagining themselves to be practitioners who uphold their *samaya* or tantric commitments.

In the second case, the young gelong condemns monastic pretensions to virtue. He blames sectarianism on three factors: (1) the lack of understanding of those monks who only pretend to be virtuous in their conduct, (2) misguided ngakpas who miss the main point of meditation, and (3) lamas who are more concerned with prestige than with knowledge. Accordingly, the three trainings of conduct, meditation, and knowledge are thereby corrupted, leading to schism, a sure sign that Buddhist doctrine and its realization are waning. The impassioned critique, voiced by the gelong after his brief schooling by the old ngakpa, denounces his contemporaries' preoccupation with artifice as the source of troubling sectarianism. By placing his critiques in the first-person voice of his characters, first the ngakpa and then the gelong, Do Khyentsé deftly avoids the taint of sectarianism himself. In an ecumenical spirit, he satirizes the foibles he observes in tantric practitioners and monastics alike, representing the "old" and "new" schools, respectively. Neither is free from criticism.

In the conversion of the gelong from arrogant skeptic to devoted disciple, we see a clear assertion of yogic triumphalism. After listening to the old ngakpa's extensive practice instructions, the young gelong states with newfound respect: "Thank you very much! We monks usually think of you ngakpas as the old folks in the village. I never knew you had oral instructions like these!" This statement prompts a reassessment of the worthiness and prestige of ngakpas: one's own village lama could potentially be a great Dzokchen master! In turn, a Dzokchen master, here played by the old ngakpa, is positioned as someone who can lead both monastics and tantric practitioners alike to awakening. The text ends with just such a promise by pronouncing the young gelong's attainment of enlightenment and his departure for the pure realm of Akaniṣṭha. The once skeptical monk not only becomes a devoted disciple over the course of a single encounter with an old ngakpa; he is also liberated. The promise for the reader is left hanging in the air.

Over the course of the text, in a decidedly Nyingma schema, sectarian identities and disputes are left behind for the authenticity of the "natural state, free of mental fabrication." As the text tacitly proposes, nonsectarianism is authentically located in the realization of the ultimate nature of reality. Yet, ironically, the instructions to access such authenticity are nonetheless the purview of the Nyingma. The old ngakpa represents the best of what the esoteric tradition can offer, the promise of swift enlightenment. In the process, Do Khyentsé relegates monastic scholasticism to a lower tier of Buddhist training and positions Dzokchen as the pinnacle of tantric praxis, which is at once a Nyingma specialty and at the same time presented as a teaching available to all without regard to sectarian affiliation. In this light, nonsectarianism may best be accessed through the skillful means offered by old ngakpas like Do Khyentsé himself.

In my translation I choose to highlight the colloquial style of the work and its dialogue format. I use simple language and sentence structure whenever possible, so that the dialogue has the sound of the spoken word. For example, I use "school" and sometimes "tradition" for *druptha*, which can also mean "philosophical system." I preserve the Tibetan terms *gelong* for monk and *ngakpa* for tantric practitioner to lend the translation a more Tibetan ambiance.[4] To showcase this work's arrangement as a series of questions and answers, I structure the conversation between the gelong and ngakpa in a dialogue format akin to a script, rather than as a narrative as it appears in the Tibetan, adding bold headings to signal major topics.[5] In the Tibetan there are statements regarding the affective response of the gelong after his conversion, which I place in parentheses as one would read stage directions in a script. Along these lines, to maintain the sense of a dialogue, I use the second-person mode of direct address throughout, which is explicit in certain parts of the original work and less evident in others.

---

4. With that said, there are a number of technical terms that I render in Sanskrit, since the Tibetan would be too obscure and an educated reader of Buddhist texts will often more readily recognize the Sanskrit than an English translation.

5. In adding bold headings to mark the overarching framework of the ngakpa's explanation, I am lifting the outline straight out of the original text without adding any numbers or words. The only change is formatting the translation in a way that will allow the reader to follow along more easily.

The Call of a Sacred Drum

Unlike Do Khyentsé's allegorical dialogue, which gradually guides the reader through the Buddhist path, from taking refuge to its culmination in the Great Perfection, the second work, by Patrul Rinpoché, is far more dense and concentrated. As an extended series of verses, seventeen pages in the original, the work focuses on several themes: the faults of saṃsāra, the benefits of solitary retreat, esoteric instructions for practice, and a critique of intellectualism and sectarian bias. Neither ornate poetry nor a song of realization, its literary style might be best thought of as an exhortation set to verse. The title of the work, *The Call of a Sacred Drum: Advice for Solitary Retreat*, suggests that its function is to motivate the reader to engage in solitary retreat and to offer advice on the proper orientation to meditation practice within a retreat context. The four-line stanzas are standalone semantic units[6] that shift between topics as Patrul Rinpoché explores the motivation and approach to solitary retreat from different angles. Successive stanzas build momentum around his central theme of encouraging the reader to enter retreat and thereby leave behind a life of distraction, worldly pursuits, conceptual elaborations, and, for the cleric scholars in his audience, circuitous intellectualism.

In his exhortation Patrul Rinpoché routinely employs extreme language to condemn the commotion of worldly life and to praise the virtues of solitude. He talks about angry people as ogres whose company causes one's own negative emotions to multiply. A few verses later he challenges the reader to examine if there could be "even a pinprick of happiness" in the whole of saṃsāra. Following a brief homage and statement of intent to open the work, Patrul Rinpoché asks the reader to reflect on the nature of suffering in saṃsāra. Why pursue pleasure, like bees hoarding honey, and thereby accumulate karma in the "warehouse of the three sufferings"? According to the workings of karma, worldly concern for pleasure, praise, fame, and gain only strengthen and increase negative tendencies and bind one further into the cycle of suffering, with fearful consequences at the time of death. On this matter his tone is direct and uncompromising: "Along the road of distraction, when you meet the enemy, death, / how are you going to cheat your way out of that?" Numerous stanzas end with questions of this sort meant to provoke self-reflection in the reader about human foibles.

Patrul Rinpoché then delivers a glowing account of the benefits of solitude with an emphasis on the beauty of the natural world and the delights of

---

6. There is one exception, a stanza in five lines toward the middle of the text. While the Tibetan does not indicate breaks in the stanzas, I add them here for semantic clarity.

practice. First, he insists that solitude, in and of itself, has beneficial effects, since good qualities arise organically out of disengagement from the machinations of worldly life. He goes so far as to suggest that even if one is lazy or careless in retreat, negativity will neither flourish nor increase in the absence of others. For him, solitary retreat is the best companion, like a lovely bride who provides a delightful resting place—except that here "resting" means the opportunity to practice the Dharma. Extending the metaphor, he compares solitary retreat to a bed made long ago where the practitioner can rest in the genuine nature. As his praise to solitude begins to involve esoteric teachings, Patrul Rinpoché's tone becomes more jubilant, encouraging the tantric practitioner on retreat to enjoy "spontaneous experience" without needing to be self-conscious or self-contained, thereby "reveling in yogic conduct." In a wonderful repetition of the term "joy" (*gyepa*), he pronounces: "the adept enjoys the joys of solitude with joyful laughter."[7] Amid such celebratory stanzas, there are veiled references to Dzokchen practices that would be comprehensible only to those familiar with such practices, so I have sparingly added a few explanatory notes.

An intimate tone emerges as his descriptions of solitary retreat touch upon his direct experience, couched as advice about what the reader might expect to find in retreat. This middle section has certain resonances with Tibetan songs of experience (*nyamgur*). My translation shifts into the first-person voice here, as Patrul Rinpoché begins to describe the sights and sounds of retreat. Transported to his hermitage, with a vast open sky above the wildflower-dotted grasslands, the reader can almost hear the birds whistling and creek gurgling alongside him. The intimate tone of this section is integral to the performative dimension of shaldam: Patrul Rinpoché delivers personal and direct advice, based on his own experience in retreat, thereby positioning the reader as a close disciple lucky enough to receive oral instructions directly from a realized master. Before and after this section, I use the second-person referent to maintain this feeling of direct advice, even though the Tibetan remains ambiguous in this regard.

In the final selection, we get a taste for Patrul Rinpoché's uncompromising attitude when he ridicules overanalyzing things, warning that, in excess, thought and analysis can become sources of confusion and foster sectarian contention. Analysis and debate, the mainstays of monastic scholasticism, are lampooned as mere intellectualism. As he puts it: "You prove your pet

---

7. Throughout my translation of *The Call of a Sacred Drum*, I use "adept" for *naljorpa*, which translates the Sanskrit *yogin*, rather than *ngakpa*, which translates *tāntrika*, though the terms overlap semantically in Tibetan.

theories but have no time to practice them." For Patrul Rinpoché, the point
is to practice, and solitary retreat is the ideal setting. The rhetorical force
and aesthetic impact of his statements in this section are conveyed through
a biting directness and through a stylistic use of repetition and parallelism. I
try to replicate these stylistic elements and their effects as much as possible in
my translation. Witness his use of repetition here: "examining and examining,
everything is a lie." This line signals his view of the futility of overanalyzing
and indicates his epistemological distrust of language. As he asserts, speech
is conditional and subject to falsification, given the ineffable nature of realization. From this standpoint, it is better not to talk too much—as he says
toward the end of the work, as much to himself as to the reader: "Now, no
more talk . . . / Now, no more analysis."

What might Patrul's reflections on speech suggest about the project of
translation? In the face of such an epistemological distrust of language, what
is the point of teaching the Dharma, let alone translating it? If language
itself is not accurate, can a translation be accurate? In effect, Patrul Rinpoché
questions the project of translation *writ large*—from realization into words,
from the inexpressible into expression, from pristine truth into the vagaries
of speech. What does this imply for translation choices? Does it free us to
fumble along in the necessarily inaccurate world of words in order to approximate the meaning and style of a text? Or would one have to realize a set of
teachings to be qualified to then re-translate them from the inexpressible
domain into the idioms of a new host language and culture?

The question of translatability lies at the heart of the genre of shaldam,
especially when its advice relates to meditative experience. As discussed in the
introduction to this anthology, *shaldam* refers to direct and personal advice,
alluding to speech in the context of a direct encounter.[8] However, as a form
of literature, such advice can only mimic the directness and personal nature
of a face-to-face encounter. Patrul Rinpoché gestures to the mimesis involved
in shaldam, stating that his utterance is merely "an echo, generated by the
voice/of the precious lineage of omniscient father and heirs," here referring
to Longchenpa, Jikmé Lingpa, and subsequent masters.[9] If this is the case,
is a translation an echo at still further remove from the original utterance,
carrying its resonance but growing more dim? Or is shaldam, and perhaps by
extension translation, an enlivening and refreshing of a lineage transmission

---

8. See discussion of the etymology of this term on page 8. For a further resonance of the
term *shal*, suggesting the context of a direct encounter, see Malanova 1990.

9. Thank you to Alak Zenkar Rinpoché, who pointed this out to me at the Tsadra
"Translation and Transmission" conference in Keystone, Colorado, in October 2014.

that is otherwise fading into the distance? If as Patrul Rinpoché says, "realizing the inexpressible is the root of all expression," then we might adapt his statement to the dilemma of translation: "realizing untranslatability is the root of all translation."[10]

A Heap of Deliciously Sweet Honey

Finally, from a prominent disciple of Patrul Rinpoché comes the third and briefest work translated in this chapter. It can be found in a series of short works of advice grouped together under the heading *A Heap of Deliciously Sweet Honey: Heartfelt Words of Counsel* within the extensive literary corpus of the Third Dodrupchen, Jikmé Tenpai Nyima. This erudite turn-of-the-century master was the eldest son of the great visionary Dudjom Lingpa (1835–1904) and a prestigious reincarnate lama, the third in a line of Dodrupchen incarnations. His incarnation line originated with Jikmé Trinlé Özer, one of two disciples of the famed master Jikmé Lingpa, who was responsible for spreading the Longchen Nyingthik throughout eastern Tibet.[11] The Third Dodrupchen was renowned for his erudition and, in his prime, attracted a large following to his monastic seat, Dodrupchen Monastery, in Golok. He studied with some of the great ecumenical masters of the nineteenth century, including Patrul Rinpoché, Ju Mipham, Jamgön Kongtrul, and Jamyang Khyentsé Wangpo. His own disciples came from various traditions, including the Kagyü monk with whom he shares advice on solitary retreat in the short work translated here. No stranger to retreat, the Third Dodrupchen reportedly spent the second half of his adult life in a hermitage above Dodrupchen Monastery, receiving few visitors and dedicating his time to practice, study, and composition.[12]

I translate the first work in *A Heap of Deliciously Sweet Honey*, a letter in five pages to his disciple, Karma Ngedön Chökyi Gyatso. The Third Dodrupchen's letter is written in a more erudite style than the texts of advice by Do Khyentsé and Patrul Rinpoché. It starts off systematically by dividing the path of Dharma into two approaches, that of the householder (*khyimpa*) and that of the renunciate (*rabjung*). Not surprisingly, a hierarchy of values quickly emerges that positions the renunciate practicing in solitary retreat

---

10. This view of translation is similar to how José Ortega y Gasset describes translation as a utopian task in "The Misery and the Splendor of Translation" in Schulte and Biguenet 1992.

11. The other was Jikmé Gyalwai Nyugu, one of Patrul Rinpoché's primary teachers.

12. For a short biography of the Third Dodrupchen, see Tulku Thondup 1996, 237–50.

above the householder as well as the scholar-monk. For example, he cautions his disciple not to allow scholasticism to become a distraction by devolving into the pursuit of endless information—which he likens to birds pecking at bits of grain—while forgetting to put the Dharma into practice. Instead, one should rely on lineage blessings and oral instructions, channeling these directly into meditation practice on solitary retreat. Although textual learning lays an important foundation, he emphasizes that the oral instructions of a qualified master are instrumental for clarifying doubts and ascertaining certainty in the view prior to going into retreat.

While indicating the importance of practicing on retreat, the Third Dodrupchen is not as liberal in his presentation as Patrul Rinpoché. Sequestering oneself in solitude, away from the clamor of daily life, is not enough in and of itself to transform the mind. If one takes the Dzokchen notion of wandering carefree too far and neglects the foundation of genuine renunciation, he warns that this is no better than a herder reclining on the mountainside. For this reason he emphasizes the "four thoughts that turn the mind" (*lodok namshi*), a standard element of the preliminary practices (*ngöndro*) in Tibetan Buddhism, which inspire practitioners to renounce worldly concerns and dedicate themselves wholeheartedly to practice. In the four thoughts, one contemplates the preciousness of a human birth, impermanence and the inevitability of death, the inexorability of karmic cause and effect, and the faults of saṃsāra.

The Third Dodrupchen remarks that without renouncing worldly concerns, the mind remains fickle, sometimes oriented toward the Dharma and sometimes not. In his view, one cannot make progress in meditation practice on retreat without genuine renunciation and also constant vigilance, self-examination, and exertion. In similar terms to Do Khyentsé, he highlights the potential pitfall of pretense regarding false displays of yogic conduct. He paints a picture of the absurdity of acting haughty and putting on airs of realization, which he likens to the cause of demon possession. Better to remain a hidden tantric adept than risk this type of arrogance and duplicity. In the end, the Third Dodrupchen boils all heartfelt words of counsel down to a simple dictum. Quoting from Nāgārjuna's *Letter to a Friend*, he states that it comes down to this: "tame your mind!"

Acknowledgments

I am indebted to Ringu Tulku for helping me puzzle out countless metaphors, colloquialisms, and difficult passages in these texts. I could never have attempted these translations without his generous consultation in their original preparation and revisions for the present volume. My thanks also to Sarah Harding, Wulstan Fletcher, and Joshua Schapiro, who provided comments on these translations at various stages in the process. Any remaining errors are mine alone.

The Babble of a Foolish Man: Notes on Creation and Completion to Clarify the True Nature

by Do Khyentsé Yeshé Dorjé

> Eminent father and kind benefactor,
> my teacher Rikdzin Jangchup Dorjé,[13]
> whose compassion cannot be measured,
> omniscient one, protect me always.
>
> By the radiance of his thousand rays of blessings,
> the lotus garden of my mind has bloomed.
> In order to entice fortunate ones, like bees,
> I emit the fragrance of excellent instructions.

At one time, in a mountain hermitage called Valley of Delight, there dwelled a monk, presuming to do his seasonal tantric observances, and an old ngakpa, a lineage holder of seeing whatever arises as self-liberated and taking sensual enjoyments as the path. One day, they met in the village of Appearances Grasped as Reality.

GELONG: You, old ngakpa, in this land of Tibet, there are a lot of disputes between schools over the early and late diffusions of the Dharma and the old and new tantras. Do you know the reason why? Which tradition do you belong to?

NGAKPA: In India there were no new and old teachings by the Buddha. But you're right, gelong, here in Tibet, because of the rise and decline of the Dharma, it has been categorized like that. From the reign of Lhato Thori Nyenshal up to Lord Tri Ralpachen, there was a joyous age spanning thirteen

---

13. This is an alternative name for the First Dodrupchen, Jikmé Trinlé Özer, one of the two main disciples of Jikmé Lingpa, who brought the Longchen Nyingthik teachings to eastern Tibet. It was the First Dodrupchen who recognized Do Khyentsé as the mind incarnation of Jikmé Lingpa and served as his main teacher.

generations. The Buddhist teachings spread in Tibet during that period are called the "early diffusion of the Dharma," and the ones that came afterward are called the "later diffusion of the Dharma." All the translations of tantras into Tibetan before Lord Tri Ralpachen are called the "early translations," and the ones that came afterward are known as the "later translations." Why? In between, there was a king named Langdarma, who was responsible for the destruction of the Dharma.

These days in Tibet there are too many disputes among the schools. If you want to know what this old ngakpa thinks, all those can be subsumed into three great traditions. What are these three? The ground is the Great Seal, the path is the Great Middle Way, and the fruition is the Great Perfection. From the time of my ancestors, my family has belonged to the Nyingma school, based on the early translations. Even though I myself don't know anything about these schools, I follow the tantric teachings passed down by my father.

GELONG: All right, old ngakpa, what are the scriptures of you followers of the Nyingma? What do you hold as the teachings of the Buddha? How do you old ngakpas practice according to your tradition?

NGAKPA: Don't be ridiculous, gelong! Of course, you know that the scriptures are the three *piṭakas* and the four classes of tantra along with their commentaries. The discourses of the Buddha in the three piṭakas were translated into Tibetan during the reign of Trisong Detsen, so they are our Nyingma scriptures. What are the three piṭakas? They are the Vinaya Piṭaka, the Sūtra Piṭaka, and the Abhidharma Piṭaka. What are the four classes of tantra? Of course, you know that these four are kriyā tantra, caryā tantra, yoga tantra, and mahāyoga tantra, which is equivalent to anuttarayoga tantra.

The Buddhist teachings have two aspects: the Dharma as doctrine and the Dharma as realization. The Dharma as doctrine is the twelve branches of discourses by the Buddha, and the Dharma as realization is the intended meaning of those discourses integrated into an individual's own mindstream, and whatever qualities are attained from practicing the three trainings as well as creation and completion. If you want to follow the Buddhist teachings, it's crucial to be diligent in hearing, contemplating, and meditating. At first, you hear and contemplate the Dharma as doctrine at a monastic college (*shedra*). After that, you meditate on the Dharma as realization at a retreat center (*drupdra*). These days many from both the new and old schools reverse the application of these; this is a sign that the Buddhist teachings are degenerating.

Of course, as a monk, you understand the three trainings. The subject of the Vinaya is the training in superior discipline. The subject of the Sūtra section is the training in superior meditation. And the subject of the Abhidharma is the training in superior knowledge. All together, the three trainings make up the teachings on the noble eightfold path. How is that explained? From what I've heard, right action, right speech, right thought, and right livelihood refer to the training in discipline. Right concentration refers to the training in meditation. And right view refers to the training in knowledge. Right effort and right mindfulness apply to all three and allow them to develop. For us ngakpas, there's a way to teach and practice these in conjunction with creation and completion. If you understand how, then everything described in the sūtras can be easily realized through tantra.

In our tradition, we old ngakpas practice the "four great streams of transmission" from the early translations. What are these? They are empowerment, creation stage, completion stage, and the explanation of tantra. These should be placed in the context of the four mudrās: *karma mudrā*, the ground of practice; *dharma mudrā*, the object of practice; *samaya mudrā*, the means of practice; and *mahāmudrā*, the result of practice.

I. Empowerment

To signify that we hold the lineage of the guardians Nāgārjuna and Padmasambhava, we in the Nyingma have to be accomplished in holding the three vows. The best foundation is to become either a novice or a fully ordained monk. But this old ngakpa, under the influence of my village, didn't have the right circumstances to become ordained, and so my foundation is being an *upāsaka*. As an upāsaka, I have taken only the refuge vow. For my precepts, I endeavor in the three things to be abandoned, the three things to be adopted, and the three supports. These are the genuine upāsaka vow. Besides that, I have taken the bodhisattva vow, which at root can be distilled into the three sublime methods. Within this, I hold the tantric vow in order to engage in and practice creation and completion. To the younger ngakpas with little understanding, I explain it in this way, so that they can know a little bit about the presentation of the three vows.

To receive the actual empowerment, there are many methods for how the empowerment that ripens is given, but these can be subsumed into four main ones: the vase empowerment, the secret empowerment, the wisdom empowerment, and the word empowerment. Through the potent blessings of the compassionate lama's three secrets, the empowerment is immediately bestowed on the channels, essences, winds, and mind of worthy disciples by using the auspicious substances of the vase, *amṛta*, portrait, and crystal. Then gradually, by practicing the creation and completion stages, with one body and in one lifetime, you can accomplish the state of the four *kāyas*: the *nirmāṇakāya*, the *sambhogakāya*, the *dharmakāya*, and the *svābhāvikakāya*.

What are the three things to be abandoned in the refuge vow? The main ones are seeking refuge in worldly deities, harming sentient beings, and lacking faith in the two divisions of the saṅgha.[14] What are the three things to be adopted? These three are reverence and respect for even a broken fragment of a buddha statue, for even one letter of Dharma from a torn page, and for even the outer shell of monastic garb. And what are the three supports? These are to rely on a lama who is both learned and realized, to study and reflect on the Dharma, and to retain the monastic robes.

These days, some of my old ngakpa friends suppose that teachings by one's lama are enough. They make up stories about why it's useless to study and reflect, and so they don't learn the words or meaning of creation and completion. Practicing tantric techniques, they refuse to wear the ngakpa garb; they don't even feel the need to wear an upper garment, the cotton shawl or woolen blanket. Meanwhile, they prostrate until their foreheads are swollen with lumps, and they fumble their rosaries until their fingernails become cracked. They even refuse the feast requisites of meat and liquor. Going on like this for years, they consider themselves practitioners who hold their samaya well. In my estimation, by not even understanding the refuge vow, all they accomplish is to squander this precious human body! Now you, as a monk, need to speak up. No one listens to what an old ngakpa has to say. If they did, I would tell them about the three sublime methods of the Mahāyāna, the fundamental point of the Dharma.

What are these? As preparation, it is sublime to arouse bodhicitta. For the main practice, it is sublime to practice without reference point. To conclude, it is sublime to dedicate the merit. Whatever Dharma practice or virtuous activity you do, begin by generating the sublime motivation, thinking, "I will practice this source of virtue so that all sentient beings may attain enlightenment." To do the sublime practice without reference point, approach your undertaking without fixation on the three spheres of subject, object, and action as real. As soon as you have finished, do the sublime dedication, thinking, "I dedicate this so that all sentient beings may attain enlightenment." If you don't frame your practice with the three sublime methods, you will only gain the virtue conducive to merit, which leads to rebirth as a god or human.

---

14. The twofold division of the saṅgha refers to monastics, both novice and fully ordained, and ngakpas or tantric practitioners.

If you do, you gain the virtue conducive to liberation, so that you can attain the state of buddhahood. Without a doubt, this is very important. Especially among us ngakpas, if we don't understand that we should adopt the three sublime methods, we can deviate into rudrahood,[15] a state of total egohood associated with incorrect tantric practice. You monks, if you don't know how to practice these, you have sunk to the Hīnayāna level. So don't forget this!

For us ngakpas, the crux of the vows is the creation stage, and the crux of the samaya is the completion stage. So the basis of the vows and samaya can be found in creation and completion. Even if they understand this, the lamas don't talk about it. Even if they know how to apply this, none of the disciples put it into practice. But if you want, this old ngakpa can tell you as much as I know.

II. Creation Stage

The creation stage is connected with the three samādhis. The four types of creation stage—elaborate, medium, concise, and very concise—are associated with the latent tendencies of the four types of birth and are methods to purify them. Understanding the rationale for these, you should know the seven aspects in the path of visualization: the five preliminaries through which to train, familiarize, and stabilize in direct application; the main practice; and the subsequent integration into daily life.

What are the three samādhis? The ground is called the *suchness samādhi*. Let your mind rest evenly within its uncontrived natural state. The path is called *all-illuminating samādhi*. Great compassion arises out of the unobstructed radiance, intrinsic to the uncontrived mode of being. The fruition is called the *seed samādhi*. The sublime and vibrant manifestation of inseparable emptiness and compassion transforms into a seed syllable such as *Hūṃ* or *Hrīḥ*.

In terms of the four types of birth, these are birth from an egg, birth from the womb, birth from heat and moisture, and miraculous birth. To purify them, there are four types of creation stage: the elaborate, medium, concise, and very concise. To purify latent tendencies of birth from an egg, there is an elaborate process for the creation stage, which includes visualizing the five generated from yourself and the three generated from something else. To purify the latent tendencies of birth from the womb, there is a medium-length process of creation stage. You generate the visualization through the

---

15. On the myth of Rudra, see Kapstein 2002 and Dalton 2013.

five awakenings, the four awakenings, and the three vajra rituals.[16] To purify the latent tendencies of birth from heat and moisture, there is a concise process of creation stage. As soon as you recite the seed syllable and mantra, you generate the complete form of the deity. To purify miraculous birth, there is a very concise process of creation stage. By merely recollecting the deity, you instantly give rise to the complete form. You should understand its mode of being just how it is described.

Principally, there are seven facets in the path of visualization: (1) to concentrate on the deity, (2) to amend the visualization of the deity, (3) to separate from the deity, (4) to bring the deity to the path, (5) to assimilate the deity within your mind, (6) to actualize the deity, and (7) to integrate into everyday activities.

1. To Concentrate on the Deity

Allow the form to arise of whatever deity of the three roots you intend to practice. When it first arises, an appearance without reality, meditate concentrating on that image. Sometimes stare intently at the form of the deity. At other times, allow it to reflect in mind. When you visualize by alternating these, initially the mind is turbulent with discursive thoughts. This is called the "experience of movement." After some time, there will be intervals without many thoughts, and the image of the deity will appear crystal clear. This is called the "experience of attainment."

2. To Amend the Visualization of the Deity

Whatever color, gesture, symbol, or expression is vague in the form of the deity, concentrate on that so it becomes clear.

3. To Separate from the Deity

In one session visualize by concentrating intensely on the deity without distraction. And in the next, without visualizing the form of the deity, simply attend to the natural state of mind of the meditator. Practice by alternating these two.

---

16. These refer to different steps in the visualization process. The four awakenings involve a moon disk, seed syllable, symbolic implements, and the fully formed body of the deity. The five awakenings add an acknowledgment of emptiness at the beginning, and the three vajra rituals refer to the body, speech (in the form of the seed syllable), and mind of the deity.

4. To Bring the Deity to the Path

Sometimes visualize the deity as large and sometimes as quite small. You can visualize the deity in different modes of actions and with various expressions. As a result, the presence of the deity becomes continuous whether or not you are meditating. This is called the "experience of familiarity like a flowing river."

5. To Assimilate the Deity within Your Mind

This is the key point. Meditate by letting your mind rest evenly altogether without differentiating between the deity as a meditation object and the mind of the meditator. When the vivid presence of the deity is constant in every respect, this is called the "experience of stability like a mountain." It's the culmination of stability. You should meditate until eight signs of clarity and stability manifest. The signs of clarity are *salé*, brilliant; *sing-ngé*, sharp; *lhakgé*, vivid; and *lhangé*, total. The signs of stability are unwavering, immutable, utterly immutable, and flexible. As a result, whatever appears definitely arises as the form of the deity. This is called the "experience of perfection," when appearances become the maṇḍala of the deity.

These five points are the preliminaries through which to train, familiarize, and stabilize in terms of the five aspects of successive experience: movement, attainment, familiarity, stability, and perfection.

6. To Actualize the Deity

When you reach the section for reciting the mantra, first apply the "approach," which is the nail of samādhi. Up until now, the deity has been visualized in front of you. At this point, you visualize yourself as the deity. Look at a *thangka* or statue if the visualization is unclear, and then meditate until it doesn't waver for even an instant.

Second, apply the "close approach," which is the nail of mantra. Meditate remaining in the pride of the deity until the eight signs of clarity and stability occur. Within that, the training in mantra involves visualization and recitation, whether recitation by number, such as 100,000 mantras; recitation by time, such as the four intervals; or recitation by signs, such as seeing signs in dreams.

Third, apply the "accomplishment," which is the nail of immutable realization. At a certain point, you realize that the deity to be visualized and the mantra to be recited are just mental constructs. You genuinely resolve that accomplishment comes from within and not from elsewhere. Then the Dharma to be practiced is cast off! The meditator disappears on its own! The rope of mindfulness is cut! Putting effort into antidotes falls apart! Hope and fear are released from within! Dharmatā without concept—spacious and free, peaceful beyond expression, wisdom transcending mind—becomes manifest. This is the supreme accomplishment, called *mahāmudrā*. It is seeing the face of the preeminent deity directly.

Fourth, apply the "great accomplishment," which is the nail of emanating and gathering. By means of this one preeminent deity, the only one you need to know how to emanate, you can engage in countless activities, such as pacifying, enriching, magnetizing, and destroying.

These four nails are crucial; they are points to apply in the main practice.

7. To Integrate into Everyday Activities

There are two aspects of the integration: what is to be understood and how to integrate it. First, you should understand the "three spheres" of the maṇḍala of peaceful and wrathful deities. The spheres of the five male and five female buddhas are the five aggregates and five elements. The spheres of the eight male and eight female bodhisattvas are the four sense organs of eye, ear, nose, mouth, their four sense consciousnesses, their four sense objects, and the four times. The spheres of the four male and four female wrathful deities are tactile consciousness, the tactile sense faculty, tangible objects, the cognition of touch, the view of eternalism, the view of nihilism, the view of self, and the view of defining characteristics.

Since the beginning, the objects to be purified are primordially pure. The resulting purity is intrinsic to the natural state. This is the special teaching of us ngakpas. But it's rare to find anyone who comprehends it. At any rate, if you don't understand this, when you refer to food and drink as a *gaṇacakra*, you run the risk of straying into deception.

Now, the second aspect, how to integrate this, has three parts: the nirmāṇakāya integration in life, the dharmakāya integration at death, and the sambhogakāya integration in the intermediate state.

First, from early in the morning until late at night, never stray from the play of the preeminent deity arising out of vivid presence. This is the infinite purity of the environment and its inhabitants or the three spheres of the maṇḍala of peaceful and wrathful deities, called the "nirmāṇakāya integration in life."

Second, as you go to sleep, dissolve the manifest aspect of the creation stage into the unmanifest space of the completion stage. Rest evenly in the basic ground free of concepts. This is taking sleep as luminosity, called the "dharmakāya integration at death."

Third, when you arrive in the dream world at night, recognize it as being a dream. Merge together the creation and completion practices you do during the daytime with the appearances of dreams. This is called the "sambhogakāya integration in the intermediate state."

These are the points regarding the postmeditation integration. In this way, it is necessary to integrate life, death, and the intermediate state as the three *kāyas*. By accomplishing the dharmakāya integration at death, you'll be liberated as soon as your breathing stops. By accomplishing the sambhogakāya integration in the intermediate state, even if you're not able to be freed at the moment of death, you attain the level of coemergence in the self-arising *bardo of dharmatā*. At the very least, accomplish familiarity with the nirmāṇakāya integration in life to ensure traversing to a pure realm like Akaniṣṭha or Khecara during the self-arising *bardo of becoming*.

This is the distinctive teaching of the unsurpassable secret mantra. Up to this point was a short description of the creation stage according to us ngakpas.

III. Completion Stage

Now, there are two types of completion stage—with an object and without an object. For the completion stage with an object, there are many categories, but they can be briefly summarized as the profound six dharmas: the root as inner heat, the ground as the illusory body, the essence as luminosity, the sign of progress as dreams, the escort as the intermediate state, and the assurance as the transference of consciousness.[17] You should practice these six.

As for the completion stage without object, according to the practice of us Nyingmapas, followers of the early translations, it is called the "section of esoteric instructions on the Great Perfection."[18] Through the kindness of the Indian *paṇḍita* Vimalamitra, this was translated in Tibet. If you realize it in the morning, you're able to meet the mind of the Buddha in the morning. If you realize it in the evening, you're able to meet the mind of the Buddha in the evening. This is its distinctive feature. For the method, ascertain the view of *trekchö*, which is the ground, and practice the four visions of *thögal*, beyond speech and concept, which is the path.

---

17. This list summarizes the main practices in the so-called six yogas of Nāropa, a specialty of the Kagyü lineage and often practiced within the context of the traditional three-year retreat.

18. The Sanskrit for this term is *upadeśa-varga*, and the Tibetan is *mengakdé*.

IV. Explanation of Tantra

There are ten subjects in tantra: (1) empowerment, (2) samaya, (3) maṇḍala, (4) mantra recitation and mudrās, (5) sādhana, (6) offerings, (7) activities, (8) view, (9) meditation, and (10) conduct. For each of these, you should understand its essence, definition, categories, divisions, brief and elaborate explanations, and the summary. You should also know the reasons for needing to understand these subjects, the pitfalls if you don't understand them, the benefits of understanding them correctly, and their fruition. You need to anchor these in experience just as described by examining them with scripture and logic. Being feeble-minded, this old ngakpa is sorry to say that I haven't put many of these into practice.

GELONG (with newfound respect for the old ngakpa): Thank you very much! We monks usually think of you ngakpas as old folks in the village. I never knew you had oral instructions like these! Now please give me some condensed instructions that can help at the moment of death, whatever you think is appropriate.

NGAKPA: You monks need to rely on the three trainings, especially the three disciplines. These days, few practice these exactly as the Buddha taught. Even if some may, you should know that the only way to actually attain Buddhahood in one lifetime, within sūtra and tantra, is the unsurpassable secret mantra.[19] So you should understand how the three trainings, as taught by the Buddha, can be practiced within tantra.

To do so, during the preparation for an empowerment, you take the vows of *prātimokṣa*, bodhisattva, and tantra. Observing these vows is the essence of the training in discipline. Within the main practice of creation and completion, the creation stage is the essence of the training in meditation, and the completion stage is the essence in training in knowledge.

When you combine creation and completion together and view the environment and its inhabitants as the maṇḍala and deity, this is the discipline of refraining from misdeeds. The creation stage is the accumulation of merit, and the completion stage is the accumulation of wisdom. Meditation that combines both is the discipline of consolidating virtue. The four activities are

---

19. Ringu Tulku suggested that this phrase refers to all tantra, hence my translating "the unsurpassable secret mantra," rather than referring specifically to the anuttarayoga tantra. This reading makes sense, given the Nyingma orientation of the text.

the discipline of benefitting others on the basis of emanating and gathering and so forth.[20]

Therefore, if you understand that all the essential points of sūtra are completely included in tantra and then practice accordingly, you can attain liberation in one lifetime.

GELONG (speaking in the honorific as his faith in the old ngakpa increases): Indeed! What you have explained until now is easy to comprehend, but there is still a doubt that I can't resolve. What is it? These days some say that concentrating on reciting liturgies leads to enlightenment, but I don't hear anyone say that meditation leads to enlightenment. Is this true? Please help me to resolve this doubt.

NGAKPA: You are right, gelong. If you realize the special implications of view and meditation internally, your conduct need not be so strict. This is the specialty of us ngakpas. Nowadays people don't understand the point and concentrate on the minutiae of performance. Putting effort only into reciting liturgies, they engage in techniques without understanding them and, caught up in useless activity, completely misconstrue what creation and completion are. For that reason, most ngakpas are ngakpas in name only, more careless than worldly householders. Not understanding even when explained, they sit there unpersuaded like an imbecile. They'll never attain enlightenment in this life or the next just by reciting liturgies or repeating mantras. It's not even enough to only meditate! Instead you must concentrate wholly on creation and completion. Ultimately, it all crystallizes in the completion stage. The main point is to let your mind rest evenly in the natural state, the inexpressible truth.

GELONG (in a voice quivering with devotion): Oh, thank you! Although you appear in the ordinary body of a ngakpa, you hold oral instructions that can perfect the mind as dharmakāya. You are what they call a "hidden buddha." Now, please give me some advice for swift enlightenment that encompasses a hundred words into a single meaning. If you instruct me, the gelong, I earnestly wish to stay here to meditate.

NGAKPA: The mind of the Buddha is dharmatā, untouched by concept. It is the perception of nowness, the natural state, free of mental fabrications. Just that! What distinguishes buddhas from ordinary beings is whether they real-

---

20. The four activities are pacifying, enriching, magnetizing, and destroying as mentioned earlier in the text.

ize that. The 84,000 teachings of the Buddha, the countless tantras of secret mantra, together with commentaries on sūtra and tantra consist of skillful means and an introduction to realize that crucial point.

Not letting your busy mind chase after words, rest in the meaning. Seize the primordial mode of being—beyond contrivance. When you do so, there can be an experience of bliss, unbearable to part with. Don't grasp after it! There can be an experience of clarity, so brilliant and sharp that it can be presumed to be the genuine continuity. Don't grasp after it! There can be a state of nonthought, which seems like the elimination of mental activity. Don't grasp after it! Don't remain in a state imagined to be free from conceptual mind. Turn inward toward the knower who perceives it that way.

Rest evenly with nothing to be laid to rest. This is the natural state beyond concept. When you are meditating there is no focal point. When you are not meditating there is no distraction. Mind is self-liberated, completely at ease. The knots of hope and fear are loosened. The shackles of doubt are cut. Bondage and freedom are primordially pure. Freed from antidotes, this is wisdom. With nothing more to relinquish, this is dharmatā. This is the realization of your own nature as the mind of the primordial buddha.

Having received this introduction to the nature of mind, the gelong was instantaneously liberated. At that time he attained a realization equal to his master. Then he sang this song to expose the faults and weaknesses of himself and others:

GELONG: On the surface, you appear like an ordinary man;
in reality, you're the utmost deity of the three spheres,
who unerringly lives up to the name *secret mantra*.
Father, the old ngakpa, Khyemé Dorjé, protect me.

Since childhood, I have pretended to practice Dharma,
no need to mention my aspiration to renounce.
While a novice monk, I wasted my life in dalliance;
foolishly, I didn't understand the three trainings.

Kyé ma! In these degenerate times,
many monks, concerned only with appearances,
put on the facade of interest in the teachings.
But pure discipline is as rare as a daytime star.

Most lamas and monks presume to practice tantra
but don't train in the view of creation and completion

or the noble pursuits: to hear, contemplate, and meditate.
They're distracted by who gets a high or low rank.

In this potent place, the golden valley of Repkong,
some with the pretense to be ngakpas in name
are confused, not knowing the real purpose of life.
And it's not just the disciples who are to blame.

In the region of Do Kham, there's one able to explain
how to accomplish the paths and *bhūmis* in one lifetime
by distilling the intention of sūtra and tantra into one.
He is the protector and Dharma king, Dodrupchen.

In the land of snows, some pretend to be learned.
Not knowing the distinction between new and old schools,
they create factions of us and them within the Buddha's teachings,
a sign that the Dharma as doctrine and realization is waning.

Thinking of this again and again, I get depressed.
Those who are intelligent should consider this:
you have no idea where life is headed—
if you died right now, what would you do?

If you have a faulty lama teaching you the path,
then even if you have a vajra name, what's the point?
Without realizing the profundity of creation and completion,
what's the benefit in seeking further profound teachings?

If you strive for liberation in one lifetime,
why not maintain the natural state without contrivance?
To speak of "maintaining" is just an expression;
if there's something to maintain, that's not view and not meditation.

Looking everywhere, since nothing can be found,
the terminology of "view" is itself a deceit.
Since there's no one even to maintain meditation,
how ridiculous to speak of an experienced meditator.

Even ethical discernment is your own projection.
Uprooting conceptual mind, doubt is extinguished.

The ripening of view, meditation, and conduct
is the instantaneous awareness of dharmatā.

This I realized due to the kindness of Khyemé Dorjé.
By the merit of singing this song of realization,
may the realms of confused beings, yet to understand,
attain the level of my father, a primordial buddha.

Saying this, the gelong instantaneously departed for the true, inner realm of Akaniṣṭha.

The realized master, Jamyang Gyatso, the teacher who instructed me in painting, and several among the devoted community of ngakpas asked me to write something allegorical to elucidate how to practice the view and meditation of our ngakpa tradition—namely, creation and completion along with their result. Concerned that an extensive explanation would be too difficult to comprehend, I condensed this into an amusing discourse, using the colloquial expressions of villagers. May the gathering of new tantric adepts attain the eye of wisdom!

This was composed by the Dzokchen practitioner, the youthful Yeshé Dorjé. Virtue, virtue, virtue!

The Call of a Sacred Drum: Advice for Solitary Retreat

by Dza Patrul Rinpoché

Namo Guru Lokeśvaraya

I pay homage to the bodhisattvas,
regents of all buddhas, lords of the three families,[21]
who strive with affection for infinite beings
in deeds of boundless wisdom and power.

Relying on them, one is never deceived.
The precious Vinaya, Sūtra, and Abhidharma,
all three trainings are the peerless teacher's word.
Guard these instructions as the essence of amṛta.

Since it brings delight to the minds
of those fortunate to enjoy the path to peace,
this advice for solitary retreat is like the call
of a sacred drum. What I utter here, please put to use.

Kyé ho! In the illusory city of saṃsāra,
appearing but not existing, the merchandise of karma
accumulates in the warehouse of the three sufferings,
while ignorant beings swarm around it like flies.

With more beings than dust motes in the cosmos,
since the state of happiness is rarer than a daytime star,
who is not discouraged in these realms of existence?
Why not kindle the Sugata's joy in the Dharma?

---

21. This refers to the three main bodhisattvas: Mañjuśrī, representing wisdom; Avalokiteśvara, representing compassion; and Vajrapāṇi, representing power.

The problem is overreliance on degraded people,
who have an angry disposition akin to ogres.
Befriending them, the mass of afflictions will multiply.
In dark times, who's not disheartened by such friends?

Wealth amassed and amassed like honey by bees,
you don't use for yourself, let alone for the Dharma.
When you die, it becomes iron shackles
of attachment, only serving to bind your being.

While still alive, abandon the distractions
of abundant good fortune and all its conceits.
At the time of death, what's the use of wealth,
if you consider the state of anguish that arises?

Acting as lord of the three worlds for hundreds of eons,
even so, you'd be far from quenched by desirable
    objects,
since craving increases more, experience after experience.
However much craving—you can be sure it's the cause of
    saṃsāra.[22]

Luxury provides comfort, but the result is suffering;
the fleeting pleasures of life only lead to lower realms.
Surely if you examine, within the realms of saṃsāra,
it's impossible for even a pinprick of happiness to exist.

Even those puffed up with pride, bowed to
and revered by thousands of the high and mighty,
become the lowest of the low. At the time of death,
what use are vanity and pride to you?

At the end of this dark age, the Buddha's teachings
are just a glimmer. If you're smug in this life,
you won't make effort in scripture and realization.
So seize the vital teachings, the three trainings, in your being.

---

22. The term for saṃsāra here, *sipa*, can technically refer to "becoming" in the twelve links
of the dependent origination. More generally, its valences include "existence" and saṃsāra.

If you mix your intention with the Dharma,
it may be hard to find like-minded people.
Taking the purity of mind as your witness,
it's good to minimize trying to please everyone.

A thousand buddhas cannot tame beings in dark times,
let alone ordinary people like us trying to do so.
With others' welfare as your aim,
nurture yourself on the noble path.

Distractions and deluded activities proliferate,
while your life, by nature, continually dissipates.
Along the road of distraction, when you meet the enemy, death,
how are you going to cheat your way out of that?

Taming the mind which is difficult to tame
is the footprint of the wise, none other than that.
There's no higher mark of attainment—
just that alone is the way of discipline.

Even if you mouth praises to please others,
observing their contrived mannerisms, so lovely,
without removing worldly concerns from your mind,
there's much to drag you into the stream of common folks.

If you take pleasure at the sight of degraded friends,
it's surely a sign that your mind is far from Dharma.
As soon as you cross the threshold into honor and gain,
you arrive at the doorstep of the lower realms.

Fools, upon seeing childish mirages, are deceived
by the fine riches of saṃsāra, like a deer ensnared.
Breaking free from the snare of attachment,
the wise should strive to practice in solitary retreat.

In lonely mountain ranges, praised by sages,
the preserve of buddhas, their heirs, and great hermits,
lies a precious gold mine of all good qualities.
Rely on such a place; the path to freedom is near.

Not bound by passion and aggression toward peers,
nor appeasing those higher, overseeing those lower,
aglow with the white light of renunciation, like the moon,
you're alone in a relaxed place of solitude.

In solitary retreat, a thousand rays of erudition shine
like the sphere of the sun in the sky of nonattachment.
Even when it sets, the stars circle like a hundred deities.
There's no distraction, only support for Dharma practice.

Once you abandon the viewpoint of foolish folk,
keenly apply the vision of supreme noble ones.
Then buddhas, bodhisattvas, and great warriors
will accept you, considering you their kin and heir.

Avoiding pleasurable objects like poison,
you'll find the supreme medicine of Dharma,
sublime, more delicious than the celestial elixir
of immortality, amṛta to heal the heart.

Escaping far from the enemy of commotion,
you'll find superb meditative concentration.
Good qualities will blossom all around you,
placing the power of higher perception in your hand.

Practicing Dharma, virtues proliferate;
so don't become prideful in solitary retreat.
With no one to compete with or impress,
the buddhas and bodhisattvas will bear witness.

Even when careless and overcome by laziness,
passion and aggression won't increase in solitude.
So if you diligently examine your mindstream,
anger and lust based on others will cease.

There are many distracting activities and diverting friends—
go far from these sources of passion and aggression.
In solitary retreat, there's nothing but Dharma;
what else is there for you to think about?

The capacity for joy in renunciation, strength
in compassion, and tears of faith and devotion
is naturally roused in solitary retreat
when resting, not too tightly, in meditation.

Counting on others in the long or short term—
whether a ruinous home, wayward friends,
or desirable things—definitely keep far from these;
the mass of negativity then naturally diminishes.

The varied rocky peaks are lovely like a bride,
providing thousands of delightful places to rest.
As a support for freedom in the precious Dharma,
this alone is the dwelling place of fortunate beings.

Atop the rustling leaves and bowing vines,
birds intone melodies to inspire renunciation,
calling out to me like a flock of wise celestial birds
as if to vanquish the pride of heavenly drums.

A bundle of finely shaped, fragrant flowers
blazing in a luster of a hundred red and white hues
are the enjoyment of merit by resourceful bodhisattvas,
as if deftly placed on the ground as requisites before a buddha.

Amid that, the melodious hum of bees—
as if joyfully entering a lotus grove—
inspires me to study, reflect, and meditate
in the lotus garden of faultless Dharma.

Tasting and tasting again sweet drops of nectar,
the bees get intoxicated while flying around.
Tasting the Dharma of reflection and meditation
likewise reveals a joy without clinging, isn't it so?

The expanse of sky, brilliant with the light of sun and moon,
displays thousands of beautiful, spontaneous spheres,
plundering the beauty and splendor of Akaniṣṭha
as if spread out before me as my inheritance.

The natural radiance of emptiness in the unstained sky
is enchanting like the beauty of a lapis-colored ocean.
Saying, "I signify the primordial ground, vast original space,"
it imparts the hidden meaning of "pointing out" on the secret
    path.[23]

Gushing and gurgling, a creek descends from on high,
providing the sublime gift of serenity and cool nectar.
Its melody encourages me with these instructions:
"Follow me, with sustained effort, to the ocean of omniscience."

With no provisions, the tastes from fruit trees and roots
sustain me, quelling the pride of the wish-fulfilling tree.
Whoever is satisfied with the food of austerity
surpasses the wealth of gods by a thousand times.

Slaying torpor and cutting proliferating thoughts,
I sing of naked experience, reveling in yogic conduct.
In solitary retreat, no need to be furtive or self-contained;
you can enjoy the pleasures of spontaneous experience.

Within the display of unimpeded awareness, awaken
the latent deeds of saṃsāra and nirvāṇa as a purification.[24]
In solitary retreat, there are thousands of pleasant spots
to enjoy carefree experience, blazing up in ceaseless wonder.

Entering the meditation that purifies as illusion
perceived objects and the grasped material body,
the illusory adept intones a resounding *Hūṃ*
and revels carefree in illusion's sphere.[25]

---

23. This last line refers to the "introduction" (*ngotrö*) to the nature of mind, sometimes called "pointing out" instructions.

24. This is a reference to *rushen* exercises intended to release habitual tendencies. They involve, according to David Germano, "going to a solitary spot and acting out whatever comes to your mind" (1994, 262).

25. This verse refers to the "yoga of illusion" (*gyumai naljor*) that uses the seed syllable *Hūṃ* to destroy fixation and reveal phenomena as illusion. Here the term is personified as the one who engages in that practice, hence "the illusory adept." The next verse continues on the same theme.

In solitary retreat, you can proclaim without inhibition
the fierce sound of *Hūṃ*, filling the earth and sky,
the weapon that shatters to pieces apparent phenomena,
which are the myriad guises of unimpeded awareness.

Rivaling the scepter of thousand-eyed Indra,
arrange as a vajra the supreme indestructible body,
signifying the wisdom of the *trikāya* in your own being—
no chance to be seen by unsuitable vessels here.[26]

In solitary retreat, the bed where the adept rests
is the genuine nature, as if made ready long ago
to invite the renouncing meditator back as a guest.
This is useful as a pleasant support, isn't it so?

The way to invoke the *śrāvaka*'s peaceful meditation
is the unwavering sevenfold cross-legged posture.
In the pose of wrathful dance with a bodhisattva gaze,
the adept enjoys the joys of solitude with joyful laughter.

Keeping to snowy ranges, like the king of beasts,
intrepid and fearless, never lose sight of *dharmadhātu*,
which outshines saṃsāra and nirvāṇa.
In solitary retreat, you are a lion among men.

Roaring, devour the wild game of discursive thought
and mangle the head of the Hīnayāna fox.
Sporting the lush turquoise mane of direct perception,
how could you get lost in the city of distraction?

Experiencing the display of wisdom and space,
spontaneous presence, retract the limbs of duality
in the proud physical form of the lord of elephants.[27]
From that, enjoy true comprehension in solitary retreat.

---

26. This posture is not meant to be seen by the uninitiated, making solitary retreat an ideal setting for its practice.

27. This verse—and several above and below it—relates to the *trikāya* poses: the lion, the elephant, and the hermit (*ṛṣi*), which correspond to *dharmakāya*, *sambhogakāya*, and *nirmāṇakāya*, respectively. In the elephant pose, the limbs are retracted to signify withdrawing from dualistic fixation. The gaze for this pose is described in the next verse.

In the manifesting rainbow patterns of *sambhogakāya*—
the radiance of lamps of self-existing wisdom and awareness—
with the gaze of far-reaching sideways glances,
enjoy the state removed from discursive elaborations.

Solitude of body, the blazing of wisdom's blissful heat,
solitude of speech, beyond expression, the skill of hermits,
and solitude of mind, none other than the six lamps,[28]
this is enjoying the display of the four visions, isn't it so?

Seeing with the all-knowing eyes of *nirmāṇakāya*,
which apply the gaze of compassion, narrowing the eyes,
this is the vital point to clear away impure habits,
like a divine hermit on solitary retreat.

The supreme Buddha, his heirs, and *siddhas*
all relied completely on solitude,
the beautiful pleasure grove of gods.
In this divine place, who wouldn't feel inspired?

If you remain in this place, you'll get disgusted
with craving and never lament saṃsāra.
With serene meditation, through the force of aspiration,
you'll combine the two benefits of self and other.

Dredging the depths of saṃsāra to benefit beings,
the mind pacifies elaborations into space, completely free.
Within that wisdom, the fault of seeing things as saṃsāra
naturally ceases; that is called "emptying saṃsāra."

Unimpeded awareness, beyond the scope of intellect,
is the essence of dharmakāya, ever-present.
When left alone, uncontrived and unaltered,
it's the luminous nature, the vast primordial ground.

In the space of equality, boundless and unobstructed,
the expanse of vajra essence, there's no view, meditation, or action.

---

28. The six lamps and four visions have to do with the practice of *thögal* or "direct crossing," which follows *trekchö* or "cutting through" in the Dzokchen system.

Striving on the paths and stages is worn out as child's play.
Left alone, awareness is Vajrasattva, indestructible being;
if contrived and fabricated, it descends down the path of confusion.

Awareness-wisdom, devoid of conceptual elaboration,
is the supreme essence of all solitude.
Fortunate ones who delight in this kind of solitude,
even when staying in town, act as if utterly alone.

Bound by fixation and the demon of self-preoccupation,
undeluded mind is cast into the abyss of delusion.
Remaining without fixation or grasping, saṃsāra
and nirvāṇa self-liberate in the expanse of dharmakāya.

Meditative stability, attained through various methods,
is compounded and thereby unreliable, due to circumstance.
The mind of dharmakāya, left alone without effort,
is uncompounded, so adverse circumstances arise as aids.

Fixation, the fetter that binds, imagines, "This."
Conviction, the cause of confusion, imagines, "I am."
Effortful action, a childish mindset, imagines, "It's done."
Utterly abandoning all that is dharmatā.

Transcending empty and not empty is the great emptiness.
Neither looking nor not looking is the vital point of outlook.
If you break the bounds of meditation and nonmeditation,
however you act, even so, it's just the play of illusion.

The enumeration of vehicles into stages and reverse order,
and all the philosophical assertions, true and false,
are like arguing over good and evil in a city of *gandharvas*.[29]
Without fixation, they fall apart like a knotted snake uncoiling.

The expanse of equality is unimpeded awareness without end;
even if it moves with thoughts as its expression, like waves on water,
without the animating factor of grasping, it is akin to a dead snake.
Thus the adept can act, enjoying whatever is desirable.

---

29. The *gandharva* is a class of spirit in Indian cosmology, and "a city of gandharvas" is a standard analogy for illusion.

With awareness in its own bed, on the ground of dharmatā,
the instruction for meditation is "resting freely like the ocean."[30]
In the play of dharmatā, the spontaneous expression of awareness,
the instruction for action is "mastering appearances."

High up the rocky precipice of lustful and angry thoughts
and in the dense forest of confused conceptuality,
here the king of *garuḍas* enjoys natural freedom,
and the gazelles of empty awareness frolic in play.

If you don't exhaust the conviction that imagines "that's it,"
however much you practice, you're on the path to confusion.
Recognizing all that, if led astray by reference points,
how will you ever find the paths and stages to traverse?

Whatever you do, just that is the path to freedom.
However much you practice, the natural expanse of dharmakāya is
    there.
Good and evil are child's play; the meaning is the same.
Without goal-orientation, the mind is continually at ease.

Since all phenomena are conditioned, moment by moment,
how can momentary appearances help or harm the mind?
Right and wrong are etchings on water; there is no gain and loss.
Without hope, the eight worldly concerns fall apart on their own.

Since it's within yourself, what are you searching for?
Left alone, dharmakāya is there, so what are you accomplishing?
Whoever knows that striving for realization is bondage
will be free from the shackles of philosophical theories.

Resting within the dharmakāya, nothing to be done,
there's no time to count the atoms in the universe.
In the vast open blissful expanse, left alone,
it's good to avoid lectures on philosophy.

While some compose treatises and others teach
and a few get distracted by the cycle of debate,

---

30. "Resting freely like the ocean" is one of three *chokshak*, or ways to rest the mind, in Dzokchen as referenced in this text. The last line of this stanza may refer to another of the chokshak, "resting freely with appearances."

when examined, everything is true and everything is false.
What's the use of circumstantial truths and falsehoods?

You prove your pet theories but have no time to practice them.
Since everything's true, refutations and proofs are superfluous.
Examining and disputing the treatises of others,
like harmless mirage water, what's the point of damming it?

Whether the nature of appearances is true or false,
whether the nature of mind exists or not,
whether the nature of confusion is empty or not,
why analyze according to your own system?

If thoughts and analysis have confused you so far,
with still more analysis, you'll be more confused!
Resting without fixation in nonthought,
the spontaneously perfect basis has never wavered.

Hundreds of noble ones and ordinary individuals in the past
have established their own philosophical systems thoroughly,
but to immature minds, it appears as mere contention;
further assertions are just more of the same.

Whatever you do, undertake to reject contention.
Whatever you say, recognize it as circumstantial truth.
Ultimately "it is" and "it isn't" don't really exist.
Abandon personal opinions. Left alone, there's no problem.

When you renounce the confusion of saṃsāric activity,
what nirvāṇa is there to attain later?
If you understand the nature as primordial buddhahood,
why would you wish for buddhahood all over again?

The path and result, the view and conduct,
every right and wrong, have the same basis.
Within the sphere of effortless discernment beyond thought,
deliberate activity and grasping should naturally purify.

Now, no more talk. There's no true or false in conversation.
Now, no more analysis. There's no "is" and "isn't" to things.

Everything has the same taste, whether true or not;
it's nothing but spontaneous chatter, whatever arises.

Examining and examining, everything is a lie.
Practicing and practicing, nothing to grasp in Dharma.
However much you say, there's no end to talking.
Realizing the inexpressible is the root of all expression.

Who knows the true nature? Certainly not me.
This utterance is like an echo, generated by the voice
of the precious lineage of omniscient father and heirs.[31]
What I express here is beyond my own experience.

At heart a rogue, I wear the shell of holiness;
seeming mature but immature, I am an idle boy.[32]
The words set forth here, like the color of bitter fruit,
how lovely they appear when you gaze at them.

Though the poison of faults has spread in my mind,
it's not mixed up, even a little, in what I've said here.
To inspire joy, eloquent speech consistent with Dharma
is worthwhile to adopt, even if spoken by a child.

Though the fire of negativity burns in my being,
and, like an incense stick, I hold the ashes of lowly deeds,
this eloquent speech emits fragrance in all directions;
may it delight the noble ones someday.

Though my own qualities fade day by day,
like a butter lamp with frayed wick, going out due to bad karma,
I am still able to provide illumination for others;
may I stand at the end of the line of omniscient ones.

May I remain as the victorious regent of the Buddha.
May the assembly of bodhisattvas flourish,

---

31. At the Tsadra "Translation and Transmission" conference, Alak Zenkar Rinpoché identified the "father and heirs" as Longchenpa, Jikmé Lingpa, and subsequent masters.

32. This translates one of Patrul Rinpoché's pen names, Abu Lhöpo. *Abu* is a term of endearment for a young boy, and *lhöpo* means someone who is idle and carefree in a slightly pejorative sense.

as in the time of the Buddha. May all attain buddhahood.
May the noble Buddhist path spread throughout the world.

Life after life, may I never part from the jewel of faith.
In an atmosphere of single-minded conviction,
may I, the fortunate one with folded palms,
touch a speck of dust at the feet of the Jetsun Lama.

May it be virtuous!

A Heap of Deliciously Sweet Honey:
Heartfelt Words of Counsel

by the Third Dodrupchen, Jikmé Tenpai Nyima

I pay homage to the benevolent root guru.

Generally, as the basis for practicing the sublime Dharma, there are two approaches: that of the householder and that of the renunciate. According to the first, the method for leaders as well as subordinates and ordinary people is to maintain their own household without contravening the path of Dharma. This is done by relying on the five foundations of comportment and the seven foundations of merit-making based on material goods.[33] Although there are numerous such methods for attaining provisions for this world and the next, now is not the occasion to elaborate.

The second is the method for renunciates. Whether you are a novice or a fully ordained monastic, first and foremost exert yourself in studying: taking in worthy counsel and guarding it with great diligence. Even though there are general topics of knowledge—such as grammar, poetry, and astrology—in this short life during degenerate times, to be distracted by minutiae of this sort is akin to birds pecking at tiny bits of grain while a pile of feed slips away and is lost.

What is the essential point to grasp—solely and unmistakably—on the complete path to enlightenment? You need to obtain the unbroken blessings of the Dharma transmission traced to our teacher, the Buddha. It is not sufficient to read books alone. Rely on a master and thoroughly clarify your doubts regarding the instructions.

---

33. The Third Dodrupchen does not mention what these five and seven categories entail. The term for "comportment" (*tulshuk*) usually implies yogic conduct, but that is not likely the case here, given the context of ordinary householder practice under consideration in this passage. In that case, it could refer to the five precepts of an *upāsaka*. The seven kinds of materials for merit-making may refer to the daily offerings that a Tibetan householder makes in seven bowls on the shrine in their home, including offering water (all seven bowls or just two), flowers, incense, butter lamps, perfume, and food. On the symbolic meaning of these, see Beer 2003, 56–58.

Then, without casting about and chasing after outwardly oriented knowledge, you should one-pointedly hold steady to practice and take to heart what you've learned. Don't waste your life on misdeeds like appeasing corrupt associates and saving face amid turmoil. Don't waste your life on the triad of enmity, contention, and spite. Don't waste your life on commerce and agriculture, plans and projects, nor on the round of endless gossip.

Doing all that, the opportunity for even one day of genuine practice won't arise! So remove yourself from such clamor and remain in solitude. Even so, if when residing in solitary retreat you spend your time in carefree distraction, idle at leisure, doing whatever comes to mind, you're no different from a herder reclining on a mountain slope.

For that reason you must constantly train yourself in the four thoughts that turn the mind.[34] If you're distracted even for a moment, wavering between a Dharmic view and non-Dharmic thoughts, spur yourself to regain a sense of urgency. Without prior training, you'll only generate a fickle hair-tip of renunciation—which at times arises even though you're not meditating, and at times doesn't arise even when meditating. For renunciation to be reliable and arise when needed, contemplate the four thoughts that turn the mind according to explanations from oral discourses and the textual tradition.

Each morning, forge the intention: "Today, instead of performing ordinary activities in this hermitage, I will sustain only my spiritual practice." If you have Dharmic thoughts within a practice session but negative states of mind arise in the break between sessions, you'll make no progress and gradually grow insensitive. Instead consistently cultivate mindfulness, examining yourself at all times and never forgetting the continuity of your spiritual practice.

In that way, maintain tremendous exertion. With excessive effort, however, you may get fed up and not want to stay in retreat. For this reason you should know how to engender diligence like a lute string that remains tight but relaxed. Occasionally listening to or reading the life stories of various past masters will enhance your diligence. For inspiration, read the life stories of the founding fathers of the Kagyü lineage such as Jetsun Milarepa, the lineage masters of Shijé and Nyungné,[35] and the heart-essence lineage of Dzokchen, the Great Perfection.

---

34. The "four thoughts that turn the mind" (*lodok namshi*) make up a standard set of contemplations to encourage renouncing worldly concerns and turning toward Dharma practice. They are regarded as outer preliminaries to tantric practice. The list of four is given in the introduction to this chapter.

35. *Shijé* or "pacification" is a practice lineage generally considered to have been transmitted to Tibet by Pha Dampa Sangyé in the eleventh century. *Nyungné* is a fasting practice ascribed to Gelongma Palmo, who may have lived in the tenth or eleventh centuries.

Vowing to emulate the masters, each evening assess whether your spiritual practice improved or deteriorated on that day. Enumerate your faults to yourself if your practice seems to be deteriorating and ardently forge the intention: "Tomorrow won't go this way." If your practice is improving, reflect that this has occurred on the basis of solitary retreat, and eventually you'll take delight in solitude. Recall the kindness of the Three Jewels and seal the day with pure aspiration.

If you assume the appearance of a recluse and adept, you may become tainted by arrogance. Holding others in contempt and belittling them, you may hope for people to admire you and show off whatever good qualities you've developed. Even if no realization arises, you may still wish to teach the Dharma. Not achieving meditative heat, you may exhibit inappropriate and crass behavior. Far from accomplishing the Dharma, this is the cause of demon possession. For this reason, hide your yogic conduct like a treasure underground or like a fire beneath a pit of ashes.

Generally, by turning the mind toward the Dharma, Dharma does progress along the path.[36] Relying on the kindness of the lamas and Three Jewels, it's vital to always make an effort to offer supplications and rouse devotion, to purify obstacles to realization through confession and the four powers,[37] and to cultivate favorable conditions through the many methods of accumulation.

By grasping the pith of the pragmatic instructions, and by engaging wholeheartedly in practice in solitary retreat, gradually corrupted views will diminish, and the pure, uncorrupted view will grow stronger and stronger. That is called "taming the mind." Apart from taming the mind, there is no other point to such instructions. According to the eminent master Nāgārjuna:

What more to say to one free from fear?
The point of beneficial instructions is this:
Tame your mind! The Bhagavan stated:
"The mind is the root of Dharma."[38]

---

36. This is a reference to the first two of the "Four Dharmas of Gampopa," a well-known Kagyü chant.

37. The "four powers" (*topshi*) are integral to confession practice and purifying negative deeds in Tibetan Buddhism. The four are: (1) the power of reliance or support, such as taking refuge in Vajrasattva, (2) the power of regret over the negative deed, (3) the power of resolution not to do a deed again, and (4) the power of remedial action, which can be any number of meritorious deeds. For an explanation of the four powers, see Patrul Rinpoche 1998, part 2, chapter 3.

38. This quote is from Nāgārjuna's *Letter to a Friend* (Sanskrit: *Suhṛllekha*), verse 117. For a translation of this work, see Padmakara Translation Group 2005.

Once the root of Dharma is firmly planted through going for refuge and contemplating the four thoughts that turn the mind, you should train by holding the twofold bodhicitta—the heart of the general path of Mahāyāna—as the main point of practice.[39] There's no point in me writing something brief and makeshift here about the method to do so; you should already know in detail from the *Way of the Bodhisattva*, the *Great Chariot: A Treatise on the Great Perfection*, and Gampopa's *Ornament of Precious Liberation*.[40]

Specifically, if you engage in yogic practices of the uncommon method to meditate on ultimate bodhicitta—namely, the Great Seal and the Great Perfection—you must hold the foundational empowerment and tantric vow of samaya. Then put into practice the discourses of past masters—scholars and adepts—and the elixir of speech of an experienced lama regarding the introduction to these: the divisions into view, meditation, and action; the removal of hindrances and enhancement of practice; and so forth. By doing so, before long the qualities of the paths and stages will quickly blossom like a sprout in summer.

According to the request made in a letter and accompanied by a present, sent from a descendant of the Yilhung Lharu family with sublime qualities and magnanimous character named Karma Ngedön Chökyi Gyatso, I hope this personal advice will also benefit a few others who strive to acquire it. Although I myself, Jikmé Tenpai Nyima, have no experience practicing the Dharma, this is written as mere drops from the stream of speech of those sublime accomplished masters who brought the Dharma into experience, such as the bodhisattva Śāntideva.

May it be supremely virtuous! Virtue! Virtue! Bhavantu śubha!

---

39. *Bodhicitta* means "awakened mind" and has two aspects, relative and ultimate. Relative bodhicitta involves (a) aspiring to save all sentient beings from suffering as expressed in the bodhisattva vow and (b) entering the bodhisattva path, encapsulated by the six *pāramitās*: generosity, discipline, patience, exertion, meditation, and superior knowledge. Ultimate bodhicitta is synonymous with the Mahāyāna teachings on emptiness.

40. See Shantideva 2006, Longchen Rabjampa (forthcoming), and Gampopa 2017.

Translated Works

Do Khyentsé Yeshé Dorjé (Mdo mkhyen brtse Ye shes rdo rje). 2009. *Bskyed rdzogs kyi zin bris blun gtam de nyid gsal ba.* Collected Works, vol. 8 (*nya*), 524–56. Chengdu: Rdzogs chen dpon slob rin po che.

Dodrupchen Jikmé Tenpai Nyima (Rdo grub chen 'Jigs med bstan pa'i nyi ma). 2003. *Bslab bya'i snying gtam zhim mngar sbrang rtsi'i gong bu.* Collected Works, vol. 1, 328–33. Chengdu: Si khron mi rigs dpe skrun khang.

Dza Patrul Orgyen Jikmé Chökyi Wangpo (Rdza Dpal sprul O rgyan 'jigs med chos kyi dbang po). 2003. *Dben pa'i gtam lha'i rnga sgra.* Collected Works, vol. 1, 351–65. Chengdu: Si khron mi rigs dpe skrun khang.

Suggested Readings

Jamgön Kongtrul. 1996. *Creation and Completion: Essential Points of Tantric Meditation.* Translated by Sarah Harding with commentary by Khenchen Thrangu Rinpoche. Boston: Wisdom Publications.

Ngawang Zangpo, trans. 1994. *Jamgon Kongtrul's Retreat Manual.* Ithaca, NY: Snow Lion Publications.

Tulku Thondup. 1996. *Masters of Meditation and Miracles: The Longchen Nyingthig Lineage of Tibetan Buddhism.* Boston: Shambhala Publications.

Additional References

Beer, Robert. 2003. *The Handbook of Buddhist Symbols.* Boston: Shambhala Publications.

Dalton, Jacob. 2013. *The Taming of Demons: Violence and Liberation in Tibetan Buddhism.* New Haven: Yale University Press.

Gampopa. 2017. *Ornament of Precious Liberation.* Translated by Ken Holmes, edited by Thupten Jinpa. Boston: Wisdom Publications.

Germano, David. 1994. "Architecture and Absence in the Secret Tantric History of rDzogs Chen." *The Journal of the International Association of Buddhist Studies* 17.2: 203–335.

Kapstein, Matthew. 2002. *The Tibetan Assimilation of Buddhism: Conversion, Contestation, and Memory.* Oxford: Oxford University Press.

Longchen Rabjampa. Forthcoming. *The Great Chariot: A Treatise on the Great Perfection.* Translated by Ives Waldo, edited by Constance Miller. Boston: Library of Tibetan Classics (Wisdom Publications).

Malanova, T. M. 1990. "On the Interpretation of the Term *zhal-snga-nas [mdzad pa]* as used in Tanjur Colophons." *Acta Orientalia* 44: 23–24.

Padmakara Translation Group, trans. 2005. *Nagarjuna's Letter to a Friend with Commentary by Kangyur Rinpoche.* Ithaca, NY: Snow Lion Publications.

Patrul Rinpoche. 1998. *The Words of My Perfect Teacher.* Translated by the Padmakara Translation Group. Boston: Shambhala Publications.

Ringu Tulku. 2005. *Daring Steps toward Fearlessness: The Three Vehicles of Buddhism*. Edited and translated by Rosemarie Fuchs. Ithaca, NY: Snow Lion Publications.

Schulte, Rainer, and John Biguenet, eds. 1992. *Theories of Translation: An Anthology of Essays from Dryden to Derrida*. Chicago: University of Chicago Press.

Shantideva. 2006. *The Way of the Bodhisattva*. Translated by the Padmakara Translation Group. Boston: Shambhala Publications.

7. Traversing the Path of Meditation

Bamda Thupten Gelek Gyatso
Translated by Michael Sheehy

Bamda Lama Up In Your Face

Among the prime movers in the nineteenth-century revival of Jonang scholarship was Bamda Thupten Gelek Gyatso (1844–1904), more affectionately known by Jonangpas as "Bamda Lama." One of the great powerhouse figures of his generation, Bamda Lama was critical in situating the Jonang tradition within the broader Buddhist intellectual discourse that emerged during his lifetime in the far-eastern frontiers of Tibet.[1]

Bamda Lama was born down the road from the Dzamtang monastic complex and was recognized as a prodigy early in his life. At eighteen years old, Bamda Lama ventured into the Degé district of Kham, where he found himself immersed in the rimé eclectic moment. He studied primarily with Jamgön Kongtrul Lodrö Thayé (1813–99), Dza Patrul (1808–87), and Phurtsa Khenpo Akön (1837–97) at Dzokchen Monastery.[2]

Bamda Lama went on to become one of the most widely recognized Kālacakra masters from the Jonang tradition—overshadowed only by Dölpopa and Tāranātha. His tantric and nontantric writings continue to serve as core sources for the contemporary Jonang scholastic and meditation

---

1. Ngawang Lodrö Drakpa 1992, 412–24 and Kapstein 2001, 306–13.

2. Dza Patrul was Bamda Lama's main teacher for Dzokchen, and Phurtsa Khenpo Akön, the eleventh throneholder at Dzokchen Monastery's Śrī Siṃha Academy, was his main teacher for textual studies. See Ngawang Lodrö Drakpa 1992, 184.

curriculum.[3] Bamda's literary output was tremendous. Within his twenty-two-volume collected works, we find compositions across genres and traditions. He wrote on subjects ranging from Dzokchen instructions to the sixfold Dharma teachings of both Nāropa and Niguma. He also composed a multivolume commentary on the *Abhisamayālaṅkāra* and penned a seminal work on collected topics for reasoning based on Geluk epistemology. His most influential writings, however, are his extensive expositions on the Jonang system of the *Kālacakra Tantra*. It is these writings on ritual, astrology, and yogic praxis that revivified the Jonangpa tradition of composing commentaries on various aspects of the Kālacakra. Today these works serve as primary source materials for the study of tantric systems within Jonang retreat settings. From Bamda Lama's extensive writings, I have selected two concise shaldam texts that impart his personal advice about how to traverse the Buddhist path of meditative cultivation.

Literary Features of Shaldam

Shaldam are spoken or written advice on a variety of subjects, almost always about personal transformation through Dharma practice. The term *shal* is a word for "face," suggesting an intimacy of presence, of both teacher and student, as well as author and audience. *Dam* means to explain or instruct. Hence the term denotes an interpersonal exchange wherein a disciple is up close and literally *in the face* of the master who is instructing. The term *shaldam* conjures an image of a student sitting so closely to his or her teacher that the warmth from the guru's breath can be felt, the micromovements of the guru's facial expressions can be discerned, and the intonations in the guru's voice can be heard.

This type of instruction is designed to capture an intimate exchange of knowledge that was communicated in a setting that is not repeatable. Such intimate exchanges are intrinsic to Buddhist tantric transmission whereby a disciple becomes a vessel for the knowledge of the guru. Shaldam, in particular, often offer heartfelt advice about how to shift one's habituated way of being in the world. They also include advice about the deep listening that enables such a shift to occur. The texts selected here place particular emphasis on the student's capacity to listen, think critically, and retain knowledge. The directives imparted in shaldam texts are understood to derive from hands-on experience as opposed to textbook learning, and therefore are highly customized to a particular topic.

---

3. See Sheehy 2009b.

Shaldam occur within a broader Tibetan lexical constellation that includes words that are specific not only to types of instruction, but to styles of reception and learning as well. Related literary clusters include spontaneous songs of realization (*nyamgur*) and poetic songs (*gurlu*), correspondence letters and dialogues (*drilen*), as well as comparable forms of written advice (*triyik*) and guidance texts based on personal experience (*nyongtri*). The term *shaldam* in particular relates to a sibling set of words that emphasize a first-person immediacy; this set includes pith advice (*shalta*), direct advice (*shalkö*), oral transmission (*shalgyun*), personal direction (*shalshé*), and final testament (*shalchem*). Insofar as these terms signal a kind of advice that is worth receiving, because of its transformative effect, they fall under the broad rubric of "what there is to learn" (*lapja*).[4]

The usage of the term *shal* as a prefix links itself semantically to deep-rooted Buddhist sensibilities about the power of words. The practice of repeating the sūtras or words of the Buddha has its origin among the earliest disciples of the Buddha in India. This origin is captured by the Tibetan word *ka*, indicating words that come directly from the Buddha's mouth.[5] In a similar vein, we find the Tibetan word *ngak*, meaning speech, used for spoken instruction (*damngak*), and the more esoteric expressions of direct spoken instruction (*mengak*).[6] These terms suggest content that is deliberately obscure or cryptic, giving this literature a reputation for being arcane. Shaldam, in contrast, is practical, even playful.

One value of shaldam literature lies in its importance as a historical record of exchange between two or more persons. Shaldam texts are typically composed in response to a request made in person by a disciple. This information is regularly documented in the colophon of these works, giving us a record of a particular interaction. Such information can prove to be a window into the intricacies of a relationship—like reading the prescriptions of a psychologist to his patient.

Given that these records of interpersonal exchange claim to capture the immediacy and spontaneity of the special instruction, we might ask whether

---

4. The term *shaldam* is defined as "*gdams ngag gam slob bstan/ shal gdams bslab bya/ khyed kyis gsungs pa'i shal gdams rnams sems la bcangs yod/*" and "*shal = shal nas gsungs pa / kha'i zhe sa/.*" (Dungkar Losang Trinlé 2002, 2380). On life advice and shaldam in Tibet, see Schapiro 2012, 66–75.

5. On scripture recitation and speaking for the Buddha in early Indian Buddhism, see Nance 2011, 14–35.

6. *Damngak* has a broader connotation than *mengak* and is used within a variety of contexts to specify an instruction on a given subject. *Mengak* can denote a higher degree of esotericism. On the contrast between these terms, see Kapstein 1996, 284n1.

the very act of transferring the spoken word to written text alters the message. And why have these texts been so commonly printed in the first place? The practice of writing down verbatim an oral teaching or instruction is common in Tibet. One of the recurrent methods of composition is for a learned master to speak a text, or comment on a text, for scribes to record. After transcription, the text is gradually edited, reviewed, and recomposed for further reproduction. Throughout this process the spoken word is waxed, acquiring appreciable complexity of structure and literary virtue. By modifying syntax and formalizing colloquialisms and patois utterings, teachers and their students adapt the spoken word to the written form.

These scribal and editorial procedures, coupled with an authorial desire to maintain the integrity of what was said, often result in the layering of intentionality, innuendo, and idiosyncratic expression. The product is typically a highly polished hybrid work of vernacular literature that uses figures of speech found within everyday natural language—slangy, demotic, idiomatic—yet codified by the technical speak of the particular discipline that is being instructed.[7] In the case of shaldam, one finds technical Dharma language communicated with a vernacular feel. All of this gives further rhetorical force to the written passage. So while the setting in which the instruction was imparted is gone—for the guru's warm breath has forever evaporated—there are layers of nuance and complexity written into shaldam that were not present when they were originally communicated orally.

Bamda's Shaldam in Translation

Though layered with literary features, the shaldam texts translated here bring us as close as we can get to precious face-time with Bamda Lama. Among his extensive treatises are preserved two short, sweet texts that record instructions that he spoke: *Extracting the Essence of Freedoms and Fortunes* and *Concise Personal Advice*. Stylistically, each exemplifies the intimacy, directness, and idiosyncrasy that are hallmarks of shaldam.

While my translations strive to capture some of the figures of speech and natural language of Bamda's advice, in their written form both texts employ

---

7. For a good example of a polished vernacular Tibetan text, see Ricard 2001. The vernacular is not spoken language per se but rather a literary language that is grammatically and syntactically based on the spoken language, adapted to text. It is the language used in the composition of vernacular literature. This is often in verse, sometimes fifteen-syllable or, in the case of Bamda Lama's texts, nine-syllable verse. Vocabulary of vernacular texts can draw from technical terms and learned languages. See Hinterberger 2006, 12.

stylistic and linguistic registers that lend Bamda's words a texture that is not always translatable. For instance, in his *Concise Personal Advice*, he contrasts the phrases "the way things are" (*tsulshin*) and "how things are" (*tsulyin*) with "how things are not" (*tsulmin*), and then creates a compound to express what is real and unreal (*tsulyinmin*). In Tibetan these terms not only are in literal opposition but are harmonically discordant—a quality not easily captured in English. Both texts are also metered in nine syllables, which I made no attempt to mimic in translation. For each text, I have inserted topical headers within the translation in order to provide scaffolding that might give a fuller vision of the logical structure of the work.

In *Extracting the Essence of Freedoms and Fortunes*, Bamda guides the reader through the course of the Buddhist path of transformation. He begins with the arousal of revulsion for the appetites of saṃsāra through contemplating the unlikelihood of being human. He later outlines the logic of altruism and the subtle inner gestures of Vajrayāna deity-yoga practice before concluding with the apex of Dzokchen. His advice orbits around a dyad: the "freedoms and fortunes" (*daljor*) that create the conditions that allow human beings to transform themselves into buddhas.

The Tibetan text is pithy, with a spoken syntax. Almost every line ends with a connector of one kind or another. The text thereby features a series of long, logically flowing strings of segues and run-on sentences. There is ample use of metaphor, such as Bamda's allusion to the alchemical transmutation into gold, a thematic riff on the title "extracting the essence." He also switches voices within the instructions. For instance, there is an interjection of a first-person voice over the third person in the bodhicitta section. The switch occurs with phrases where Bamda's directive in the first person is combined with instructions in the second person. I have used quotation marks to signal these shifts.

The second text translated here, *Concise Personal Advice*, structures Buddhist contemplative education as a gradual process by applying the rubric of listening, reflecting, and meditating. Bamda Lama teaches throughout his verses how to discern the way things are from how they are not, repeating the point for emphasis. A prevailing theme is that one must reverse (*dokpa*) the patterns of everyday destructive behavior—turn around the habits that reinforce an unwholesome lifestyle.

Like *Extracting the Essence of Freedoms and Fortunes*, the *Concise Personal Advice* is complex in its literary logic, interlocking syntactical connectors over several lines. This complexity is compounded by a technical vocabulary that describes precisely the stages of the path. For instance, in discussing the process of learning, he describes how even without having an abstract concept (*dönchi*) in mind, through recollection and reflection, you can bring to mind a general sense of what you have heard (*drachi*) until a particular meaning is well understood.

If the literary form of these texts is that of shaldam, the content is that of Buddhist path literature. Both texts present a gradualist approach toward enlightenment. We might therefore classify these writings as "graduated meditation" (*gomrim*) or "progress along the path" (*lamrim*) literature. Interestingly, in *Extracting the Essence of Freedoms and Fortunes*, Bamda Lama includes verses on Dzokchen within his gradualist approach. Though one might not expect a Jonangpa master to teach Dzokchen, these verses are evidence of Bamda Lama's rimé orientation.[8] They also offer an example of Tibetan strategies for synthesizing sudden and gradual approaches to the Buddhist path.

Bamda Lama was a master communicator. One of his primary accomplishments in these short texts is his capacity to lead the reader through a heightened literary experience of traversing the entire continuum of the Buddhist path. Each text strives to elicit a visceral shift in the reader. In so doing, these texts are not merely about the Buddhist path, but are instructions that transport one along the path.

---

8. On Bamda as a Dzokchen lineage holder see, Tenzin Lungtok Nyima 2004, 628–33, and Ngawang Lodrö Drakpa 1992, 412–24.

Extracting the Essence of Freedoms and Fortunes: Advice on the Precious Mind, Vajrayāna, and Dzokchen

by Bamda Thupten Gelek Gyatso

These are the ways and means to extract the essence of the freedoms and fortunes:[9]

I. Homage

To the sublime masters, homage![10]

II. Renunciation

With regard to extracting the essence of the freedoms and fortunes,
if the thought of revulsion for saṃsāra does not arise,
the stream of entanglements due to your addiction to existence
will spur you onward as the cause of saṃsāra, despite the three trainings.

So with clear understanding by means of hundreds of reasons
pertaining to the defects of these five defiled saṃsāric aggregates,[11]
which have the very nature of the three kinds of suffering,
give rise to the thought of renunciation without pretense, please!

---

9. The full phrase is *dalwa gyé jorwa chu*. This is the common list of eight freedoms (*dalwa*) and ten fortunes (*jorwa*) that constitute the prerequisite conditions for being capable of practicing the Buddhist path as a human being. For a fuller description by one of Bamda Lama's teachers, see Patrul 1998, 19–37.

10. The Tibetan term *yongdzin* can be translated as "masters." To wax the term, we might render it as "upholders of the whole." Separated into its component parts, it is defined as "the masters who completely hold or protect from the two extremes of existence and quiescence." See Dungkar Losang Trinlé 2002.

11. Here there is an implicit understanding that the defiled aggregates (*pungpo*) that make up the body are imperative for the topic of the text, the freedoms and fortunes of having a human body.

With the mindset that yearns for liberation free from addiction to
   existence
simply in order to transform their longing for all that is real,
by making it their motive to utterly extinguish existence,
all those with wholesome minds are transformed and liberated—
this is the true nature of what's real.

III. Bodhicitta

However, without the precious mind that awakens,
even a wholesome mind that is colored with the thought of
   renunciation
is not capable of transmuting into the pure gold of the supreme path
   of total omniscience.[12]
This is what the Bhagavan taught.

With measureless altruism toward measureless beings,
bearing burdens hard to measure, for the immeasurable benefit of
   others—
this precious mind that attains immeasurable supreme enlightenment
has a true nature such that its cause and fruit are equivalent.

Therefore, attentive solely to the consideration that all beings
   without exception,
as numerous as space is vast, have been your mother,
recall the kindness that they have given you, and
with the thought to repay their kindness,
gently give rise without pretense
to the love that wishes all mother and father beings
be imbued with both temporary and ultimate happiness,
and give rise to the compassion that wishes them free
from the fear of the coarse and subtle sufferings of existence and
   quiescence.

Then give rise without pretense to the pure motivation
of bringing happiness, both temporary and ultimate,

---

12. Note the reference here to the alchemical transmutation into gold that is embedded
in the text title.

to all beings who have been your mother and of freeing them
from the fears of existence and quiescence.

Think, "Since at this very moment I am incapable of liberating
    infinite living beings
from their fears of existence and quiescence
and of establishing them in omniscience,
I must attain buddhahood!" And keep the thought in mind
that you will free living beings from existence and quiescence!
Continue to think, "In order to be of benefit to others,
I must attain buddhahood!" Please give rise within your
    consciousness to this mind set on awakening
without pretense and with utter purity!

Because buddhahood cannot be attained
without training over countless eons
through the infinite accrual of the two accumulations,
with great waves of constant devotion and diligent application
to every arduous act along the Mahāyāna path that is beyond
    measure and transcends enumeration,
don't back down!
Gracefully wear the armor of a heroic mind.

By treading along the ordinary path like this,
there is no way for it not to take countless eons
to purify your mindstream
and free all mother beings from the ocean of saṃsāra.

IV. Vajrayāna

So give rise within your mindstream to the perfect aspiration
of the extraordinary mantra,
wishing along the vajra path to accomplish swiftly, in one lifetime,
the level of Vajradhāra and to liberate every single being from
    existence and quiescence.

As the ground for being ripened through the four empowerments of
    the unexcelled vehicle,
take hold of this ground with pure samaya,
and through the path of the generation process,

carefully ripen the channels, winds, and drops
to make these of prime importance, so that during the completion
   process
the pristine wisdoms are able to actually arise within your mindstream.

V. Dzokchen

While along the Dzokchen path,
all phenomena that are grasped
are understood to be merely apparent within the mind that grasps.
For even the mind that grasps
emerges, abides, and vanishes!

By knowing how things are unreal,
and by loosely nurturing uncontrived lucent empty awareness,
all the winds of karma and discursive thoughts, material and subtle,
dissolve into the unalterable seminal drop in your heart.

Appearances and experiences of the grasped and grasper dissolve into
   the expanse of phenomena.

Pristine awareness is without elaboration, blissful yet empty, without
   a grasper;
this is the ground awareness that is carefree and free from partiality.

Instead of the sūtra path's infinite two accumulations,
by meditating on this alone, again and again,
and traversing the four *vidyādhara* levels,
you will attain direct awakening on the very ground
of the original protector, Samantabhadra,[13]
and you will never be severed from the enlightened activity that
   guides infinite living beings.

VI. Summation

When you thereby extract the essence of the freedoms and fortunes,
there are mental hindrances that can create obstacles for Dharma:
In general, there is the idea that, while it is important to practice the
   sublime Dharma,

---

13. To attain the same ground as the original protector Samantabhadra is to achieve full awakening.

practicing in future lives might also suffice.
But putting this off to further future lives is procrastination,
for if you have a body of the six types of beings other
than the one that is endowed with the freedoms and fortunes,
you will not have a chance to practice the sublime Dharma.

Even to have a sublime human life, however you think about it—
from the point of view of its causes, numerical comparisons, or
    analogies[14]—
is something so extremely difficult to obtain.
So much so that in this life, I urge you to practice the sublime
    Dharma alone.
Understand the certainty of how difficult it is to find these freedoms
    and fortunes.
Turn your mind around!

Even if you understand this,
thinking in this life that there is tomorrow and the day after to
    practice the sublime Dharma
and postponing it till later is a block due to laziness.
Since death is certain, and the time of death is unpredictable,
understand the certainty of death and impermanence.
Turn your mind around!

Not believing in adopting virtues and rejecting vices is
another obstacle to putting the sublime Dharma teachings into
    practice throughout all your lifetimes.
While you still have the support of a life that has these freedoms,
understand clearly the certainty of cause and effect,
how actions and their fruits inevitably ripen in each and every person.
Turn your mind around!

The path of liberation from addiction to saṃsāric phenomena
may be disrupted by a mind that is addicted to existence.
By contemplating renunciation through understanding the entirety of
    saṃsāra to have the nature of suffering,
you must turn your mind around!

---

14. These are classic explanations found in Tibetan instructions on the subject. See Patrul
1998, 33–37.

Colophon

These are the ways and means to extract the essence of the freedoms and fortunes. Requested in person by the illustrious monk Thupal. Composed by Thupten Gelek Gyatso.

Concise Personal Advice: Listening, Reflecting, and Meditating on the Path

by Bamda Thupten Gelek Gyatso

Treasury of wisdom—you with the prowess to express
even a sliver of the thousand light rays of your wisdom—
bring the lotus grove of all there is to know beyond limit into full
  bloom at once.
To you, Mañjuśrī,
I bow down!

I. Primary Analysis

From time without beginning, your mind, deluded by not knowing,
has taken as true what is not true,
as permanent what is not permanent, and so forth.
By giving rise to such perverse thinking that interprets things to be
  what they are not,
all sorts of upsetting emotions, such as craving and the like, have
  come about.
You have confused this to be the way things rightly are, and wander
  in saṃsāra.[15]
You have been bound by the tight noose of taking things to be real,
  which is hard to snip off.
You've been tormented by the weaponry of unbearable intense
  suffering,
deprived of the wisdom-eye that discerns what to accept and what to
  reject,
deprived of the good fortune of encountering spiritual friends,
deprived of teachers who can guide you to freedom,
and because of inexhaustible karma, you have lived without a chance
  to be free.

---

15. This is a reference to the upsetting emotions (*nyönmong*) that create the saṃsāric experience.

Now, at this time when you have just a tiny bit of residual karma
    that's not too bad,
you have acquired a human life with the freedoms and fortunes that
    are capable of relinquishing suffering.
Take a thorough hold of the supreme wisdom that realizes rightly
    the natural state of phenomena,
and discard your erroneous ideas.
In this way, by accepting what is real and rejecting what is unreal
    within the natural state of what there is to know, you relinquish
    existence and quiescence and traverse to freedom.
This is what the omniscient ones have taught.

II. Renunciation

Disgusted with saṃsāra, having the thought of renunciation,
fully take the vows of individual liberation
and, thoroughly guarding your perfectly pure discipline,
engage in the practices of accepting and rejecting!
From time without beginning your mind has become accustomed
to upsetting emotions like craving; these will arise without effort.
Since your mind will chase these upsetting emotions,
if you don't restrain these habits of mind,
you will be unable to engage in the virtuous activities of accepting
    and rejecting.

If your mind is not engaged in virtuous activities,
the bounties of meditative concentration—the proper support
for relinquishing obscurations as they are by training
in the perfect wisdom that deciphers the actual state of things,
that supreme antidote that actually combats perceptual habits,
and perverse thinking that grasps at what's real in the wrong way—
    will not arise.

If there is not firm meditative stability,
wisdom—whether letting be, resting, or analyzing, whichever is
    appropriate,
to gain familiarity and mastery in analyzing and resting on
the real nature of the four truths, the absence of self and so forth,
and the relinquishment of obscurations through direct realization—
will never come about. This is why discipline is supreme!

Rely on this to be the foundational root of all enlightened qualities.
Seize hold of this discipline. Cherish it more than your life!

III. Listening

In this way, living with pure discipline,
rely on the extensive expositions that expose knowledge about the
    perverse thinking that contradicts the path
and open the doors to sūtra and mantra teachings
on the expositions about transcendent wisdom that show the entire
    path,
on the genuine expositions about the vast and profound Mahāyāna,
on the expositions of Madhyamaka that deliberately disclose
the power of the profound view, and explain in detail,
like a key that opens onto specific ground so as not to err along the
    path of Madhyamaka.
For the two divisions of Abhidharma and the four divisions of
    philosophical systems,
rely on a qualified teacher.
Listen, understand, explain, debate,
repeatedly practice, recite, and so on—
resolve to constantly be learning.

IV. Reflecting

By studying the textual expositions in this way,
reflect on whether you have reached with certainty the meaning of
    what you are studying;
inferring by reason and through mere intellectual analysis
about its unerring meaning,
consider whether you have a clear and correct abstract sense of the
    meaning.
By thinking about what you have studied, bring to mind an
    unmistaken sense of what you have heard.
Think day and night about all the reasons concerning the meaning of
    what you are studying.
Again and again, analyze and scrutinize,
reflect on it many times until you ascertain the reasons,
and you will reach a proper certainty about what is encompassed
    within that proof.

Once the valid cognition of inference arises as to the meaning,
That's when the wisdom born from contemplation is obtained.
By analyzing and resting on the meaning that has arisen through
  contemplation,
and by familiarizing yourself with this meaning over and over,
the third stage of stabilizing the mind[16] will come.

V. Meditating

At that time, because you are free of mental expressions regarding
  the meaning,
images about what you have heard are also exhausted and the
  abstract sense alone comes about.
However, at that time, what arises from meditation is not complete.
Through listening, reflecting, and meditating, you will bring it to
  completion.

Then, by again and again cultivating familiarization,
at the time of the ninth stabilization of the mind,
you will establish a special refined suppleness of body and mind,
and when you seize your understanding during meditation,
that's when meditation occurs.

VI. Summation

Thus, the exalted mind is not the mind of desire states,
for with thoughts driven by desire, meditation cannot come about.

Dwelling in these ways, all whose laziness
obstructs them from observing, listening, reflecting, and meditating,
through application of the four mind-changings,
turn your mind around!

Continually engage in listening, reflection, and meditation.

---

16. This is the third of the nine stabilizations of the mind (*semné gu*). It refers to repeated replacement of attention (*lenté jokpa*) on a single object without distraction.

Colophon

Requested in person by the enthusiastic Dharma practitioner Önpo Sherab from Sang. Composed by Thupten Gelek Gyatso. May this be virtuous!

Translated Works

Thupten Gelek Gyatso (Thub bstan dge legs rgya mtsho). *Zhal gdams dal 'byor gyi snying po len pa'i thabs tshul.* Collected Works, vol. 15, 559–62. 'Dzam thang: Rnga ba rdzong.
———. *Zhal gdams bsdus pa.* Collected Works, vol. 19, 785–88. 'Dzam thang: Rnga ba rdzong.

Suggested Readings

Garfield, Jay L. 2009. "Translation as Transmission and Transformation." In *TransBuddhism: Transmission, Translation, Transformation*, edited by Nalini Bhushan, Jay L. Garfield, and Abraham Zablocki, 89–103. Amherst, MA: University of Massachusetts Press.

Guenther, Herbert. 1977. "The Spiritual Teacher in Tibet." In *Tibetan Buddhism in Western Perspective*, 178–95. Emeryville, CA: Dharma Publishing.

Gyatso, Janet. 1997. "Counting Crows' Teeth: Tibetans and Their Diaries." In *Les habitants du toit du monde*, edited by Samten Karmay and Philippe Sagant, 159–77. Paris: Société d'Ethnologie.

Kapstein, Matthew. 1996. "Gdams ngag: Technologies of the Self." In *Tibetan Literature: Studies in Genre*, edited by José Ignacio Cabezón and Roger R. Jackson, 275–89. Ithaca, NY: Snow Lion Publications.

Sheehy, Michael R. 2009a. "A Lineage History of Vajrayoga and Tantric Zhentong from the Jonang Kalachakra Practice Tradition." In *As Long as Space Endures: Essays on the Kalachakra Tantra in Honor of H.H. the Dalai Lama*, 219–35. Ithaca, NY: Snow Lion Publications.

Additional References

Dungkar Losang Trinlé (Dung dkar Blo bzang 'phrin las), ed. 2002. *Dung dkar Bod rgya Tshig mdzod chen mo.* Beijing: Krung go'i bod rig pa dpe skrun khang.

Hinterberger, Martin. 2006. "How Should We Define Vernacular Literature?" Paper presented at "Unlocking the Potential of Texts: Interdisciplinary Perspectives on Medieval Greek" at the Centre for Research in the Arts, Social Sciences, and Humanities, University of Cambridge, July 2006. Accessed December 3, 2013, http://www.mml.cam.ac.uk/greek/grammarofmedievalgreek/unlocking/Hinterberger.pdf.

Kapstein, Matthew. 2001. "From Kun-mkhyen Dol-po-pa to 'Ba'-mda' dge-legs: Three Jo-nang-pa Masters on the Interpretation of the *Prajñāpāramitā*." In *Reason's Traces: Identity and Interpretation in Indian and Tibetan Buddhist Thought*, 301–16. Boston: Wisdom Publications.

Nance, Richard. 2011. *Speaking for Buddhas: Scriptural Commentary in Indian Buddhism.* New York: Columbia University Press.

Ngawang Lodrö Drakpa (Ngag dbang blos gros grags pa). 1992. *Jo nang chos 'byung zla ba'i sgron me*. Qinghai: Nationalities Press.

Patrul Rinpoche. 1998. *The Words of My Perfect Teacher*. Translated by the Padmakara Translation Group. Boston: Shambhala Publications.

Ricard, Matthieu, trans. 2001. *The Life of Shabkar: The Autobiography of a Tibetan Yogin*. Ithaca, NY: Snow Lion Publications.

Schapiro, Joshua. 2012. *Patrul Rinpoché on Self-Cultivation: The Rhetoric of Nineteenth-Century Tibetan Buddhist Life-Advice*. PhD Diss., Harvard University.

Sheehy, Michael R. 2009b. "The Zhentong Madhyamaka Writings of Ngawang Tsoknyi Gyatso (1880–1940)." In *Ngag dbang tshogs gnyis rgya mtsho gzhan stong phyogs bsgrigs*. Sichuan Nationalities Publishing House.

Tenzin Lungtok Nyima (Bstan 'dzin lung rtogs nyi ma). 2004. *Snga 'gyur rdzogs chen chos 'byung chen mo*. Beijing: Krung go'i bod rig pa dpe skrun khang.

8. How to Practice When Ill

Jikmé Lingpa
Translated by Wulstan Fletcher

Spontaneous Liberation in the Trikāya

R ikdzin Jikmé Lingpa Khyentsé Öser died in 1798, two years before the
beginning of the period designated for the present anthology. Nevertheless, as the immediate predecessor in the incarnational lineage of Jamyang
Khyentsé Wangpo, Do Khyentsé, and Patrul Rinpoché, he was an influential
forerunner of some of the most significant figures in the history of Tibetan
Buddhism in the early modern period, specifically in the formation of the
nonsectarian or rimé movement. In any case, his teaching on how pain and
sickness may be turned to advantage on the spiritual path is so interesting
that it would be a pity not to include it in a collection of this kind.

Given the fact that Jikmé Lingpa identifies himself in the last few lines
of his shaldam using his personal name Khyentsé Ö[ser], it is a surprise to
find that his text is not included in the edition of his collected works preserved in the archives of the Tibetan Buddhist Resource Center. Happily,
the poem was sufficiently popular, and perhaps sufficiently challenging, to
prompt the composition of a commentary on it by Rikdzin Gargyi Wangchuk (1858–1930), a disciple of Jamyang Khyentsé Wangpo, Kongtrul Lodrö
Thayé, Mipham Rinpoché, and others, which gives us clear attestation of
Jikmé Lingpa's authorship. Being short and memorable, the text must have
circulated freely among the disciples and practitioners associated with the
great names just mentioned. This no doubt explains the minor discrepancies
of vocabulary and spelling in the manuscript versions that have survived.

For the purposes of the present translation, the version embedded in Gargyi Wangchuk's commentary has been used as the final reference.

The poem is an instruction on how to understand, deal with, and even profit from the pain of inescapable sickness. Jikmé Lingpa composed his teaching when he had himself fallen ill in the course of a solitary retreat—in other words, in circumstances where palliative treatment would probably have been impossible to obtain. And although his advice was no doubt primarily intended for experienced yogins in a similar predicament, his instructions on the correct attitude to adopt and the meditative techniques to implement are of interest to any aspiring practitioner of the Buddhist path.

According to the textual outline or *sapché* devised by Gargyi Wangchuk, the instruction is divided into three sections: introduction, main part, and conclusion. The introduction is an opening salutation (lines 1–8) addressed to the Medicine Buddha, who is immediately identified with Orgyen Menla (the Medicine Buddha in the form of Guru Padmasambhava), thereby indicating the author's Nyingma affiliation. The main body of the poem (lines 9–57) is divided into "common" instructions based on the Abhidharma (lines 9–24) and "uncommon" instructions (lines 25–57) based on the teachings of the Great Perfection. The third part of the poem (lines 58 until the end) is a concluding peroration. It recapitulates the encouraging remarks given earlier in the text and closes with a colophon, incorporated into the verse itself, in which the author identifies himself and describes the circumstances of his composition.

Although Gargyi Wangchuk divides the salutation from the main teaching, Jikmé Lingpa's instruction really begins at the opening of the poem, in line 2. The saṃsāric process is described in terms of the twelve links of dependent arising, which have ignorance as their source. Saṃsāra is itself a state of sickness for which the Medicine Buddha is the cure; individual ailments are simply flagrant instances of a general malaise. And as in saṃsāra generally, so too in the experience of sickness and pain: from the point of view of spiritual training, one can either sink or swim. Sickness, especially unavoidable sickness, is a testing ground in which the practitioner must try to apply the teachings; it is an arena in which inner strength is tried and progress assessed.

In his instruction, Jikmé Lingpa does two things. First, he gives an energetic and encouraging reminder of the significance of illness and of how it is to be viewed in a positive light. Second, he shows how pain, when approached in the proper way, can be used as a means to recognize the very nature of reality, thereby releasing the sufferer into a state of naked awareness that transcends both sickness and health, both pain and the absence of pain. It is in this sense that, as a means to purification and wisdom, as a gauge of spiritual strength and proficiency, and as an urgent presence impossible to ignore, the pain of sickness is indeed a teacher.

Jikmé Lingpa's words of encouragement are typical of the Mahāyāna teachings on mind training. They are intended to instill an attitude of serenity and courage in the face of adversity. Sickness is a manifestation of karmic law. It is not a meaningless happenstance but has its roots in past negative actions. No one else is to blame but oneself. And this is good news; for if the present situation is the result of past deeds, it follows that the future will be conditioned by attitudes and behavior in the present. One's destiny therefore is in one's own hands. Furthermore, by saying that sickness happens through the kindness of the teacher and the Three Jewels, Jikmé Lingpa alludes to the idea, made explicit toward the end of the poem, that intensive practice can accelerate the ripening of karma. The results of past evil may be forced to the surface, manifesting ahead of time in the comparatively manageable form of sickness. Negativity is thus purified and exhausted instead of remaining dormant in the mindstream, where it is liable to provoke far more devastating consequences—for example, rebirth in the lower realms—at some later stage.[1] For those engaged in long retreat, this is important information. Seen in this light, sickness, far from being a misfortune, is an encouraging sign that the practice is working. It is itself a sign of accomplishment for which the *yidam* deity should be thanked.

The central section of the instruction introduces the doctrine of the *trikāya* (the three bodies of a Buddha) as interpreted in the Great Perfection tradition. Profound and difficult to understand on the intellectual level,[2] it is alluded to here in the simplest terms. Jikmé Lingpa shows that even a partial understanding of this teaching can have a mitigating effect on the experience of pain. Conversely, when properly understood, sickness itself makes manifest the nature of the trikāya and thus the nature of the mind.

The three kāyas are correlated with the well-known tripartite description of the mind given in the Great Perfection teachings. The mind's nature is empty (*dharmakāya*); its character is luminous display (*saṃbhogakāya*); its cognitive

---

1. This argument is based on the idea that karmic seeds accumulated and stored in the mindstream have a tendency to proliferate over time, eventually producing effects of disproportionate magnitude compared with the original acts themselves. The longer the seeds are stored, the greater the fruits will be. See Jigme Lingpa 2010, 136.

2. See Jigme Lingpa 2013, 278–317.

potency is unobstructed (*nirmāṇakāya*).[3] This opens up three possible ways of relating to physical suffering. When sickness strikes, the general tendency is to apprehend the pain as something objectively real, and to be carried away by it. But if, instead of being overwhelmed, one is able to recognize the state of pure and naked awareness, the sickness itself becomes a manifestation of the nature of the mind, the dharmakāya.

Alternatively, one may have the strength and determination to conduct an analysis, searching for the pain within one's body and mind. One quickly finds that the body, taken in isolation, is nothing but inert matter. It cannot in itself be a feeling subject, for in that case, it would follow that a corpse could feel. The painful experience requires the presence of an animating consciousness. This is, after all, the basic premise of anesthesia. One therefore comes to the conclusion that the experience of pain is essentially a state of mind, a "thought." If one then searches for that thought, trying to see how it arises, remains, and subsides, the thought itself—which seemed so clear until one started to look for it—falls apart. If the thought is left to dissolve without residue, that is, without allowing it to proliferate sequentially into "chains of thought," the pain, which is the thought itself, disappears, if only for a moment, replaced by a state of awareness "empty, vast, and clear." The pain of sickness is seen to be a mirage, the luminous display of the empty mind, appearing in the manner of the saṃbhogakāya.

Finally, it is an easily verifiable fact that the intensity of physical pain arises in proportion to the degree to which one identifies with the aggregates of the psycho-physical continuum. For most people this identification is instinctively very strong, with the result that they suffer helplessly when

---

3. The Tibetan terms are *ngowo* (nature), *rangshin* (character), and *thukjé* (cognitive potency). The last of these three terms is usually translated as "compassion," but this is misleading in the context of the Great Perfection. *Thukjé* is the honorific equivalent of the Tibetan word *nyingjé*, and in those situations where it denotes the inability to tolerate the suffering of others, it certainly comes close to the English word "compassion." Etymologically, *thukjé* means the "lordship" or "power of the mind," and this gives the word a range of possible meanings that the English word "compassion" cannot possibly cover. In his commentary on Jikmé Lingpa's *Treasury of Precious Qualities*, Khenpo Yönten Gyatso defines *thukjé* as "pure and unadulterated awareness that has not yet stirred from its own true condition or state (but that has the potential to do so)." This being so, the term "cognitive potency," albeit rather clumsy and unattractive, is provisionally suggested as a not altogether inadequate English equivalent. It should be remembered, of course, that whatever meanings it may bear in a given context, the Tibetan word never loses the nuance that had originally prompted its translation as "compassion." And indeed, the outflowing, so to speak, of the mind's cognitive potency may well result in actions in relation to beings that can only be described as "compassionate."

sickness occurs. Practices like *chö*, in which one imaginatively offers one's body to harmful spirits, or the technique of viewing one's body as a hollow and insubstantial network, are meditative devices aimed at attenuating this identification. Logically speaking, what one can give away is not an intrinsic part of oneself. A space thus opens between the mind and its experience, between oneself and one's discomfort. The pain of sickness is not ourselves; it does not even belong to us. The suffering body-mind is simply an externalized display, a "body of manifestation," like the nirmāṇakāya. And if, as Jikmé Lingpa says, we are able to rest in that discovery, in a state of clear and stable awareness, the physical pain will, if only for a short moment, disappear.

To be convinced of the intrinsic reality of pain, and to be caught up in it, is the sign that the nature and character of the mind have not yet been recognized. The appearances that, according to the teachings of the Great Perfection, emerge from the "ground," the most fundamental dimension of the mind, are not seen for what they are.[4] Beings take them for objective reality separate from the mind itself; and thus they wander, suffering in the ordinary, unenlightened state. The failure to understand—this "loss of the view"—is none other than the coemergent ignorance (*lhenchik kyepai marikpa*) that sets saṃsāra in motion.

Ignorance thus imparts a thematic unity to the entire poem. It is the source from which the links of dependent arising unfold, and is the underlying basis of saṃsāric experience generally. It is also the key to understanding the metaphor that Jikmé Lingpa uses to refer to his own illness at the conclusion of his instruction (lines 73–74). His sickness occurred, he seems to say, in a moment of confusion, when "the triple kāya was disturbed," that is, when he momentarily lost sight of the emptiness, luminosity, and cognitive potency of the mind's nature. Written from his bed in solitude, Jikmé Lingpa's text functions both as a reminder to himself and as an instruction to his disciples: by correctly understanding the pain of sickness in the moment that it manifests, the view of the Great Perfection may be (re)established and suffering dispelled.

The profundity of the content of this instruction is offset by the simplicity of its form. Shaldam literature frequently makes use of colloquialisms, elliptical expressions, and unusual metrical forms redolent of folksong. Engaging and easily understandable to the intended audience, they are nonetheless often extremely obscure to the non-native speaker. In the present case, however, Jikmé Lingpa adopts the plain, traditional format of nine-syllable lines. On the whole his meaning is quite straightforward, falling naturally into a

---

4. See Jigme Lingpa 2013, 234–40.

simple quatrain structure. The language is not particularly complicated, and technical and abstruse terms are kept to a minimum. The overall tone is that of essential advice given with warmth and simplicity in a time of pressing need.

Content is of paramount importance in a practical instruction of this kind, and any translation, if it is to succeed, must convey the meaning as clearly as possible. Yet Jikmé Lingpa's text has a poetic charm that greatly enhances its persuasive power. Therefore, although the translator's first duty is to capture the meaning, the importance of stylistic expression in the target language cannot be overlooked.

Directness, brevity, the simple and uncluttered arrangement of ideas, the lyrical effect of repeated constructions—these are all characteristics of the original that should in some measure be present in the translation. Fortunately in this case, the task is facilitated by Jikmé Lingpa's stylistic simplicity. His syntax, the area in which Tibetan and English diverge most markedly, is not complex; for the most part, the sequence of ideas can follow the same order in both languages. Moreover, many of the linguistic configurations of the original, particularly the repetitions ("your sickness . . . your sickness," "this sickness . . . this sickness"), are easy to reproduce in the translation.

In the attempt to convey the almost lyrical simplicity of the original, I felt justified in abandoning the four-line stanza structure of the Tibetan in favor of a looser form in English, with the text separated into sections according to subject matter, and couched in the natural, mostly iambic, rhythms of English verse. Inevitably, the verbal economy of the original was lost. The translation is seventy-seven lines long, compared with the forty-four of the original. This would of course be unacceptable if one were aiming at interlineal translation of the kind used in certain prayer books. Here my aim is not to produce a liturgical text suitable for chanting, or a parallel text to help students decipher the Tibetan. Rather it is to create a version that I hope will faithfully echo the original—evoking in the mind of readers something of the emotional impact that the original has on Tibetans.

Acknowledgments

I would like to take the opportunity to thank Khenpo Yeshe Gyaltsen and Ven. Gelong Sean Price for their help in deciphering and reconstructing damaged sections in the blockprint of Rikdzin Gargyi Wangchuk's commentary.

How Sickness Naturally Subsides in the Three Kāyas: An Essential Instruction for Bringing Sickness onto the Path

by Jikmé Lingpa Khyentsé Öser

To Awareness Wisdom, the Great Sage, I bow.

Of the twelve dependent links
the root is ignorance.
And for the sicknesses that come as they unfold
the Medicine Guru of Orgyen is the cure.
To him I bow.
May he relieve
the pain of the three poisons.

Your sickness is the broom
that sweeps away your sins and obscurations.
Take your sickness as your teacher—
meditate and pray to him.
Your sickness is the ripening
of your own violent actions.
No one else can feel this ripening
but you alone.

If you accept it as the karmic lot befalling you,
your mind will be serene.
It comes upon you as the kindness
of your teacher and the Triple Gem.

Your pain is an accomplishment:
so thank the deity!
It is a sign foretelling
the conclusion of your evil karma.

Don't look at the sickness.
Instead, look at the sufferer!
Instead of letting pain weigh on your mind,
place awareness nakedly upon your pain.
For causing sickness to arise as the dharmakāya,
this is the instruction.

The body in itself is inert matter;
the mind is emptiness.
What can injure matter and by what can emptiness be harmed?
Search the nature of discomfort:
where does it arise, and stay, and go?[5]
Your pain is just a thought, occurring just like that.
When the thought dissolves,
there and then the pain is gone—
released into awareness, mind-transcending,
empty, vast, and clear.
For causing sickness to arise as the sambhogakāya,
this is the instruction.

Sins and obscurations gathered in a vast expanse of time
are purified by sickness.
It's the messenger that brings
experience, realization, and accomplishment.
Set aside the clinging love you have for your own body,
and practice *chö* while still in bed.
Visualizing clearly, shout:
Take my body! Take my blood!
And let them go.
Sometimes see your body as a hollow network, like a sieve,
and strongly force the wind through the affected part.
Then rest within the space
of your awareness, unobstructed, omnipresent.
For causing sickness to arise as the nirmāṇakāya,
this is the instruction.

This pain of sickness is the Three Roots' loving power.
This pain of sickness is the kindness of the Triple Gem.

---

5. In Tibetan, *jung né dro sum.*

This pain of sickness is past negativity—
the power of practice brought it to the surface:
there's no better kindling wood to burn away
the veils of obscuration.

So don't indulge in rituals
that demonstrate the wrong view of despondency![6]
Your sickness is the sign
that evil karma is exhausted.
Cultivate a happy state of mind!

By binding body, speech, and mind
with the three solitudes,[7]
this practice, chief of the three ways to serve,[8]
can satisfy the Three Roots, pleasing them.

Once when the meeting of awareness and expanse,
the triple kāya, was confused,
I, Khyentsé Ö, delivered this instruction
from my bed in solitude.

From the pain of the three poisons,
through this virtue, may we all be freed!

---

6. As Rikdzin Gargyi Wangchuk points out in his commentary, this does not mean that one should neglect medical treatment when it is possible and appropriate. It means that one should not give way to the fear and unhappiness that comes from reacting to sickness in the ordinary way, seeking a cure by any means and overlooking the positive aspects of one's predicament as Jikmé Lingpa describes them.

7. The three solitudes are the three limits that the practitioner accepts and aspires to while remaining in retreat. *Outer solitude* consists in physical isolation: the retreatant undertakes not to see, or be seen by, any other human being aside from the helpers appointed before the retreat begins. *Inner solitude* consists in binding the sense powers: the commitment to renounce irrelevant sensory stimuli. *Secret solitude* is the commitment to avoid mental wandering and to remain in the state of awareness.

8. Of the three ways to serve one's teacher, the first and least important is the offering of material goods; the second is the service of practical assistance in the teacher's activities; the third and most perfect service is to practice the teacher's instructions.

Translated Work

Work appears embedded in:
Rikdzin Gargyi Wangchuk (Rig 'dzin Gar gyi dbang phyug). n.d. *Kun mkhyen 'jigs med gling pa'i nad gdon gegs sel gyi rgyab skyor lung gis gsal bar byas pa dam pa'i lam khyer 'chi gsos lha yi bdud rtsi.* Collected Works, vol. 3. Nyag a 'dzin rong: Nyag dpal ldan byams 'byor dgon gyi par khang (TBRC W19884).

Suggested Readings

Jigme Lingpa. 2010. *Treasury of Precious Qualities: Book One.* Translated by the Padmakara Translation Group. Boston: Shambhala Publications.
———. 2013. *Treasury of Precious Qualities: Book Two.* Translated by the Padmakara Translation Group. Boston: Shambhala Publications.

9. An Intimate Exhortation

Tokden Śākya Śrī

Translated by Amy Holmes-Tagchungdarpa

Experiential Advice for Escaping Saṃsāra

This chapter represents a form of shaldam known as "practical advice" (*lapja*). Like shaldam more generally, this type of advice is characterized by its pithiness, which it retains from its original context as personal advice that was orally transmitted from teacher to student and transcribed at a later date. This advice does not originate in a teacher's academic study in a monastic institution but instead emerges out of experience in retreat. This emphasis on experiential knowledge is the major theme of the text translated in this chapter, which reflects the experience and lifestyle of its author, the yogin Tokden Śākya Śrī (1853–1919).

Unlike many of the other authors in this volume, Śākya Śrī was neither a hierarch nor even a member of one of Kham's many monasteries. He spent most of his life in retreat in caves and as head of large encampments (*gar*) in the mountains of Chamdo and later at the sacred mountain of Tsari in southwestern Tibet. These establishments welcomed all types of tantric practitioners, including monks, nuns, and ngakpas—nonmonastic tantric practitioners—some of whom brought their entire families with them.[1] Śākya

---

1. The term *ngakpa* is difficult to translate. It can be rendered as "tantric practitioner," translating the Sanskrit *tāntrika*, thereby including monastic tantric practitioners along with nonmonastic ones. In Śākya Śrī's setting, however, it mostly referred to noncelibate tantric practitioners. This meaning is reflected in its use here. For more on popular perceptions of ngakpas and their reputations, see Holly Gayley's translation of Do Khyentsé's *The Babble of a Foolish Man* in this volume.

Śrī was himself a family man, heading up a lineage promulgated by his six sons and four daughters, as well as by thousands of students who came from throughout the Tibetan cultural world to study with him.[2]

His nonmonastic lifestyle exemplifies the diversity of Kham's Buddhism, in contrast to the monastic identities of most of the other masters included in this volume. However, Śākya Śrī was a student of many of these great scholars, and the intent of their messages can be understood to have been the same: an exhortation for students to practice in order to gain their desired results. The text translated here, "Beyond Talk and Into Action," represents the type of advice Śākya Śrī was renowned for: pithy, to the point, and practical. In it, he encourages the listener or reader to practice, arguing that understanding words alone will not bring any results on the Buddhist path. The stakes for accomplishing these results are high—escape from saṃsāra and suffering altogether. No less.

Translating Meditation Instructions

The urgency of Śākya Sri's message is captured in a number of ways in "Beyond Talk and Into Action." The work has an accessible, even playful tone, though it includes a number of imperative sentences and exhortations as well as strongly affective descriptions of experience. So, for example, he writes that it is not enough to express thankfulness toward one's lama; one's entire body should feel gratitude, with hair standing on end and tears flowing down one's face. Should the listener be uncertain such intense practice is possible, Śākya Śrī confirms that his instructions are based on his own experience and encourages the listener to practice energetically until her or his "sense of self and other dissolves into primordial space." As an extra incitement he reminds the listener that not only will they benefit, but so too will all sentient beings, as the basis of the experience of selflessness is compassion, which is inseparable from emptiness. He thereby reframes his instructions to elevate the social motivation for practice above the private concerns of the solitary practitioner.

Translating Śākya Śrī's impassioned language brings with it a number of challenges. While the structure of the text is straightforward, the brevity of his phrases and the deceiving simplicity of his message make it more difficult to capture the multilayered meaning of his words. This is partly due to the original context of the source: Śākya Śrī delivering personal advice to his student Drung Mipham Chokdrup (or perhaps Drung Mipham and a larger

---

2. Śākya Śrī's biography has been published in translation (Kathog Situ 2009). For a study of his biography and community, see Amy Holmes-Tagchungdarpa 2014.

group of other students). The advice may well have been tailored to contain specific advice especially for Drung Mipham.

As Sarah Harding discusses in chapter 10, the rare use of personal pronouns in Tibetan can also make it difficult to decide how to engage with the audience when translating the text. I have decided to alternate between interpreting Śākya Śrī to be discussing his own experience, on the one hand, and to be exhorting his students to properly cultivate their own experiences, on the other. With that said, the entire text could be rendered as an instruction to the student, without any authorial reflection. The layered nature of the text also led me to translate it into prose rather than verse. In order to convey the complexity of the message within, it was necessary to break apart the patterns of the structured verse. This unfortunately renders the text less poetic than in the original and likely veils some of its spontaneous flavor. Given the unfortunate trade-off, however, I chose to focus on meaning over style.

A related problem concerns translating meditation instructions, particularly those containing multiple levels of meaning. In the fourth paragraph, Śākya Śrī tells his student to practice in the clear light (*ösal*) in order to dissolve the states of meditation and nonmeditation into one. The "clear light" here refers to a form of dream yoga, but the text could have the alternate meaning of instructing the listener to visualize luminosity in a more abstract sense. This particular text is accessible due to its ultimate message, that compassion and emptiness are one, but many of its specific instructions can be understood in multiple ways, depending upon the listener or reader's level of experience. The issue of the assumed knowledge of the audience can be complex for the translator to negotiate.

Crazy Cave Dwelling: Practicing beyond the Monastery

As mentioned earlier, Śākya Śrī was not part of any of the monasteries that acted as religious, cultural, economic, and political centers in Kham. However, he participated in interpersonal and visionary networks that were found there, and he acknowledges his position in these broader networks by referring to himself as the "crazy cave dweller" in the colophon to this text. He began his religious education in a monastery in the kingdom of Lhathok, where he worked in the kitchen and practiced meditation at night. He eventually left the monastery to live with his consort in caves nearby. He slowly began to gain a reputation for his yogic experience, which emerged under the guidance of many of the luminaries of his day, including Jamgön Kongtrul Lodrö Thayé (1813–99), Jamyang Khyentsé Wangpo (1820–92), Adzom Drukpa Pawo Dorjé (1842–1924), Ju Mipham (1846–1912), and Khamtrul

Tenpai Nyima (1848–1907). From these masters he received instructions in both Great Perfection or Completion (*dzokchen*) and Mahāmudrā (*chakchen*) forms of meditation.

Later, Śākya Srī became renowned for his ability to cater his instructions to individual students, with the encampment that grew around him in the mountains of Kham divided into two halves: Dzokchen practitioners living on one side of the valley and Mahāmudrā practitioners on the other. Students from all walks of life gathered to study in this community, including monks, nuns, ngakpas, incarnate lamas, and laypeople, all inspired by Śākya Srī's example. The community operated on a strict schedule, with time demarcated every day for meditation, study, and Dharma lectures. His encampment was a self-sustaining community, with select practitioners caring for yak and sheep that provided milk, butter, and meat, as well as wool for tents and clothing.[3] The community was by no means isolated, however, or exclusive. Śākya Srī actively encouraged his students to take teachings from other lamas. His own diverse network of teachers further points to his pansectarian acceptance. His attitude was pansectarian, not nonsectarian, insofar as he was still affiliated with one specific tradition, the Drukpa Kagyü, though he did hold lineages from across a number of traditions. His pansectarian position served his community well in expanding beyond Kham into other parts of the Himalayas, where many of Śākya Srī's students would travel to establish new centers and institutions, regardless of their formal affiliations.

The transregional growth of his community was also facilitated by the creation of a textual corpus, Śākya Srī's *Collected Works*. This corpus was created from texts written, spoken, and sung by Śākya Srī and compiled by his students. The vibrant scribal cultures of Kham's meditation communities were consolidated by the strength of local printing presses, particularly at Degé. Textualization—involving scribes, editors, woodblock carvers, printers, and many others—allowed for personal advice texts, such as this one, to survive beyond an oral context. They remain available today as strong reminders of the diverse religious and literary landscape of the region, and speak to the moving interpersonal relationships between teachers and students that characterized the Buddhism of Kham.

Acknowledgments

I am grateful to Sindrang Yab Gomchen Dorlop Chewang Rinzin for kindly reading the text with me, and for so generously drawing on his own experi-

---

3. For more on encampment communities, see Jacoby 2014. Holmes-Tagchungdarpa 2014 describes Śākya Srī's communities in detail.

ence and knowledge in explaining its most important themes. Kalzang Dorjee Bhutia graciously illuminated difficult points. I also thank my colleagues from the "Translating Buddhist Luminaries" conference in 2013 for their advice, and especially Ringu Tulku, Sarah Harding, Holly Gayley, and Joshua Schapiro for their helpful comments.

Beyond Talk and Into Action: Understanding Emptiness and Compassion as One and the Same[4]

by Tokden Śākya Śrī

A ho!

To the unrepayable kindness of the most gracious Teacher,
from whom I have received such love:
with a pure mind, I pay homage.

Now at this time you have the opportunity to enter the doors of the
    profound paths of Mahāmudrā and the Great Completion.
Instead of being stuck in saṃsāra
recognize the opportunity and focus on the treasury of sublime
    Dharma.

I pay homage to the kindness of the lord lama that can never be
    repaid!
Unable to bear the separation from him, I keep him in mind as I
    meditate.
Thinking of the lama, I get goosebumps, trembling as the hairs on
    my body all stand on end.[5]
I pray that my mind is never separated from his,
as ultimately our minds are one.
Right now I have this awareness,
and if delusions or the five poisons arise,
these will dissolve into me and I will remain undistracted.

---

4. In Tokden Śākya Śrī's *Collected Works,* this text is simply titled "Advice" (*shaldam*). I have adapted several lines from the text to serve as an unofficial title.

5. The text contains a number of lines that can be understood in divergent ways. This line, for example, can be read to be referring to a specific meditation practice that stimulates the senses.

So that you can also understand this inseparability for yourself, you
   should again and again practice energetically.
All of saṃsāra and nirvāṇa may be realized through this.
Distractions and deception will dissolve into space.
Mind and phenomena become undifferentiated.
Practice in the clear light,[6] and like day and night becoming one,
   the states of meditation and nonmeditation will meld into one
   expanse.

Thinking of the limitless beings dwelling in saṃsāra, I repeatedly
   generate great compassion, until I am moved to tears and am
   overwhelmed.
May boundless compassion be continuously generated!
Do not let your prayers and bodhicitta be weakened,
and finally, let all sense of self and other dissolve into primordial
   space.
Keep this in your heart, and always practice like this.

Indeed, with great devotion to the lama, you should revere the
   instructions here, always holding the lama as the Buddha in
   person in your thoughts. When I remember the great kindness
   of my teacher, my hair stands on end, and I am moved to tears.
   You should try to attain this intense devotion, which will lead all
   delusion to disappear by itself.

If you are all talk and no action,[7] there will be no blessings.
   Without blessings, you will not be able to make out the natural
   state of reality and will remain in delusion.
Keeping respect for the lama in your mind and devotion in your
   prayers will resolve this.

Pay homage to the lama, for through his immeasurable kindness,
   you have had access to this great oral advice, which will allow

---

6. The "clear light" is one of the six yogas of Nāropa. I thank Ringu Tulku and Sarah
Harding for pointing out this possible reading to me. This is another example of a section
in the text that can be interpreted in several ways, depending on the previous yogic
experience and education of the reader.

7. This is a colloquial translation for this sentence. More literally, the sentence can be
translated as "If you just supplicate and do not practice, no blessings will be received."

you to understand the wisdom of your own mind to integrate
into your heart. Pray single-mindedly that you will attain wisdom
that shines like the sun, automatically doing away with self-arisen
ignorance.
The essence of emptiness is never-ending. Without being confused by
illusion, primordial purity beyond conception will be attained.

Do not stray into confusion! Do not allow the delusions of the past,
present, and future to obstruct your view. Just call out "Phat!"
and all of these delusions will dissolve. They will fade away,
and when you look for them, there will be only clear space. Do
not block this sensation—it will allow you to know the play of
all-emptiness.

Having realized the nature of this power, when I recall the sufferings
of saṃsāra, I am moved to tears. It is essential you do not lose
this sense of awareness.
Observe the natural state of emptiness. From the play of emptiness,
compassion is born.
Compassion is the essence of emptiness;
there is no difference between emptiness and compassion.
Once you have understood this, you have attained buddha nature.
To attain this, meditate!
If you do not practice, you will continue to pursue the endless
and confusing cycle of saṃsāra and end up in the lower realms.
Thinking like that, no matter your circumstances, always pray to
the precious lama from the bottom of your heart.
Until you realize the fundamental nature of things, meditate
undistractedly.
If you maintain your practice and this realization, saṃsāra and
nirvāṇa will come to an end. You will not fall into the lower
realms—how wonderful!
A la la ho!

*This was spoken spontaneously by the crazy cave dweller Śākya Śrī at the request
of Drung Mipham Chokdrup.*

May all be auspicious!

Translated Work

Tokden Śākya Śrī (Rtogs ldan Śākya shrī). 1998. *Zhal gdams ldeb*. Collected Works, 761–64. Kathmandu: Ven. Khenpo Shedup Tenzin and Lama Thinley Namgyal.

Suggested Readings

Holmes-Tagchungdarpa, Amy. 2014. *The Social Life of Tibetan Biography: Textuality, Community, and Authority in the Lineage of Tokden Shakya Shri*. Lanham, MD: Lexington.

Kathog Situ Chokyi Gyatso. 2009. *Togden Shakya Shri: The Life and Liberation of a Tibetan Yogin*. Translated by Elio Guarisco. Merigar, Italy: Shang Shung Publications.

Nyoshul Khenpo Jamyang Dorjé. 2005. *A Marvelous Garland of Rare Gems: Biographies of the Masters of Awareness in the Dzogchen Lineage*. Translated by Richard Barron. Junction City, CA: Padma Publishing.

Additional References

Gardner, Alexander Patten. 2006. "The Twenty-Five Great Sites of Khams: Religious Geography, Revelation, and Nonsectarianism in Nineteenth Century Eastern Tibet." PhD diss., University of Michigan.

Jacoby, Sarah. 2014. *Love and Liberation: Autobiographical Writings of the Tibetan Buddhist Visionary Sera Khandro*. New York: Columbia University Press.

Jacoby, Sarah, and Antonio Terrone, eds. 2009. *Buddhism Beyond the Monastery*. Leiden: Brill.

Kathok Situ Chökyi Gyatso (Kaḥ thog si tu Chos kyi rgya mtsho). 1990. *Rje bstun bla ma rdo rje 'chang chen po Śākya Śrī dznya' na'i rnam thar me tog phreng ba*. Gangtok: Sherab Gyalsten, Palace Monastery.

10. A Meditation Instructor's Manual

Dza Patrul Rinpoché
Translated by Sarah Harding

Patrul Rinpoché's Great Completion Instructions

In the wide spectrum of teaching topics and writing styles discernible in the great nineteenth-century master Dza Patrul Rinpoché's collected works, the text translated in this chapter, *Clear Elucidation of True Nature*, represents some of his most straightforward and helpful advice on actual meditation practice in the tradition of the Great Completion (*dzokchen*). Specifically, it provides esoteric instruction on Atiyoga, as its subtitle indicates: *An Esoteric Instruction on the Sublime Approach of Ati in the Tradition of Aro Yeshé Jungné.* The most notable feature of this instruction is its specificity in addressing nine levels of practice by supplying detailed advice on how to approach the various problems and experiences of each. It thereby seems to be a manual intended for meditation instructors, an impression further enforced by its use of leading phrases such as "You should know how to guide those of the three subdivisions." Still, an individual practitioner, were she honest and astute in her self-assessment, could benefit greatly from its careful descriptions of the multilevel process of Great Completion practice.

Clear Elucidation of True Nature is said to be a summary or commentary on the teachings of the legendary but little-known Aro Yeshé Jungné, a Nyingma master of *kama* of the late tenth century.[1] Aro Yeshé Jungné is also

---

1. Davidson 2005, 75. The Tibetan Buddhist Resource Center, in contrast, places him in the thirteenth century.

said to have held the lineages of both an Indian transmission and the Chinese transmission of Hashang Moheyan, which, if true, would have far-reaching implications beyond the scope of this chapter.[2] In the table of contents of the *Collected Works* of Patrul Rinpoché, the editors tell us in a descriptive subtitle that *Clear Elucidation* is "a summary of the essential guidebooks of the mind class of the Great Completion in the Aro tradition; a way to individually guide persons of the nine levels of mental capability." Although no mention of Aro Yeshé Jungné is found in Patrul's text, this seems to be a well-known attribution continued in modern times by teachers such as Khenpo Palden Sherab Rinpoché. A short biography of Aro Yeshé Jungné, which includes a list of his teachings, does not mention any specific text that might be the source of Patrul's summary, although the biography does cite mind class (*semdé*) and Atiyoga cycles that could include such instructions.[3] Unfortunately these text cycles no longer seem to be extant. In fact, those few original teachings attributed to Aro Yeshé Jungné that are presently available do not deal with this subject.

An addendum to *Clear Elucidation* titled *Further Tidbits of Advice* is included in the same printing. There is no colophon to this section, but the descriptive subtitle calls it Jetsun Lama Dampa's "advice to know" (*shalshé*). Jetsun Lama Dampa presumably refers to Patrul Rinpoché himself, although it could also be his guru, thus making the text Patrul's notes on the teachings of his guru. *Shalshé* is a variation of *shaldam* (personal advice) that contains "the condensed essence of esoteric instructions directly from the guru's mouth (*shal*) that one should know (*shé*)."[4] In this case it is a seemingly random medley of profound advice covering a wide range of topics: meditative experiences, visualization practices of the guru or yidam, the tripartite division of ground-path-fruition, the four yogas of the Great Seal (*mahāmudrā*), dream and intermediate-state practices, and so forth.

Perhaps the most notable part of this "advice to know" is a brief section of commentary on an ancient teaching attributed to Garab Dorjé, who is the crucial link between the transcendent and the human in the lineage of Great Completion masters. The teaching is, of course, the *Three Words That Strike the Crucial Point*. Could this section of Patrul Rinpoché's advice be his crib notes for his famous and brilliant commentary on that teaching, the *Special Teaching of the Wise and Glorious Sovereign*? As we do not have the

2. Roerich 1988, 167.

3. Khenpo Jamyang 1999, 341–42.

4. Tseten Zhapdrung 1987, vol. 2, 238.

relevant dates for Patrul's two texts, it is impossible to know. Still, the fact that a commentary on Garab Dorjé's teaching is included in *Further Tidbits of Advice* suggests a comparison with *Clear Elucidation*. Both are summaries of crucial expositions attributed to towering figures in the ancient lineage of the Great Completion. Both contain distinctive schemes for progressive stages of meditation. And both *Clear Elucidation* and Patrul's commentary on the *Three Words* deal almost entirely with the same subject matter—the nitty-gritty issues of implementing nondual meditations in the Great Completion system. One thing can be said for certain of both summaries: no one could have written them without intimate experience of the subject matter, with or without a source text.

Given the far-reaching acclaim of Patrul Rinpoché's *Three Words* commentary and his renowned exposition of the preliminary practices of the Great Completion, *The Words of My Perfect Teacher*, it is surprising how little of his literary corpus is actually dedicated specifically to this subject. In a table of contents to his *Collected Works*, if one excludes preliminary practices, then a mere ten titles out of some two hundred are listed in the volume entitled *Teachings on the Practice of the Great Seal and the Great Completion, the Path of the Fourth Empowerment.* This would seem to suggest that he was most interested in bringing basic Buddhist teachings to the general populace. Patrul Rinpoché seemed to enjoy slipping profound instructions into the simple language of eminently readable narratives and poems, and having much fun scolding the audience along the way. The few serious discussions of Great Completion meditation that we find in his *Collected Works* were no doubt supplemented to a large extent by his oral instructions. Those would be his true shaldam, emerging out of actual interactions with disciples whom he considered to be worthy. It is the intimacy of these transmissions that would ensure the effectiveness of shaldam.

Clear Elucidation seems more structured than most shaldam, however, and identifies itself as *mengak*, "esoteric instructions." Sometimes translated as "oral instructions," vast tracts of mengak exist in written form. Mengak form the content of eighteen volumes of Jamgön Kongtrul's *Treasury of Precious Instructions*, for example, and are the basis of his arrangement of the eight practice lineages. We might also classify *Clear Elucidation* as a commentary. But with much fluidity and overlap between all of these genre terms, it is reasonable to include *Clear Elucidation* with the other shaldam that constitute this volume.

Patrul Rinpoché begins by establishing the foundation of the practice to be the introduction to, or revelation of, the nature of mind. This occurs once the practitioner has thoroughly searched for that mind (*semtsöl*).

Then the actual way to cultivate or maintain the revelation in meditation (*kyongtsul*) is laid out in the rest of the text according to the three broad categorizations of practitioners' capabilities: best, average, or lesser, each of which is further divided into subcategories of best, average, and lesser. Those of the best capability simply recognize that no matter what happens, one is never apart from the pure awareness of mind. This experience is the true nature of awareness as it is and always was. It should take only a week or a month to recognize. While he mentions the three subdivisions of the best—best of the best, average of the best, and lesser of the best—he does not elaborate on the separate instructions for each group, saying only that one should apply the appropriate guidance. Patrul uses equivalent terminology from multiple different teaching systems in his explanation and quotes Indian luminaries such as Padmasambhava, Mitrayogin, and the "Shijepa" (presumably Pha Dampa Sangyé).

Patrul Rinpoché spends more time on instructions for those of average capability. He says they should be guided by means of the combination or union of calm abiding (*shiné*) and superior insight (*lhakthong*). First, the continuity of thought is interrupted through calm abiding, and the practitioner can achieve various results, such as the "five eyes" and clairvoyance of meditative concentration, the four concentrations, the four spheres of perception, and the nine equilibriums of abiding.[5] However, this in itself is not sufficient, so one must watch intently the very thought that is aware of nonthought, which will then dissipate. This is the union of calm abiding and superior insight. The emphasis in this section is on mindfulness, which is not free of effort. In the threefold subdivision, those who are average of average and lesser of average may not accept that the regular thought process can itself be meditation, so they are advised to continually watch while each thought disappears. Ultimately, the true nature will reveal itself. In this section, Patrul Rinpoché quotes several masters of the Drukpa Kagyü lineage, though he ends with a citation from the mind class of the Great Completion. With its emphasis on the union of calm abiding and insight, the teachings here are more reminiscent of the Great Seal than the Great Completion, though his many cross-references reveal that Patrul Rinpoché was comfortable in both systems.

Practitioners of lesser capability—whether best, average, or lesser—do not "believe" in superior insight with its experience of emptiness and have difficulty generating calm abiding. For them, Patrul Rinpoché gives more detailed instructions on calm abiding, including sitting posture and breath-

---

5. These are defined in the notes to the translation itself below.

ing exercises, and then takes them through the five meditative experiences. However, this may work only for the best of the lesser. For the average of the lesser and the lesser of the lesser capabilities, something more tangible is required. These practitioners should focus on props, whether actual or visualized, such as a stick, a pebble, letters, or spheres of light. Mindfulness and nondistractedness are again the emphases. Patrul Rinpoché here graces us with the kind of anecdote for which he is so loved. He tells the story of a swordsman distracted by a beautiful woman and shot down by his opponent. At the moment of death the swordsman laments:

> I am done in not by the arrow but by distraction.
> Henceforth, all you swordsmen,
> do not be distracted for even an instant.
> In distraction life is lost.

After completing his instructions on calm abiding, Patrul Rinpoché offers advice on superior insight. But he chooses to cap the section off with advice typical of the Great Completion: to simply rest in mind's nature without rejecting thoughts and appearances or feeling aversion toward them. If that does not work, then the lesser of the lesser types might have to watch all of their thoughts, looking at where they arise, abide, and go, until the thoughts are recognized as naturally pure. He rounds out the section with a discussion of "ordinary mind" (*thamalgyi shepa*) and advocates indifference to mind when still or mind when active.

Before concluding, Patrul Rinpoché discusses the qualities that are important for all practitioners to cultivate, such as forbearance and compassion. He defines and compares quite a few phrases that may well come from the original Aro text(s). Finally he discusses what should happen to those individuals who are not fit for Great Completion practice at all. He seems to include himself in this category, describing himself as "without meditative experience" and yet "ready for it." We know better than to believe him, but it is still a charming affect.

The question of Patrul Rinpoché's contribution and influence on the rimé group of masters in nineteenth-century eastern Tibet is best understood from a thorough investigation of his whole life, not to be accomplished here. Still, from this one text one can discern both his unbiased appreciation of diverse teaching traditions and the wide scope of his study by paying attention to the range of masters that he chooses to quote and to the equivalencies he makes of terms from different traditions. For instance, he identifies the natural Great Completion with both the Great Seal and the perfection of transcendent intelligence (*sherab, prajñāpāramitā*). While this may seem common, some Dzokchen masters have been unwilling to make such a statement. And yet no matter his respect for other practice lineages, Patrul Rinpoché is himself, undeniably, a pure Dzokchen master. This, I believe, is the true manifestation of rimé: to unflinchingly follow one path while appreciating all of them without bias. The famous story of Patrul Rinpoché flashing his "secret parts" to interlopers desiring his "secret name" in an attempt to identify his religious allegiance is told over and over again as the example par excellence of an unbiased attitude.[6]

The Translation

This translation was originally made at the request of the two Nyingma masters Khenpo Palden Sherab Rinpoché and Khenpo Tsewang Döngyal Rinpoché—"the Khenpo brothers"—and supported by their benefactor Joan Kaye.[7] Transcripts of their teachings on Patrul Rinpoché's text are now available. I worked very closely with the late Khenpo Palden Sherab Rinpoché on every aspect of *Clear Elucidation,* and he clarified my many questions to the limited extent of my comprehension. I feel and hope that this kind of collaboration maintains the true spirit of shaldam. I am deeply grateful for the opportunity to engage such a great text with such a learned teacher.

The most difficult decision in the translation was the question of audience. If the text is, as it seems to be, a guide for teachers to best serve their students, then it should have a particularly instructive tone for a rarified audience. But this would have entailed making every statement into a recommendation, such as "Advise the student to . . ." or "Guide the student in . . ." Although there are such statements in the text, more commonly the direct imperative is used. There would be much added verbiage to maintain a third-person "them" throughout the translation or an aloof "one." I decided to use a direct second-person approach in keeping with what seems to be Patrul Rinpoché's intention of direct communication. Although "you" as a pronoun is never used in the Tibetan, I have occasionally added it to enhance a sense

---

6. "Secret name" is the name one receives in an empowerment, and the name would normally reveal the lineage of that empowerment. "Secret parts" refers to the genitals. Both meanings are expressed in Tibetan by the same word: *sangtsen.* Chapter 2 recounts the well-known story referenced here.

7. This translation was originally published by Sky Dancer Press and more recently in *The Nature of Mind: The Dzogchen Instructions of Aro Yeshe Jungne* (Boulder, CO: Snow Lion Publications, 2016). Reproduced here with permission.

of receiving the spiritual advice of a master directly. This admittedly shifts the nature of the text to one that aspiring practitioners might read for help in understanding their experiences or might use to discover questions to ask their living gurus. This is the kind of intimidating decision that a translator must make in the hopes of ensuring the greatest possible benefit from the translation.

CLEAR ELUCIDATION OF TRUE NATURE: AN ESOTERIC INSTRUCTION ON THE SUBLIME APPROACH OF ATI IN THE TRADITION OF ARO YESHÉ JUNGNÉ

by Dza Patrul Rinpoché

Homage to all genuine gurus.

This is the way to cultivate the true nature in the natural Great Completion according to three specific processes for persons of best, average, and lesser capabilities. The foundation is laid by receiving the proper introduction to the nature of the ineffable, having first applied finely honed discernment in the process of searching for the mind. The actual way to cultivate it is as follows:

Best Capability

For a person of best capability, mind itself is mind when it is still and it is mind when it moves. Once you are convinced that mind is empty, there is no difference at all between stillness and movement. Whatever thoughts arise, whatever appears, is all the play of pristine wisdom. This is the emptiness that is the profound perspective of all victorious ones. Rest within that itself without adulterating it in any way. Although occasionally there are regular thoughts, since they are liberated automatically or within that state, it is only meditative absorption. It is dharmakāya. It is innately occurring pristine wisdom. It is the Great Seal. It is the perfection of transcendent intelligence. It is like a burned rope: it cannot tie you up because it is empty of essence.[8] The thought-like occurrence is actually the shining radiance of emptiness. There is no difference between thought and emptiness. The Great Orgyen[9] said:

---

8. A burned-up rope may maintain the appearance of a rope while its ashes stick together. But as soon as one attempts to use it, the ashes disintegrate because there is no pith or essence to them. (This and all subsequent comments are based on oral commentary given by Khenchen Palden Sherab Rinpoché, henceforth KPSR.)

9. The Great Orgyen (Orgyen Chenpo) is one name for Padmasambhava or Guru Rinpoché.

Since the essence of thought is empty, know it as dharmakāya.

If you were to meditate, it would be conceptual, so be without anything on which to meditate. Rest in regular thought. If you meddle, then it becomes the deluded chain of ordinary thought, so don't contrive in any way. When you wander from resting in that immediacy there is real delusion, so there must be no wandering. Just that is enough: a nondistractedness without focus on any reference point. Dzokchen Guru Shiwa said:

> Not experiencing meditation, not experiencing departure from it:
> do not depart from the meaning of no meditation.

That is to say, since whatever arises is meditation, there is no mind-made thing to meditate on, hence "not experiencing meditation." Since there was never any way to deviate into meaninglessness, resting in that immediacy is "not experiencing departure." "Do not depart" ever from that kind of "meaning of no meditation."

Persons of special capability need not pursue this undistractedness for more than seven or fourteen days or one month. Without striving, there will come an ability to rest without effort in whatever arises. In the Great Completion this is called "the perspective of eternally free open space." It is like "the minding of innate clarity" in the Great Seal. When you cultivate its continuity without interruption, there won't be a speck of difference between the manifestation of ordinary mind and the regular thoughts of a worldly person. However, the clarity and transparency of not grasping at an essence there relieves the sitting meditation of an object, and the postmeditation will be empty of basis. Mind polished of habitual conditioning, even without recognition, still experiences thought-like occurrence. That is the actual dharmakāya. In the mind-class teachings of the Great Completion, the phrase "without having thoughts, anything is clearly knowable" refers to this. The accomplished Mitrayogin[10] said:

> When one rests directly in whatever occurs, it is spontaneous presence free of activity.

In this way, if thoughts are naturally freed by themselves, then the objective, external objects, such as form, sound, and so on, will also be liberated as a

---

10. Mitrayogin was a great adept (*drupthop chenpo, mahāsiddha*) from Radha in Orissa, eastern India, who later came to Tibet (Roerich 1988, 1030–43).

natural consequence of this innate freedom. Thus the visual objects of good
and bad forms, the pleasant and unpleasant sounds in the ears, and similarly
good and bad smells, tastes, objects of touch, mental attachment to happiness
and aversion to suffering, enemies, friends, earth, water, fire, wind, and so
on—in short, whatever arises, whatever appears—the point is to rest without
fabrication in that very thing. As is said in the Great Completion:

> When the clinging thoughts of mind do not enter
> the clarity of the five sense consciousnesses—
> that is exactly the perspective of the victorious ones.

And from the standpoint of Pacification:[11]

> Knowing how to unlock the secret of thought:
> when thought arises, it is the great stillness;
> when blatant afflictive emotion, it is illuminating wisdom.

Therefore the perspective of the Great Completion is not to reject whatever arises but also not to follow after it. Resting in that itself without med-
dling is exactly it. That being so, there is no thing to reject, no remedy, no
dos and don'ts, no keeping and discarding, etc. Since there are no mind-
made phenomena whatsoever, "nonconceptual dharmakāya suchness" is also
this.

This is according to the level of best capability. You should know how to
guide those of the three subdivisions of the best—best, average, and lesser—
by applying it to their individual mental abilities.

Average Capability

People of the three kinds of average capability should be guided by means of
the combination of calm abiding and superior insight. Gyalwa Yangönpa[12]
said:

---

11. Pacification (*shijé*) is a lineage of teachings originating with the Indian Pha Dampa
Sangyé (ca. 11th–12th centuries).

12. Gyalwa Yangönpa, a.k.a. Gyaltsen Pal (1213–58, alt. 1153–98), was the primary
disciple of Götsangpa, and one of the main masters of the Upper Drukpa Kagyü lineage
and its subsect, the Bara Kagyü.

In pristine meditation, do not meditate with the intellect.
Do not contrive an undisturbed state through fabrication.
Do not regard thoughts as faults.
Do not meditate for the sake of nonthought.
Rest in mind's own way, and keep watch from a distance.
Meditate, and you will arrive at the core of calm abiding.

By becoming adept at just that with persistence, the movement of mind will decrease and mental stillness will become more stable. When mindfulness is applied to this, it is the combination of calm abiding and superior insight. Maintaining that continuity and meditating, all subtle and blatant thoughts are stopped. The essence of that absorption is empty of any existence whatsoever. In that clarity without thought there is no sensation of having a body and mind. There arises an experience of bliss in which you can scarcely bear to be parted from that absorption. If that is prolonged in meditation, the qualities such as "five eyes" and clairvoyance will occur.[13] This is called *meditative concentration*. Meditating in that deep calm abiding, four concentrations and single-pointed absorption in four spheres of perception will occur.[14] Ultimately, what are called the "nine equilibriums of abiding" will occur.[15] These nine are also possessed by heretics,[16] and so this meditative concentration is the common path of both Buddhists and non-Buddhists.

---

13. The five eyes or five levels of clairvoyant vision are the physical eye, divine eye, eye of knowledge, dharma eye, and buddha eye. Clairvoyance or super-knowledge or actual knowing (*ngönshé*) refers to the six super-knowledges: the capacity to perform miracles, divine sight, divine hearing, recollection of former lives, cognition of the minds of others, and the cognition of the exhaustion of defilements.

14. The four meditative concentration states are (1) joy and reflection, (2) joy and absence of reflection, (3) being free of joy, and equable concentration states, and (4) supreme equanimity. The fourfold spheres of perception are mind states or absorptions that constitute the four formless realms: infinite space, infinite consciousness, nothing whatsoever, and neither presence nor absence of conception. They are also called the immaterial states.

15. Usually the *nyamjuk gi samten gu* are translated as the "nine concentrations of equilibrium," but KPSR suggests that it is best to call them the "nine equilibriums of cessation." These are the four concentrations, the four formless states, and the śrāvaka's absorption of peace.

16. *Mutekpa* (*tīrthika*) is the term for teachers of non-Buddhist philosophy who adhere to the extreme views of eternalism or nihilism.

But if there are too many active thoughts and you cannot reduce them, you should first pursue calm abiding. However, without superior insight[17] there can be no progress in the stages and paths. Therefore, when you practice with just the aspect of mental abiding, and you feel pleased that thought is not emanating, just recognize *that* thought and look at its very own essence. Then it will dissipate. It has become one with the abiding. This, then, is called the unity or combination of calm abiding and superior insight. The Dakpo Kagyüpas call this "collapsing the boundary between stillness and movement." Essentially, it is a mind-made meditation. You need to have mindful recognition constantly, and so the Kagyüpas call it "mindful holding of emptiness." Maintaining the continuity of this itself in meditation, that mindful holding will become the mindfulness of innate clarity. Just being undistracted in that is very important. In just one month you will be able to integrate it with daytime appearances. Gyalwa Götsangpa[18] said:

> Do not meditate on the emptiness of all appearances,
> nor meditate on their nonemptiness.
> If you are mindful and hold whatever arises,
> then just one month is sufficient.
> The innate abiding in the first stage of freedom from embellishment[19]
> will come.

To wrap it up: the self-recognition of the initial absorption of calm abiding is the combination of calm abiding and superior insight. That is the Great Seal and the Great Completion. It is summarized in this quotation from Yangön:

> The movement of conceptual thought is the door to true nature.
> Self-recognition of it is the crucial point of practice.

---

17. Khenpo Palden Sherab's definition of superior insight (*lhakthong*) is interesting here: *lhak* means "special" and *tong* means "seeing," and what is seen is nonself. The *tīrthikas* strive to realize the great self (*brahman*) or the individual self (*ātman*), but their accomplishments are essentially no different than those of ordinary people, since everybody has a sense of self and (falsely) perceives a self. Therefore the *tīrthikas'* mode of seeing is not special (*lhak*). Only Buddhists see nonself, and therefore their insight is special or superior (*lhakthong*).

18. Gyalwa Götsangpa Gönpo Dorjé (1189–1258). Götsangpa—literally, "Vulture Nest Dweller"—was a great master in the Drukpa Kagyü lineage who was named after a cave where he did intensive practice.

19. *Trödral* is the second of the four levels or yogas of Mahāmudrā: one-pointed (*tséchik*), unembellished (*trödral*), single flavor (*rochik*), and nonmeditation (*gomé*).

The Average and Lesser Subdivisions of the Average

The average and lesser of the average type may not be able to accept that the regular thought process *is* the meditation, so you should look at whatever thoughts arise and they will all disappear in emptiness. Within that disappearance, while one thought subsides another arises. Again watching that, it disappears as before. It is maintaining the continuity of just that, as in the song:

> Mind, unidentifiable, is the expanse of emptiness.
> The variety that arises is the door of awareness.
> Free of concept; stark, empty, clear.
> Resting within this, regard the expanse.
> You will arrive at the pith of superior insight meditation.

Practice accordingly. In this regard Mitrayogin also said,

> By identifying whatever arises,
> awareness is liberated in its own ground.

This is simple but of great impact.

All Three Subdivisions of Average

The meditation held in common for the best, average, and lesser of the average capability is as taught in this song:

> No distraction: sharp mindfulness is not lost.
> No meditation: true nature is not fabricated.
> No desire to speak of unthinkable awareness.
> Continuing, uncorrupted by permanence or nihilism.
> Meditating, the union of calm abiding and superior insight will come.

This is easily understood. With undistracted mindfulness, do not meddle with whatever arises. Although it arises, do not regard it as existent. Although it disappears, do not grasp it as nonexistent. Without suppressing them, just let the thoughts go, sustaining mere recognition. As is stated in the mind class of Great Completion:

> From within the very expanse of original purity,
> mindful each moment of the immanent arising of awareness,

it is like finding a gem in the ocean's depths.
Nobody has contrived or tampered with dharmakāya.

In this way it is revealed.[20]

Three Kinds of Lesser Capability

Calm Abiding

The three types of individuals of lesser capability for the most part do not
believe in superior insight[21] and are not able to generate calm abiding alone.
They alternate between torpor and agitation, and meditation does not arise.
Therefore you should complete the entire preliminary practice. Then sit in
cross-legged posture on a comfortable seat with hands in meditation position, tongue touching the palate, eyes falling in front of the nose, and so
on—all seven positions of meditation. Do the nine-breath exercise to clear
away stale breath, and pray while meditating on the guru above your head or
in your heart. Within a state of relaxation of body and mind, look right at
whatever thought arises and relax directly in that itself. When another arises,
relax directly into it as before. Do not rejoice when thought has vanished
into emptiness, and do not see it as problematic when it multiplies. Do not
entertain either hope for meditation to go well or fear that it will not occur
well. Relax right into whatever arises. If you are too relaxed, there comes an
experience of no conscious thought process whatsoever, a lack of thought
similar to nonthought.[22] Then you should tighten up your attention with
mindfulness, because without recognition you will not feel the discursive
undercurrent, which is like rivulets of water underneath husks of grain. It will
not cause any harm immediately, but eventually it will win out and withhold
genuine meditation, so close attentiveness is necessary.

Obvious discursiveness is the time for the identification of the conscious
thought process, so stay relaxed directly on that. At some point thoughts

---

20. I use the words "reveal" and "revelation" throughout this translation to render the
Tibetan term *ngotrö* (*ngo sprod*), which literally means to "introduce." This phrase is
generally used in the context of a teacher revealing or introducing a disciple to the nature
of his or her own mind.

21. In other words, they cannot believe in emptiness. (KPSR)

22. This is explained to be a dull or dark unconscious state without thought. It is similar
to—but not the same as—the genuine meditative experience of nonthought that is the
result of effective calm abiding practice.

might proliferate, and you will get irritated with yourself. You think, "Meditation is just not happening for me." No problem. That is the first meditative experience, "like a waterfall off a steep cliff." The Kagyüpas call it "undivided attention that is distracted by the waves of thought." It is the occasion of the lesser undivided attention.[23] If you bear with that and continue meditating, sometimes the attention will stay and sometimes be active. It is like a little bird in the water, sometimes slipping in and out of the water, sometimes resting for a bit on a rock. This is how the second meditative experience arises. If that is prolonged further in meditation, from time to time there will be occasional mental activity, but for the most part there is abiding. For example, it is like an old person who sits still most of the time. This is how the third meditative experience arises. When that is prolonged continually, at some point mental activity will not be in evidence, like water in the small rivulets of the underbrush. At that time, mindfulness needs to be somewhat tightened. This is how the fourth meditative experience arises. If the continuity of that is prolonged in that way, eventually the mind will be still day and night without budging. Thirst and the desire for clothes won't even arise. As you abide without any movement, days and months will pass. The example is that of a mountain. If this goes wrong and gets excessive, it becomes the absorption of a hearer.[24] If it goes well, after you attain the total refinement of body, it will be supreme calm abiding. This is how the fifth meditative experience arises.[25]

This description, however, is according to the majority. It is likely that the process varies according to the individual's energetic constitution and capability.

That process will certainly occur for the best level of the lesser type of capability, but for those of the average and lesser levels of the lesser, it is difficult for stillness to occur. Therefore such individuals should assume the physical posture as described before, and then plant a stick at the level of the eyebrows about four cubits in front of them. Mingling the mind, the visualization, and the subtle wind, focus on the stick. In making just this support

---

23. This is the lesser of the three phases (lesser, middle, and greater) of the first level or yoga in the Mahāmudrā tradition, called one-pointed or undivided. See note 18.

24. The state of the cessation of all sensation and conceptualization is considered to be the highest stage of meditative absorption (*tingedzin, samādhi*) for a hearer (*nyentö, śrāvaka*). In explanations of superior insight according to Mahāmudrā and Dzokchen, as found here, such a state of absorption can be seen as a trap.

25. These five meditative experiences of absorption are also called, respectively, wavering, attainment, familiarization, stability, and consummation (*yo, thop, gom, ten, thar*).

for deactivating the mind, if you are too tight you will become easily jaded, and if too loose, the meditation will go astray. So practice with moderation, doing many short sessions. Then gradually change to fewer, longer sessions. Once the mind begins to dwell over there, imagine a white letter *āḥ* on the tip of the stick and meditate as before. Then exchange the *āḥ* for a white sphere, a yellow sphere, and so on, meditating accordingly on each visualization support for one or three days or for as long as you do not become jaded. Again, replace the stick with a pebble and go through the meditation process as before. Then, using the visualization support of letters and spheres, meditate on the three places of your body, and in the inner forehead, throat, and heart in the appropriate way. Gradually, the abiding will become stabilized. It is important not to become impatient but to keep up the process until you establish familiarization without becoming jaded.

At this time of calm abiding do not push too hard—just remain undistracted in the initial way of placing the attention, like the proverbial swordsman at battle. There was a swordsman who was not distracted even for an instant and could deflect all the arrows shot by an archer with his sword without being struck. But then for one instant the movement of a beautiful woman distracted his eye and an arrow struck him. At the moment of death he said:

> I am done in not by the arrow but by distraction.
> Henceforth, all you swordsmen,
> do not be distracted for even an instant.
> In distraction life is lost.

Saying that, he died. As in this example, it is extremely important not to be distracted.

Superior Insight

Now the presentation of superior insight: What is called "superior insight" is the perfection of transcendent intelligence. Without it there is no progress through the levels and paths, so it is explained that without it the other perfections are as if without eyes. For instance, when Lord Gampopa told Milarepa that he could remain for seven days in a single meditative equipoise, Milarepa pointed out the gods' absorption of the fourth concentration.[26]

---

26. Milarepa (1040–1123), the great yogin of the Kagyü lineage, was showing his disciple,

Superior insight has three divisions. The superior insight of fully discerning phenomena is said to be the cognizance of unmistaken superior insight, the main perspective of all sūtras and tantras. Superior insight that knows the manner of the naturally pure mind is the meditation on what has now been revealed. Once this is familiar, the superior insight of actualizing the unmistaken true nature arises in the fruition of attaining buddhahood.

Now, as with calm abiding, there is an explanation of meditative equipoise concerning thoughts. However, it is sufficient to rest in mere recognition. Even when various thoughts move, just rest within the state of mere recognition. In short, whatever arises and whatever occurs, rest within the state of merely recognizing it. That's it!

Meditating, there is absolutely no meditation subject. Looking for a remedy by rejecting something or pursuing any kind of accomplishment does not get beyond the cause and effect of cyclic existence. The antithesis of meditative absorption is discursive thought, but there is no need to reject it. Rather, let it rest in itself. Resting, it will become naturally pure. As is said:

Do not avert or reject fixation on deluded appearances.
The antithesis itself is complete in the remedy.

The lesser type of those of lesser capability might do that, but if your mind is not ready you should identify whatever thought arises and look at how it exists and where it goes. Then it will become pure naturally. By maintaining that continuity, afterward you will not need to purposefully pursue it—the thought will liberate itself. This is called innately occurring pristine wisdom. That is what is meant by

When mental movement is minutely investigated, thoughts will
    vanish into the expanse by that alone.

In general, what is called "ordinary mind" means not to meddle with whatever thought arises. If you are not distracted from this, it alone is sufficient. This will not work for those of lesser capability, so you should cultivate the sitting practice with effort. Though you look at whatever thought arises, without the ability to calm it down there will be greater mental activity, and the body posture will collapse. The one that is emanating thought—let that one

---

the monk Gampopa (1079–1153), that the accomplishment of the four absorptions, though much touted in Gampopa's Kadam sect, was nothing special without intelligence (*prajñā*), even when lasting for years or eons. In fact, the four absorptions were commonly achieved even by non-Buddhists.

emanate. Then look back at its own state.[27] It calms down in its own bed. Since mental activity and stillness are both the mind, they become one in their own bed. By engendering forbearance in meditation, it will be planted deeply. It is taught in this example:

> Like the crow that takes off from a ship:
> circling, circling, again it lands on board.

The crow that was tied with fine wire to its feet when the ship was near the coast must be sent off after arriving in the middle of the ocean. Flying upward, it finds that the sky is empty, and flying back down, the space between is empty. Below, there is nothing but water. Flying up and down and in all directions, it finds no place to go, no place to land. So it returns to the same ship and lands there.[28]

It is fine if a thought emanates—it is empty. It is fine if it does not emanate—it is empty. It is fine if it abides, fine if it moves—it does not get beyond empty. Whatever way it arises, it will fall back on itself. So even those of lesser capability who practice the technique of placement meditation[29] of the best capability will do well with this training if they persist fastidiously and develop discernment.

Conclusion

This is how the practice methods are taught, divided into the nine parts of the three capabilities of best, average, and lesser. The perspective in the aural lineage of the Great Completion is described thus:

> Best capability can meditate directly with view.
> Average capability can meditate directly with meditation.
> Lesser capability can practice directly with activity.

---

27. In other words, the person thinking the thought turns the attention on his or her own mind, the source of the thought.

28. Khenpo Palden Sherab comments: In early times when ships sailed the seas, there were sea-monsters. Sailors were scared and uncertain. So they sent out a crow or a pigeon from the ship. There was no land nearby, so if the bird did not return, it meant that it had landed on a sea-monster's head. If it did return, all was clear.

29. Placement meditation (*jokgom*) refers to placing the attention or settling the mind without distraction on an object or on mind itself. It is contrasted with analytic meditation (*chegom*), in which one actively investigates mind's nature employing the thought process.

In any case, one must engender fortitude in meditation. The old adage is certainly true: "Though the Dharma be profound, without meditation the profound instructions are left behind in the scriptures." Even though meditation affects your mind at present, if you do not meditate continually, your mind becomes stubborn. Then practice becomes stubborn and it will not help at the time of death. So take care. Gyalwa Götsangpa said that six things are needed:

> Outer retreat is to stay put in isolation.
> Inner retreat is to stay put in the retreat hut.
> Secret retreat is to stay put on the mat.
> Stay put upon the nondual view.
> Stay put upon undistracted meditation.
> Stay put upon unattached conduct.

Generally in meditation there is both "to take hold" and "to be held."[30] In the mind that is not ready,[31] one needs to take hold of the meditation subject and not lack mindfulness. Then when you are held by the thought itself, whatever arises all becomes meditation. Then that becomes a state of no-fixation in ordinary mind itself.

> Though a great meditator gives up meditation,
> meditation does not give up a great meditator.

To bring that about, you have to meditate continuously. Without meditation, even if a few minor experiences occur now, they will dissipate. This is the "rainbow meditation." "The hook" is when you hold with mindfulness. Without holding, there will be nothing. You must tighten the watch guard of nondistraction. "Separation of two" is when there is mindfulness but it is not combined with compassion. For that, you should think, "I will meditate for the welfare of all sentient beings" at the start of every session, and dedicate at the end of the session with "May all sentient beings attain awakening."

---

30. "To take hold" is in the beginning. Since the mind is so perturbed, you think that you need to meditate, calm the mind, and so on. It means making meditation a distinct object. "To be held" is when the essential empty nature of thoughts is automatically seen and meditation is natural and inseparable. There is no longer an object of meditation, only the meditator (subject). (KPSR)

31. "The mind that is not ready" is a mind that is not independent: a person who has no control or ownership of his or her own mind. (KPSR)

The Great Orgyen said, "Without compassion the root of Dharma is rotten." This is extremely important.

"Nonownership" is to engender meditation and then not maintain it but discard it. Draw the mind inside and enter meditation. "Intermittent placement" means that sometimes the meditation goes well and sometimes not. For that, practice by focusing directly, indifferent to whether it is happening or not. "Around the clock" is when the mindfulness that is applied in the daytime also occurs at night. This is when you are held by meditation.[32] The "sublime yoga" is when one is free from acting and striving in the Great Completion. In the Great Seal it is also called "no meditation."[33]

Moreover, there are the individuals of the "cut-off family" who are not appropriate recipients of trekchö and thögal. Those types should receive empowerments, train in practices of the channels and winds, and focus on the action seal.[34] The proper sequence of the four pleasures that arise from the intercourse of the two organs will reveal the essence of bliss as empty. This is said to be entering the mind-guidance as described above. However, those who cannot do it should engage in the ways of gradual liberation through skillful means, such as liberation through wearing, liberation through seeing, and liberation through tasting.

In the general mind class of Great Completion and in the Great Seal teachings there is what is called "general clarity of pristine wisdom." It is explained as "the view that holds mental examination until stability is attained."[35] However, for Great Completion practitioners, once there has been the revelation, and meditation upon it, all externally appearing objects and the active or still inner mind that grasps them arise as pristine wisdom. This is the famous "perspective of unbiased self-display" of the Great Completion.

In any case, cultivate the practice directly upon appearances from the time that mind has been revealed. When you enter into thögal practice from the dark retreat guidance or appearance guidance, innately occurring pristine wisdom will become manifest when practice is maintained directly upon lucent empty form. Thus liberation in the intermediate stage (bardo) of dharmatā is assured.

For someone like me without meditative experience and even without experience of the esoteric instruction that I have heard but mostly forgotten,

---

32. "Around the clock" means that mindfulness is naturally present during dream states, thus totally integrated at all times (the level of "to be held"). (KPSR)

33. Gomé is the fourth of the four levels of Mahāmudrā. See note 18.

34. "Action seal" (karmamudrā) refers to sexual yogic practices.

35. It is called view, even though it is a meditation, because it maintains some degree of mental examination. (KPSR)

it is as Lord Barawa[36] said:

Devoid of meditational experience,
feigning meditation instruction
based upon the black letters of the scriptures
becomes a walk down the wrong road.

And:

Even without the qualities of attaining the stages,
attaining forbearance, and doing the four activities,
with the firm root of compassion
one may yet work for the welfare of beings.

Even without attaining forbearance,[37] it is appropriate because I have some
compassion in my stream of being and especially, having mixed my mind
with the Dharma, I am ready for meditative absorption and established in
whatever I recall of the teachings of the buddha-like holy gurus. Master Śrī
Siṃha said:

First, reach the meeting point.
Next, rest in the resting place.
Finally, let go to where it goes.

That is, first of all meet the guru who knows how to give guidance, minutely
investigate the mind, and reach a level of refinement. In the middle, rest
in whatever arises without any contrivance or fabrication. Finally, let it go
without fixated attachment in the play of experiential meditative absorption.
This is culled from the guidance manuals of the Great Completion mind
class. May it benefit all.

Further Tidbits of Advice

Various signs of meditative experience may arise—the handprints of meditation—that result from the force of a positive mind-frame. But since they

36. Barawa Gyaltsen Palsang (1310–91) was founder of the Bara Kagyü, a subsect of
Drukpa Kagyü.
37. "Forbearance" (*söpa*) in this case refers to the meditative stage of forbearance on the
path of application.

are not permanent, do not be trapped into clinging to their validity. This is crucial. Now, without regard for mindful holding, whatever arises becomes stark innate freedom. Know that those experiences are completely pure, the right path.

Though there is the visualized appearance of the guru's body, creation phase of the yidam, and so forth, it is all just open, stark nonappearance. When you are doing recitation and such within that state, those appearing forms are appearances without intrinsic existence, clarity without thought, and bliss without attachment. With those three characteristics, the natural radiance of emptiness appears vividly without obstruction. If you do recitation and so forth within that state, you do not particularly need to meditate on the guru on the crown of your head and such in order to make it more effective.

As for the configuration of ground, path, and fruition in terms of the path: At the time of the path, the ground is mind-as-such: rootless, unbiased, pervasive. Within that state, the path is maintaining innate clarity without resting in clarity as an object. As a result, the concurrent natural arising of the deity's body and the melting and bliss of the completion phase is counted as the fruition of the path.

A classic scripture of the Great Completion[38] teaches "introduction directly to one's own nature." The mind of nowness is free of thoughts of the three times. Within that unadulterated natural state, recognizing the open transparent pervasiveness in a forthright manner reveals the innately occurring pristine wisdom.

"Decide directly upon one thing" means that while the previous thought has ceased and the next one has not yet arisen, in that mind of nowness when the mind of conceptual thought ceases and the intrinsic awareness is free of three parts out of four, you abide in fresh, totally nonconceptual pristine wisdom—wakeful, vibrant, immaculate openness. It is this very thing. "Free of three parts out of four" refers to past, future, and present, the three times of conceptual thinking, and to the nonconceptual present, that freshness uncorrupted by thoughts of the three times. So of these four times, it is the totally nonconceptual time that is free of the three conceptual times.

---

38. The following is a brief commentary on the famous teaching attributed to Garab Dorjé called *Three Words That Strike the Crucial Point* (*Tsiksum Nedek*). Patrul Rinpoché himself composed a well-known commentary on this teaching, the *Special Teaching of the Wise and Glorious Sovereign* (*Khepa Śrī Gyalpoi Kyechö*). See Khenpo Palden Sherab 1998 for a translation by Sarah Harding, with commentary by Khenpo Palden Sherab and Khenpo Tsewang Dongyal.

That is known as "free of three parts out of four." It is the perspective of dharmakāya beyond intellect.

"To have confidence directly in liberation" means to look nakedly at whatever arises without corrupting it, and then relax into that state. By that, the thoughts will disappear without a trace like the swells subsiding in the sea. Have confidence in whatever arises as innately liberated without rejecting it or using a remedy.

∼

The crucial points of both the mind class and the space class of the Great Completion are contained in the esoteric instruction class. In meditative equipoise within primordial purity, all appearances of the world and beings are determined to be mind-as-such,[39] innately occurring pristine wisdom, the indescribable dharmakāya. That summarizes the crucial point of the mind class. Determining that itself as being the space of true being, altogether free of effortful action, summarizes the space class. Therefore all the practices of the mind and space sections are contained in the trekchö practices of the esoteric instruction class. Thus the pinnacle of the sublime path of Great Completion is the esoteric instruction class. The method of hitting directly on the crucial point of reality without rejecting or accepting saṃsāra or nirvāṇa instantly arouses the innately occurring pristine wisdom beyond intellect. This means that it is the supreme sublime method that manifestly confirms the innate clear nature of the true being of all phenomena and thus reveals the spontaneously present clear-light pristine wisdom that abides as the basic ground.

Of these two—integrating the innate freedom of whatever arises to the six sense groups into the spiritual path and applying the seal of deity and mantra to those appearances—the former is certainly more effective. Yet to know how to integrate effortlessly on the path the dynamic appearance of the innately free, natural state as the natural radiance of deity and mantra is indeed the special approach of unity.

Various experiences arise in stark awareness, yet whatever arises does not shift from mindfulness itself and can be maintained without depending on mindful holding. This is basically similar to the "abiding experience" of the four stages of experience in the Great Completion tradition and the "one-pointed abiding" of the Great Seal tradition in that there is certainly a

---

39. "Mind" (*sem*) refers to dualistic conceptuality. "Mind-as-such" (*semnyi*) refers to the true being (*chönyi, dharmatā* or "dharmaness") of mind: emptiness. (KPSR)

glimpse in the direction of mind's essence. However, you may think that other than just attainment or lack of stability, there is no special thing to be seen or realized. In terms of personal understanding of reality in an appropriate way, mind is similar to undeluded awareness. But if you wonder about whether there is not something more, it becomes the conceptuality of intellectual clinging to the identity of phenomena. When you look nakedly and starkly at innate awareness, that basic character is free of embellishment with no clinging whatsoever. That and the emptiness that is merely understood are two different ways of experiencing. You must understand this.

Moreover, the phrase "to see the essence of mind" refers to merely the general seeing of symbolic pristine wisdom that is skillfully introduced. Other than that, the authentic essence of totally nonconceptual pristine wisdom of natural intrinsic awareness is realized only by those who have attained the level of noble ones. If even those who have applied total control in meditation results and reached ascertainment on the path of application do not have it, then there is no need to talk about those meditators on the path of accumulation or those who have not entered the path at all. Therefore these need to be differentiated.

There is a training to practice within the state of mindful recognition of dreams and a training without the mindful awareness of thinking "it's a dream" that brings greater clarity than the daytime practices. In terms of recognizing, refining, increasing, and changing your dreams, when the former training is ineffective, the latter will greatly enhance the stability of the practice. Mere appearances of experience occur as a consequence of daytime virtuous practices. Since they will be exhausted, there will be little effect on the vital points of developing stability in recognizing and refining dreams. Usually it is during the time of deep sleep that clear, empty intrinsic awareness is free of the tarnish of conceptual thought and you can maintain its true nature. From its dynamic appearance comes the ability to arouse the emanations and transformations of dreams. It can then be counted as recognizing the clear light of sleep. If that is the case, then when you arise in the dream, even if you do not recognize it with mindfulness during dreamtime, it is still effective.[40]

At the time of thögal, many people think that remaining in and habituating to a state of nonthought in regard to the appearing signs of empty form

---

40. The practice is effective because you are always abiding within dharmatā (KPSR). In other words, tapping into the intrinsic awareness of deep sleep, which is the ever-present nature, may be more effective than the typical dream-yoga practices geared toward recognizing and controlling dreams.

that are drawn from deity appearance is merely calm abiding and not the discernment of discriminating intelligence, so it is not considered superior insight. However, it is explained in the *Kālacakra Tantra* and other teachings that nonconceptual pristine wisdom is born from habituating to absorption without conceptual thought, and just that is the birth of the superior insight of discriminating intelligence.

In particular, in the tradition of Great Completion itself, with the three unmoving states[41] of the physical postures, visual gazes, and winds as the basis, gradually the channels and winds will reach the crucial point and discursive thought will cease. Since this is the field of actual clear perception, there is freedom from the added designations of discernment. Abiding in the nature of true being, mother and child combine. Since this is the decisive leap into the original expanse, unblinkingly focusing with the visual gazes on the appearing signs of spheres with vajra chains, rest without distraction or fabrication within the transparent nature of those appearing signs themselves. Only through this does it become effective.

During the dharmatā intermediate state, the measure of a day of meditative stability is difficult to determine. Once you integrate sitting meditation and postmeditation, the arising of the experience of spontaneously present pristine wisdom goes beyond an allotted period for meditative absorption. So you cannot say just where it ends. But to generalize, while sitting in meditative stability, however long you stay without interruption from discursive thought is how long you have meditated.

It is important to know that the potential for your ability to be liberated in the dharmatā during the four visions of clear light is present in you now. You can certainly determine this by whether or not the practice of dreams has measured up.

Even though mental activity arises in the face of meditative equipoise, if you can just barely carry through with mindfulness, it arises endowed with the bliss-clarity experience. If you do not fall into clinging to that experience or the desire for experience, then it will become effective.

With absolute conviction that whatever arises is your own mind, mind-as-such—rootless, clear, and empty—arises without fixation. In the face of sitting meditation, body, appearance, mind, and all fixation on distinctions are naturally purified and you dwell in stark wakeful openness without outside,

---

41. The three unmoving states are: (1) without moving from the postures of the body, the energy channels and currents are relaxed of their own accord; (2) without moving from the gazes of the eyes, appearances are enhanced; and (3) without moving from the state of the unfabricating mind, the expanse and awareness are integrated.

inside, or in between, without holding on to regular conceptual thoughts. Though they arise, merely recognize them and let them appear. That is the combining of appearance and mind. Though appearances seem to arise as meditation, from this point on you have to differentiate whether or not you need to depend upon the mindful holding of emptiness. When it happens that this fresh appearing awareness arises as innate, aware clarity free of attempts to achieve or stop something, then appearance has arisen as meditation and indeed there is no longer any need of mindful holding. Therefore, even with effort, if you do not fall into fixation, whatever occurs arises in the expansiveness of innate freedom and it has become effective.

Again, cultivate the continuity of virtuous practice by the threefold "freely resting."[42] Look at the essence of the ensuing realization with directly liberating perception (cherdröl). Outwardly looking at conditioned phenomena (chöchen), you can relax without attachment or fixation in the state of realizing that the deluded appearances appear without validity, like an illusion. Inwardly looking at true being, you can relax without attachment or fixation in the state of realizing objectlessness, like the sky. Secretly looking at the essence of intrinsic awareness and realizing emptiness, clarity, and unimpededness, you can relax without effort in that state.

The immediate benefit from that meditative equipoise is to be in complete control of immeasurable qualities such as the "eyes" and clairvoyances, and the afflictive emotions will be freed in their own ground without difficulty. The qualities that arise from the initial thorough training and subsequent actualization will gradually increase and become a profound method of accomplishing buddha-wisdom. This I heard many times directly from my true Lord Guru. Thus, with confidence, I hold it to be the truth. And since others also advise thus, keep it in your heart.

The essence of the view is the realization of intrinsic awareness, without individual reference to all dualistic phenomena, as free since forever, spontaneously present, empty, clear, unembellished, vast, unbiased, and the single flavor of the multitude. Then anything at all can appear without worry or anxiety. However, until the mind of self-fixation subsides, when something like anger or desire seems to arise in response to objects, even though the theoretical view is excellent, the direct experience may appear in contradiction to it. This is natural. So when that happens, you should directly integrate the natural freedom of whatever arises into the path and it will become effective.

Therefore the crucial point is just to maintain the state, as if abiding since

---

42. The threefold "freely resting" (chokshak sum) are: (1) freely resting mountain, (2) freely resting ocean, and (3) freely resting awareness.

forever in the great wide vast expanse which is naturally free of limitations, transcending the investigations of philosophical schools, the objective appearances of attachment, and mental operations. In any case, just like anything might sprout from the ground in summertime, the experiences of a yogin might be high or low—they are not all of one type. There is no need to even mention the overall thought patterns that include good and bad thoughts.

The view is free of limitation, the expression of the natural radiance of nonthought. The meditation is not bound up with antidotes. The conduct is letting whatever arises be in its natural freedom. The fruition is free of the dualistic fixation on hopes and fears.

If you fall into the mind-frame of desiring to experience whatever appearance arises, then it has become like medicine that does not dissolve and turns to poison. So at that time remain in the state of total conviction without getting bound up by fixation and attachment. You will be well satisfied if you always proceed at the natural pace of undistracted nonmeditation.

Though you may always recognize your obvious dreams, just recognizing them is not enough. Henceforth, having purposely tamed the appearances of the six consciousness groups in the daytime without falling into fixation, when it is time to go to sleep, fall asleep without losing the force of the daytime mindfulness. Then the progression of experience and realization of the clear light will arise.

Whatever kinds of experiences occur, do not corrupt them with thoughts of practicing or preventing, accepting or rejecting. Rather, remain in the face of whatever arises. The hosts of dualistic thought clear away like the dispersed clouds in the sky and the seed of cyclic existence is exhausted. In the expanse of naturally pure space, naturally pure intrinsic awareness dissolves and mother and child combine. Then unchanging nondualistic pristine wisdom is transcribed in space. Like waves dissolving into water, thoughts are purified into the expanse and the gap between saṃsāra and nirvāṇa collapses. The five paths and ten levels are traversed all at once, and you are free.

Translated Work

Dza Patrul Orgyen Jikmé Chökyi Wangpo (Rdza dpal sprul O rgyan 'jigs med chos kyi dbang po). 1970–71. *Theg mchog a ti'i man ngag gnas lugs gsal ston,* including *Gzhan yang zhal shes 'thor bu.* Collected Works, vol. 4 (*nga*), 709–35. Gangtok: Sonam T. Kazi.

Suggested Readings

Dilgo Khyentse. *The Heart Treasure of the Enlightened Ones.* 1992. Translated by the Padmakara Translation Group. Boston: Shambhala Publications.
———. *Primordial Purity: Oral Instructions on "The Three Words That Strike the Vital Point."* 1999. Translated by Ani Jinba Palmo. Halifax: Vajravairochana Translation Committee.
Khenchen Palden Sherab and Khenpo Tsewang Dongyal. 1998. *Lion's Gaze: A Commentary on "The Special Teaching of the Wise and Glorious Sovereign" by Patrul Rinpoché and "The Three Words That Strike the Crucial Point" by Vidyadhara Garab Dorjé.* Translated by Sarah Harding. Boca Raton: Sky Dancer Press.
———. *Pointing Out the Nature of Mind: Dzokchen Pith Instructions of Aro Yeshe Jungne.* 2012. New York: Dharma Samudra.
Patrul Rinpoche. *The Words of My Perfect Teacher.* 1998. Translated by the Padmakara Translation Group. Boston: Shambhala Publications.

Additional References

Davidson, Ronald M. 2005. *Tibetan Renaissance: Tantric Buddhism in the Rebirth of Tibetan Culture.* New York: Columbia University Press.
Dza Patrul Orgyen Jikmé Chökyi Wangpo (Rdza Dpal sprul O rgyan 'jigs med chos kyi dbang po). 1999. *Dpal sprul bka' 'bum gyi dkar chag zhib rgyas su bkod pa.* In Collected Works, vol. 8. Chengdu: Si khron mi rigs dpe skrun khang.
Khenpo Jamyang (Mkhan po 'jam dbyangs), ed. 1999. *Slob dpon a ro ye shes 'byung gnas kyi lo rgyus.* In *Bka' ma shin tu rgyas pa (Kaḥ thog),* vol. 107, 323–50. Chengdu: Kaḥ thog mkhan po 'jam dbyangs.
Roerich, George N., trans. 1988. *The Blue Annals,* 2nd ed. Delhi: Motilal Banarsidass.
Tseten Zhabdrung (Tshe tan zhabs drung 'Jigs med rigs pa'i blo gros), ed. 1985, 1987. *Bod rgya tshig mdzod chen mo,* 2 vols. Beijing: Mi rigs dpe skrun khang.

PART III: ESOTERIC INSTRUCTIONS

11. Pointing to the Nature of Awareness

Ju Mipham Rinpoché
Translated by Douglas Duckworth

Turn On, Tune In . . . Don't Space Out!

The following short text is in the genre of raw, direct advice for meditation. It is a concise instruction on cultivating open presence—the nature
of awareness—and points to a simple and profound practice for recognizing
and sustaining this awareness in the tradition of the Great Perfection. This
practice is a hallmark of what has been called the "ecumenical movement,"
in general, and of the Nyingma tradition to which Mipham was heir in particular. While Mipham is renowned as an erudite scholar, this text reveals
his ambidexterity. It shows him capable both of elaborating on philosophical
topics with the best of scholars and of laying out an unelaborate practice of
letting go of all such conceptions.

The text translated in this chapter is representative of the genre of quintessential instructions. This genre serves as the backbone of Buddhist meditative traditions across Tibet, as quintessential instructions are oriented toward
personal experience, not abstract philosophy. Differences among sects fade
away when the fundamentals of practice are in focus, despite the fact that
conflicting interpretations are vigorously debated and dissected in other contexts. For this reason, the genre of quintessential instructions has a special
place in an ecumenical approach to Buddhism.

The teaching in this text is particularly significant for Mipham's tradition,
as it highlights the fundamentals of the practice of the Great Perfection. His
text is organized around three short instructions, which is representative of

the direct style of the genre. Quintessential instructions are often structured around three or four key points of practice. This style of teaching enables the instructions to be easily brought to mind and keeps the essential points from getting lost in the details.

The first of the three instructions shows the way to rest naturally and look to the nature of awareness, which Mipham calls "the quintessential instruction that cracks open the egg of ignorance." This initial directive is reminiscent of the injunction to "recognize your own nature" in *Three Words That Strike the Crucial Point*, a famous set of three quintessential instructions by Garap Dorjé upon which Patrul Rinpoché famously commented.[1] Beginning his first instruction, Mipham advises to "let the mind rest naturally without thinking anything at all." Yet letting be in this way is only the first step in unfolding the nature of wisdom. Mipham next shows how to recognize the nature of awareness by looking at experience itself.

The recognition of the nature of awareness is the main message of the text. It is the crucial moment when practitioners ascertain the view, which is the ground and path to freedom. Mipham likens this self-recognition, which dispels the darkness of ignorance, to "the light of dawn illuminating your house." Like turning on a light, recognition is to "turn on," or to directly engage the nature of mind. In this way, Mipham's first of three instructions resembles the first part of Timothy Leary's motto, "turn on, tune in, drop out," an injunction for American hippies in the sixties (although with different results, and indeed, different causes!).

According to Mipham's instructions, without "turning on," or turning attention to uncontrived awareness, one will remain in the darkness of ignorance, always chasing after what is external and peripheral—namely conceptual constructions. It is like the Buddhist parable of the dog that only chases after the stones thrown at him in contrast to the lion that turns to the person who throws the stones.[2]

Mipham's second instruction, "the quintessential instruction for cutting through the web of existence," concerns the practice of familiarizing oneself with this view. It corresponds with the stage of meditation or the path, or in a more contemporary idiom, the act of "tuning in." In the context of this instruction, Mipham lays out two cognitive modalities: the extrinsic, conceptual mind, which is to be distinguished from intrinsic, nonconceptual awareness. Similarly, he distinguishes between two types of "inexpressible" (*jödral*)

---

1. See Dza Patrul 2009.
2. See Kunzang Pelden 2010, 162.

modes of being: (1) the nonconceptual and inexpressible state of confusion or ignorance and (2) the nonconceptual and inexpressible state of clarity or awareness. While both are said to be "inexpressible," it is inexpressible *clarity* that is the nature of awareness. Clarity is what is to be recognized and sustained. Without clarity, there is simply dullness or ignorance.

Being aware, "clarity," is who and what we fundamentally are, so simply *being* it (without alteration or distraction, or needing to capture or contrive it) is the way to sustain it. Clarity, or awareness, is not identified in the way that an *object* of knowledge is known—such as knowing that "this is empty" or "this is clear." Of course awareness can be known to be empty like any other object in the world, but awareness can also be known in a unique way—from within, by attunement to its nature. The act of knowing awareness from within—of recognizing the nature of awareness—lacks any separate objective content. The nature of awareness is not known as an extrinsic object is known because it is not found somewhere *out there*. It can, however, be recognized from within, or *intrinsically*, as the basic nature of all things (subjects and objects). Thus, the nature of awareness can be said to be "known" by recognizing it *as it is* or by attuning to its nature, or rather by attuning to one's own nature.

The third and last of Mipham's threefold instruction is called "the quintessential instruction of space-like equanimity." In this instruction, Mipham gives the example of looking at various scenes while traveling; they are always only fleeting moments of passing spectacles. Yet equanimity is not indifference to the world. So rather than "dropping out," the third part of Leary's motto—which connotes disengagement, quietism, and isolation—equanimity is a dynamic gesture of presence and embrace. Whether there is joy or sorrow, pleasure or pain, Mipham's advice is not to waiver from equanimity, which is the accommodating, open presence of awareness. That is, everything is vividly present in equanimity; and since it is vast, open, and empty, it is "space-like." The space-like quality is not a rejection of appearances or a denial of life but the affirmation of the empty and equal nature of all things.

"Space-like equanimity" is not about being indifferent, disengaging, or spacing out. So rather than "drop out," "don't space out!" makes for a better counterpart in adapting Leary's motto for Buddhists. It is an injunction to be mindful and not distracted. Mindfulness in this context is a reminder or touchstone for reality; it serves as a prompt to not confuse contrivance for the natural, nor conflate nonconceptual dynamism with a dead idea or an amorphous void.

Mipham's first instruction, the method of resting naturally, relates to the practice of calm abiding, while the second step of his first instruction, looking to the nature of uncontrived awareness, relates to special insight. In his second and third instructions, Mipham highlights the union of these two modes in meditative practice. His advice in the second instruction chiefly concerns the practice of meditation, or the path, while his third instruction gestures at the result of the practice. Indeed the Buddhist triad of ground, path, and result are all integrated within the Great Perfection's unique approach to cultivating the nature of mind.

Like the first instruction, in the third instruction Mipham's advice to sustain the recognition of awareness is to leave awareness as it is. In the context of this practice, he states that ideas gleaned from studying meditation texts, and even acts of introspection, disturb the recognition of awareness's uncontrived nature. Using the metaphor of water becoming clear when it is not stirred, he shows how natural awareness becomes clear when undisturbed by fixation and directed thought. To conclude the text, Mipham affirms the efficacy of this simple yet comprehensive path, claiming it to be a complete path to becoming a buddha and a path without difficulty.

Since the nature of awareness is supposed to be inexpressible, and cannot be adequately described or directly shown, we might wonder about the intent of instruction manuals like this. What is the point of trying to describe the indescribable? The content of these instructions, however, is not traditionally read as descriptions of awareness but as guidance manuals to a practice in the context of the path of awakening. Instruction manuals like this serve as prompts for practical knowledge and personal experience. As with learning any skill, it is not enough simply to read the manual, for a manual is only a directive for the actual endeavor. The task of understanding and mastery is to be discovered in the endeavor itself—in the skill of the performance of the task. For example, in the case of learning to ride a bike, it is not enough simply to read a manual on bike riding. One must practice riding, which brings familiarity, experience, and mastery. Learning to experience the nature of mind from quintessential instructions is comparable.

Mipham tailors his instructions to students who seek to experience the nature of awareness. As he says in the colophon, his explanation is "in a language that is easy to understand for village practitioners who are interested in experiencing the nature of awareness but have not put much effort into study and reflection." His audience is neither scholar-monks nor hermits but villagers, who may be married or have families to support and do not necessarily have time for in-depth scholarly analyses or scholastic pursuits. In any case, he presents a concise and powerfully evocative text for anyone interested in understanding the nature of awareness, and the way to cultivate it, in the tradition of the Great Perfection.

While addressing the heart of his tradition, Mipham's short text reveals a style that is uniquely his own. With carefully chosen words he shows the way to undirected awareness, the nonreferential referent of his prose. As with teaching effortless action, instructions that purport to guide students to unguided awareness might seem like a lesson in performative contradiction. But this genre is not meant for scholars or logicians, as Mipham clearly states. This text is meant to be applied and experimented with. As the lifeblood of the living tradition of the Great Perfection—"the way of the realized masters of the past"—it is to be tried and tested. The text calls for reader participation, for getting one's feet wet and one's hands dirty.

A Beacon to Dispel Darkness: Instructions in the Way of the Old Masters Pointing to the Nature of Awareness

by Ju Mipham Rinpoché

Homage to the teacher and the wisdom-being Mañjughoṣa!

Without needing a lot of study, reflection, or training,
the way of the quintessential instructions for sustaining the nature of
   mind
brings most village practitioners to easily reach the stage of an
   awareness-holder—
this is the power of the profound path.

Rest your mind naturally without thinking anything at all. When you sustain the continuity of mindfulness within that state, there is a dull, blank state of neutral awareness—indifference. Teachers have called this state that lacks insight into knowing this or that "ignorance." It is called "neutral" from the aspect of its not being identified or expressed in a determinate way. It is called "ordinary indifference" because anything you think or however you abide cannot be formulated. It is remaining in the state of the universal ground— abiding in an ordinary, default mode.

You should cultivate nonconceptual wisdom based on such a method of resting, yet without the presence of wisdom's recognition, it is not the main part of the meditation. It is said in the *Prayer of Samantabhadra*:

The blankness of not thinking anything
is itself the cause of delusion and ignorance.

When the mind is experiencing this kind of cognition—a blankness without thinking anything—look directly at the one who knows this, the one who remains without thought. This awareness, free from the movement of thought, is open—without inside or outside—and clear like space. Although there is no separation between the experiencer and the experience, through reaching a firm conclusion yourself as to your own nature, you will come to see that there is nothing other than this. This cannot be expressed by word or thought—as like this or that—but can be called "freedom from extremes," "inexpressible," "innate luminosity," or "awareness." As the dark haze of oblivion is dispelled by the dawning of wisdom's self-recognition—like the light of dawn illuminating your house—you gain confidence in the basic nature of your mind. This is called "the quintessential instruction that cracks opens the egg of ignorance."

When understood in this way, this basic nature is known to be the natural way things have been from the beginning—unconditioned by causes and conditions, and not modified in the past, present, and future. Other than this, no "mind" is observed whatsoever. The previous dark oblivion was inexpressible, but the utter inexpressibility was not decisively ascertained. While the essence of awareness is inexpressible, too, the inexpressible meaning here is ascertained without a doubt, so the difference between these two ways of inexpressibility is great, like that between a blind and sighted person. Herein lies the essential point of the difference between the universal ground consciousness and the body of reality, too. Thus, there are two meanings—authentic and inauthentic—for terms such as "ordinary mind," "mental nondoing," and "inexpressible." Through ascertaining the essential point of shared terms with exalted values, you'll find the experiential realization of the profound truth.

When one is resting freely in the natural state of mind, some people maintain that mere clarity or mere cognition is to be sustained, and one rests in a state that is thought to be a clarity derived from the mental consciousness. Others hold in mind a blank void, like a mental absence. Both of these are just fixations on experiences of an apprehended and apprehender that are aspects of mental consciousness. When these occur, look directly at the lucid continuity of the fixated attention to clarity and the apprehender of clarity, or to emptiness and the cognition apprehending emptiness. By uprooting the stakes that hold the mind's dualistic fixations in place, there comes a clear ascertainment that its nature is free from center and edge—empty, clear, and vividly naked. This is called the essence of awareness. The dawning of this naked wisdom is awareness free from the crust of fixated orientations. This is called "the quintessential instruction for cutting through the web of existence."

Moreover, awareness is like husked rice separated from the chaff of mentally conceived experiences. Recognize this basic nature as it is through self-luminosity. Yet it is not enough simply to recognize the nature of awareness; you need to stabilize its abiding aspect through familiarity within this state. It is extremely important to sustain the natural continuity of awareness without distraction. When sustaining in this way, sometimes there will be a darkness of nonconceptuality that is nothing at all, and sometimes the clarity aspect of insight will shine forth unobstructed by thought. Sometimes there will be grasping to an experience of bliss, and sometimes there will be no holding on to the blissful experience. Sometimes various experiences of clarity will be held on to, and sometimes there will be immaculate, pure clarity without clinging. Sometimes there will be unpleasant, harsh experiences, and other times there will be pleasant, tender moments. Sometimes, due to thoughts being overwhelmingly powerful, you will follow after them and give up your meditation. At times, there will be all kinds of confusion that come out of a dullness undifferentiated from clarity. There will be uncertain and unpredictable waves of various habitual thoughts and karmic winds from beginningless time. Sustain your path without deliberately fixating on whatever arises, as when observing the various bustling sights along a long journey.

Manifold thoughts blaze like fire—especially when not accustomed to recognizing awareness. Don't be frustrated by the experience of thought activity. Sustain the continuity without losing it, with a balance between tightness and looseness. Through this, later experiences like "attainment" progressively come about. Generally this is the time to find certainty in recognition experientially from your teacher's instructions on the difference between awareness and ignorance, the universal ground and the body of reality, consciousness and wisdom. As water becomes pure when it is left undisturbed, leave consciousness as it is when sustaining this recognition. Thereby its basic nature manifests as self-existing wisdom—you should mainly apply this quintessential instruction. Do not proliferate a bunch of ideas about the meaning understood from texts, nor consider what to accept and reject, wondering, "What is the content of my meditation—consciousness or wisdom?" Doing this will just obscure both calm abiding and special insight.

A familiarity sets in within the way of the natural integration of (1) the aspect of stability in calm abiding, which is the steady continuity of mindfulness while resting naturally, with (2) special insight, which is recognizing your own self-luminous nature. When this happens, there dawns the viewpoint of the Great Perfection—self-existing wisdom—the natural way from the beginning and the natural luminous clarity that is the original indivisibility of calm abiding and special insight. This is "the quintessential instruction of space-like equanimity."

Moreover, the glorious Saraha expressed this method of resting as follows:

Completely leaving behind thoughts and objects of thought,
remain like a small child, thought-free.

And he said,

When you strive diligently in the words of the teacher . . .

With the quintessential instructions that introduce the nature of awareness,

. . . There is no doubt that the coemergent[3] (*lhenchik kyepa*) will arise.

This is the arising of self-existing wisdom—awareness—the basic nature of mind that is coemergent with your own mind from the beginning. This is not different from the basic nature of all phenomena and is also the innate, actual luminous clarity. Therefore the way of resting naturally and the way of sustaining the awareness that is recognized—sustaining the nature of mind or reality—is the quintessential instruction that comprises a hundred essential points in one. This is what is to be sustained constantly.

The signs of familiarity are that luminous clarity is held through the night, and the signs that this path is authentic can be known by the spontaneous growth of such qualities as faith, compassion, and insight. This path is easy and without hardship; this can be known through your own experience. That this is vast and swift is certain because the realization is the same as for those who make great efforts in following other paths. By cultivating the luminous clarity of your own mind, the result that is achieved too is self-purified of the defilements of thoughts and their habitual tendencies. When this happens, the two wisdoms effortlessly expand and the primordial seat of existence is seized—the three bodies are spontaneously accomplished. Profound. *Guhya. Samaya.*

---

3. "The coemergent" here refers to coemergent wisdom.

Translated Work

Ju Mipham Gyatso ('Ju Mi pham rgya mtsho). n.d. *Rtogs ldan rgan po rnams kyi lugs sems ngo mdzub tshugs kyi gdams pa mun sel sgron me.* Collected Works, vol. 32, 375–80. Chengdu: Nationalities Press.

Suggested Readings

Dilgo Khyentse Rinpoche. 2011. "Commentary on 'The Lamp That Dispels Darkness.'" In *The Collected Works of Dilgo Khyentse Rinpoche,* vol. 3, 668–92. Boston: Shambhala Publications.

Duckworth, Douglas. 2011. *Jamgön Mipam: His Life and Teachings.* Boston: Shambhala Publications.

———. 2008. *Mipam on Buddha-Nature.* Albany: State University of New York Press.

Pettit, John. 1999. *Mipham's Beacon of Certainty: Illuminating the View of Dzogchen, the Great Perfection.* Boston: Wisdom Publications.

Schmidt, Erik (Erik Pema Kunzang), trans. 2012. *Perfect Clarity: A Tibetan Anthology of Mahamudra and Dzogchen.* Hong Kong: Rangjung Yeshe Publications.

Additional References

Dza Patrul Orgyen Jikmé Chökyi Wangpo (Rdza dpal sprul O rgyan 'jigs med chos kyi dbang po). 2009. *Tshig gsum gnad du brdeg pa'i man ngag mkhas pa shrī rgyal po'i khyad chos kyi 'grel pa.* Collected Works, vol. 6, 419–36. Chengdu: Nationalities Press.

Jikmé Punstok (Mkhan po 'Jigs med phun tshogs). n.d. *Sems ngo mdzub btsugs kyi 'grel ba man ngag gter gyi mdzod khang.* Collected Works, vol. 2, 197–340. Gser thang bla rung lnga rig nang bstan slob gling.

Khangsar Tenpai Wangchuk (Khang sar Bstan pa'i dbang phyug). 2005. *Rtogs ldan rgan po rnams kyi lugs sems ngo mdzub tshugs kyi zin bris.* Collected Works, vol. 3, 139–83. Beijing: Nationalities Press.

Kunzang Pelden. 2010. *The Nectar of Manjushri's Speech: A Detailed Commentary on Shantideva's "Way of the Bodhisattva."* Translated by the Padmakara Translation Group. Boston: Shambhala Publications.

12. Putting Buddha Nature into Practice

Jamgön Kongtrul
Translated by Tina Draszczyk

Meditation Instruction for the View of Shentong

A central concept within Mahāyāna Buddhism is the doctrine of *tathāgata-garbha*, or buddha nature (*deshin shekpai nyingpo, deshek nyingpo*), the element inherent to every sentient being. Presenting this buddha nature as the absolute in positive terms, as a state of wisdom with inconceivable qualities, is the essence of the so-called shentong view. Mind as such is understood to be *shentong* or "empty of other," meaning that it is empty of adventitious stains, which are not mind's true nature. But mind is not empty of its enlightened qualities. Still, as long as sentient beings' perceptions are obscured by the temporary stains, they are incapable of directly relating to wisdom's inherent enlightened qualities. According to the relevant texts,[1] these stains constitute the only difference between normal beings and the awakened ones who have removed the stains and actualized their inherent buddha nature. From the perspective of both the doctrine of tathāgatagarbha in general and shentong in particular, proper Buddhist philosophy and spiritual training in ethics, view, and meditation have as their goal the removal of the stains of karma and afflictive emotions and their subtle tendencies of ignorance so that the mind's inherent qualities can manifest.

This chapter deals with the corresponding approach in view and meditation

---

1. For example, the *Tathāgatagarbha Sūtra*, the *Śrīmālādevīsiṃhanāda Sūtra*, and the *Ratnagotravibhāga*, also referred to as the *Uttaratantra Śāstra*.

taught by the cleric-scholar Jamgön Kongtrul Lodrö Thayé (1813–99). As one of the leading figures in the rimé movement in eastern Tibet, he worked to preserve practice traditions from the various Buddhist lineages of Tibet—in particular, practices from the Nyingma, Kadam, Jonang, Kagyü, and Sakya schools. His work exemplifies the idea that implementing philosophical understanding in meditative training is an essential part of all Tibetan Buddhist traditions. His *Immaculate Vajra Moonrays: An Instruction for the View of Shentong, the Great Madhyamaka* (abbreviated here as *Instruction for the View of Shentong*) is but one instance of the integral relationship between philosophical understanding and meditative training. The text guides meditators in a gradual practice that aims to achieve a direct realization of the true nature of mind—buddha nature with all of its inherent qualities.

As the title conveys, the instructions are given within the philosophical framework of Madhyamaka, which in Tibetan Buddhism is generally considered to be the pinnacle of all Buddhist views. Kongtrul here uses the term Great Madhyamaka (*uma chenpo*) to designate a practice-oriented synthesis of the Yogācāra and Madhyamaka schools of thought within Mahāyāna Buddhism. While the Mādhyamikas prove the unreal nature of all things, the Yogācāra school provides detailed instructions about meditative processes and the workings of mind. As evident in *Instruction for the View of Shentong*, the outcome of the synthesis of these two approaches is complex. In line with the "Great Madhyamaka" scriptures and treatises, it presents teachings on emptiness and metaphysical and epistemological theories alongside instructions for implementing meditative practice. Those sūtras that integrate teachings on buddha nature—considered to belong to the last cycle of the Buddha's teachings—and the commentarial literature associated with them form the backbone for the practice presented in *Instruction for the View of Shentong*.

According to Kongtrul, the Yogācāra-Madhyamaka teaching system communicates the final definitive meaning of the Buddhadharma, and it is in this sense that he understands Great Madhyamaka to be equivalent to shentong in its various forms. But he does not restrict shentong to the Jonang position formulated by Dölpopa and Tāranātha. Kongtrul remarks that "the teaching and study tradition known as shentong Madhyamaka arose according to circumstances in slightly different ways." This statement shows that he was fully aware of the various interpretations of shentong that had developed in Tibet. He praises a series of masters in his introduction, including Karmapa Rangjung Dorjé, Dölpopa, Tāranātha, and Śākya Chokden, emphasizing that they had all reached levels of realization. This clearly reflects his deep appreciation for all of their respective interpretations. As for his own shentong presentation, despite claiming in the colophon that he has given instruction in accordance with Tāranātha's view, Kongtrul chooses not to follow Dölpopa or Tāranātha in every regard. This becomes all the more obvious when one studies the corresponding section on shentong in his *Treasury of Knowledge.* Kongtrul shows his appreciation for Tāranātha's expositions of other-emptiness by quoting him there at length, but he simply skips over a section where Tāranātha describes self-emptiness as being contradictory in itself.[2] To the contrary, Kongtrul states that both self-emptiness and other-emptiness are effective for preparing students to access mind's true nature. In this regard, he follows more closely presentations given by Śākya Chokden (1428–1507).

The main difference between Dölpopa and Kongtrul is that Kongtrul synthesizes the "empty of other" and "self-empty" views and Kagyü mahāmudrā, a practice that Dölpopa does not approve of. Dölpopa considers saṃsāra and nirvāṇa to be fundamentally different, comparing them to the opposing natures of light and darkness or nectar and poison.[3] In his interpretation, conceptual mental activity is saṃsāra, whereas the wisdom of a Buddha is nirvāṇa. Being opposites, they cannot share the same ground. The mahāmudrā teachings in the Kagyü school, in contrast, focus on the fundamental unity of saṃsāra and nirvāṇa. They emphasize that the true nature of concepts is the dharmakāya, or the body of reality (*chöku*). Conceptualization may be the manner of saṃsāra's appearance, but the very nature of conceptualization is held to be nothing else but the true nature of phenomena, dharmatā, or nirvāṇa.[4]

Kongtrul claims that Svātantrika- and Prāsaṅgika-Madhyamaka—which together make up what many Tibetan Buddhist doxographers call *rangtong* or "self-empty" Madhyamaka—present emptiness as a mere negation of reality. These philosophical procedures convey the meaning of the middle cycle of the Buddha's teachings, which assert that all subjective and objective phenomena are inherently empty. For Kongtrul, these views help practitioners to let go of conceptual proliferations (*tröpa*) about the nature of reality. *Shentong* (or "empty-of-other" Madhyamaka), in contrast, is essential because it helps practitioners to avoid stagnating in the mere emptiness of phenomena. Shentong provokes them to proceed to actualize mind's true nature—self-aware luminous wisdom free from conceptual proliferations. Mind's true nature, buddha nature, manifests more and more clearly as the temporary stains

---

2. Kongtrul 2002a, 185. See Hopkins 2007, 90–92, for a translation of the parts left out by Kongtrul. See also Kongtrul 1982, 2:549, and Callahan 2007, 257.

3. Stearns 2010, 106–10.

4. Mathes 2008, 65.

caused by karma and negative emotions dissipate. In this sense, rangtong and shentong are complementary not contradictory. Rangtong presents reality from the perspective of what reality is not—nothing in reality has inherent, real existence. Shentong presents reality from the perspective of what it is—that mind as such is unimpeded enlightened qualities.

In one of his songs of meditative experience, Kongtrul sums up in a few verses how he integrates the perspectives of rangtong, shentong, and mahāmudrā:

All phenomena are emptiness, having never arisen,
they come nowhere to an end, and are without any abode.
They are unobstructed mere appearance, the actuality of dependent arising.
The view of me, the yogin, is rangtong.
Though inexpressible, it is the ground for all expression,
the luminous nature, encompassing all, saṃsāra and nirvāṇa,
not to be pointed out by examining, untouched by the analytical mind.
The meditation of me, the yogin, is shentong . . .
The unfabricated ordinary mind is momentary,
simultaneously realizing and liberating;
whatever appears is the dharmakāya,
nondistraction, nonmeditation, the course of the natural flow.
The practice of me, the yogin, is mahāmudrā.[5]

As Kongtrul states in his introductory verse, *Instruction for the View of Shentong* is a "condensed, short instruction for the Madhyamaka view." The theoretical background for this view is extremely complex and multilayered, and its terminology is hard to translate in a concise way. The term "distinct analysis,"[6] for example, refers to an entire process of meditation that cuts through delusions about the self and phenomena at large. It was therefore a great challenge to render the Tibetan in a way that alludes to the entire spectrum of connotations that each term carries.

Instruction for the View of Shentong is an "instruction for the view" (*tatri*) belonging to the Tibetan genre of "instruction texts" (*triyik*) or "essential instructions" (*damngak*). This term usually pertains to condensed oral or written advice meant to facilitate the integration of theory into practice. In

---

5. Kongtrul 2002b, 978.

6. See *so sor tokpa* in the glossary.

the context of the Buddhist path, essential instructions are meant to support the practitioner in developing and deepening his or her view and meditation. Even today it is common practice for Tibetan Buddhist teachers to orally counsel their students with instructions for personal meditation practice. Instruction texts thereby function as mere guidelines for structuring meditation sessions. In some cases, as with Kongtrul's *Instruction for the View of Shentong*, the text includes verses that can be recited during meditation.

Practitioners, after establishing an ethical lifestyle built upon the discipline of maintaining Buddhist vows, are advised to go through a process of study and reflection in order to generate certainty in their understanding. Meditation brings about direct realization of reality based on this certain understanding. Meditative training is twofold: calm abiding (*shiné*) and deep insight (*lhakthong*). Deep insight means to go through a process where a nonconceptual, direct vision of reality becomes possible, built as it is upon the ground of the conceptual knowledge that analytical meditation generates. This process requires the stability of shiné, however. Thus meditative training demands that practitioners unite, inseparably, two aspects of meditation: calm abiding and deep insight.

Instruction for the View of Shentong consists of three parts: the sources, the actual instruction, and the benefit. The actual instruction is the main body of the text. It first explains the view of the sūtras, meaning Mahāyāna broadly speaking, then states the view in the context of the practice of Vajrayāna. In both cases, Kongtrul first discusses the view or what a practitioner should understand prior to meditation, and then how the view is to be put into practice though meditation. His presentation of the sūtras explicates the tenets of the Niḥsvabhāvavāda-Mādhyamikas and the Yogācāra-Mādhyamikas. In the context of the tantras, no specific philosophical tenet is discussed.

The actual practice according to the sūtras involves the preparatory training, the main part, and postmeditative practices. The preparations pertain to understanding impermanence, suffering, and essencelessness. They encourage practitioners to strive for liberation and enhance their trust in their own inherent buddha nature. The main part contains guidance for taking refuge, developing bodhicitta (*jangchup kyi sem*), and increasing meditative concentration. Practitioners are advised to first generate an intellectual understanding of the essencelessness of the individual self and of phenomena in general. In that regard it is essential to comprehend that any outer or inner object of appearance is nothing but an aspect of one's own mind. For that reason, appearances and mind are inseparable from one another, just like waves in water are nothing but water. Based on this insight, practitioners abide in a clear state of mind open as space: whatever appears comes to an end on its own accord and is in this sense self-liberated. In this state of uncontrived freshness, practitioners need not identify certain states of mind to be cultivated and certain states of mind to be avoided. All experiences are understood to be adventitious mental processes, in the sense that they are all the product of imagination, and are seen to be similar to fleeting cloud formations. In this state of awareness, the true nature of mind, buddha nature, is experienced, which is nothing other than uninterrupted clear awareness as such, also called self-arisen wisdom.

As this true nature of mind is beyond words, Kongtrul quotes from sūtras. He advises practitioners to contemplate these quotations as sources of inspiration that might help them to integrate into their meditation the intuition that the true nature of one's own mind is buddha nature, imbued with enlightened qualities. The instructions for postmeditation include general advice, as well as recitations for dedication and aspiration prayers. The instructions for the actual practice according to the tantras, which are given in a very concise manner, are based on the *Kālacakra Tantra*. Kongtrul concludes the text by describing the benefit of the various practices described. To that end he cites a number of sūtras, ascribed to the middle and final cycles of the Buddha's teachings.

Understanding Kongtrul's text requires comprehensive knowledge of Yogācāra and Madhyamaka tenets, in addition to extensive familiarity with meditation. It would therefore appear that Kongtrul designed the text as a manual for teachers or as a guideline for experienced practitioners. The instruction is given in prose yet is interspersed with a number of verses drawn from various sūtras, as well as from the *Ratnagotravibhāga* or *Uttaratantra,* one of the Five Treatises of Maitreya. Kongtrul uses formal, scholarly language to make his points. While in many of his other works, such as the *Treasury of Knowledge,* he integrates entire sections of writing by eminent Tibetan masters into his text, *Instruction for the View of Shentong* is his own composition.

Instruction for the View of Shentong is found in two of Kongtrul's Five Great Treasuries. As one of Kongtrul's own compositions, it appears in volume 5 of his collected works in thirteen volumes. It is the last of twenty-four works on the essential meaning of the sūtras and tantras. Kongtrul also included the text in the massive *Treasury of Essential Instructions* (*Damngak Dzö*), which he structured according to the eight practice lineages of Tibetan Buddhism. Its most recent edition comprises eighteen volumes. Even though Kongtrul devotes one section of the *Treasury of Essential Instructions* to Jonang instructions, he nonetheless includes *Instruction for the View of Shentong* within a section (in volume 4) that consists of Kadampa texts.

The very fact that he did not place it alongside Jonang teachings indirectly confirms that, in his view, the shentong view was not exclusively transmitted by Dölpopa's tradition. Early Tibetan Kadampa masters held a transmission for the meditation tradition of the *Ratnagotravibhāga*, which they received from Tsen Khawoché, who was himself an important source for the shentong interpretation. Tsen Khawoché had received the meditation tradition of the *Ratnagotravibhāga* from the Kashmiri master Sajjana and brought the transmission to Tibet, teaching it in Kadampa circles.

The implication is that Kongtrul views shentong to have been part of mainstream Buddhism during the flourishing of the early Kadampas, from the eleventh century through the fourteenth century. At the same time, he explicitly recognizes the Jonang teaching tradition of Dölpopa and Tāranātha by praising them as holders of the shentong transmission. Indicating his affinity for the Jonang, the colophon to *Instruction for the View of Shentong* informs us that Kongtrul wrote this text at "the great Dharma seat Glorious Dzamtang," which is most probably the Jonang monastery of Dzamtang in Amdo. In his autobiography, Kongtrul does not give any additional information regarding his stay in this Jonang monastery, and no date is mentioned in the colophon. But as Kongtrul spent time there between 1846 and 1848, he must have written the text during that period of time.

In addition to being one of the most important Kagyü teachers of his time, Kongtrul was also a highly respected proponent of the Nyingma tradition. It is therefore not surprising to find some of his works included in Nyingma collections, such as the 120-volume *Detailed Instructions* (*Kama Shintu Gyepa*) published by Kathok Monastery. *Instruction for the View of Shentong* appears there in volume 49, in a section with explanations of the intent of the Mahāyāna.

Rather than drawing a clear dividing line between the views of rangtong, shentong, and mahāmudrā, Kongtrul integrates them into one progressive approach. This is one way in which the spirit of the rimé movement shines through Kongtrul's *Instruction for the View of Shentong*. His nonsectarian attitude is also clear in the references that appear in his text, where he alludes to eminent masters from all of the major traditions of Tibetan Buddhism, apart from the Geluk tradition. In other writings, such as the *History of Rimé* (*Rimé Chöjung*), Kongtrul goes even further. There he says that all scholars and siddhas of the Nyingma school, such as Longchenpa, and the scholars and siddhas of the four great and eight small Kagyü traditions, such as Marpa, Milarepa, and Gampopa, and the scholars of the Sakyapas, such as Sachen Kunga Nyingpo, Sakya Paṇḍita, Phakpa Lodrö Gyaltsen, Śākya Chokden, and Bodong Choklé Namgyal, are all proponents of the shentong Madhyamaka view, even if their individual expositions may vary in the details.[7] By mentioning these masters, Kongtrul gestures toward all of those traditions whose prominent representatives in the nineteenth century contributed to the rimé movement.

Most of these schools share in common a style of meditation practice that emphasizes a positive approach toward reality in contrast to meditating upon a mere negation, as happens in the Geluk tradition. For Kongtrul, the empty-of-other view plays an important role for meditation itself, even when it is not labeled as such in meditation instructions or in the intellectual training of practitioners. *Immaculate Vajra Moonrays: An Instruction for the View of Shentong, the Great Madhyamaka* embodies this perspective. It guides practitioners seamlessly through a systematic contemplation of impermanence and suffering through to the mahāmudrā practice of abiding spontaneously in the uncontrived mind, where there is nothing to relinquish and nothing to adopt. These instructions reflect Kongtrul's rimé attitude in that they integrate a multiplicity of aspects of the Buddhist practice into one path, regardless of their affiliation with specific tenets or schools.

---

7. Kongtrul 2002c and also van der Kuijp 1983, 41.

Immaculate Vajra Moonrays: An Instruction for the View of Shentong, the Great Madhyamaka

by Jamgön Kongtrul Lodrö Thayé

With the spiritual master and the holders of the teaching of the ultimate irreversible Dharma[8] as my heart essence, I am writing here a condensed short instruction for the Madhyamaka view. It consists of three parts: the sources upon which it relies, the actual instruction for the view, and the presentation of the benefit. The first part comprises in turn two sections, the general and the specific explanations.

I. The Sources

Generally the division into provisional and definitive[9] is made not because there is anything fallacious or untrue in the Victor's words but because of the differences that exist in the capacities of individuals to engage with inconceivable actuality or to be unable to do so. Just as with children who are progressively provided with the nourishment they require, the first teaching cycle of the words of the Buddha allows for detachment from cyclic existence, the middle one counteracts the clinging to characteristics, and with the last cycle a precise distinction is made between existence and nonexistence, being and nonbeing, and so on regarding the actuality of the mode of abiding. With the authoritative statements of the *Saṃdhinirmocanasūtra* and so on, the first cycle is established to be of provisional meaning, the middle cycle as a combination of provisional and definitive, and the last as of unsurpassable definitive meaning. Moreover, it is not only impossible to ignore these

---

8. A term used to describe the third cycle of the Buddha's teachings.

9. The provisional meaning (*drangdön*) pertains to teachings that require further interpretation, such as teachings on impermanence, while the definitive meaning (*ngedön*) directly points to the ultimate level of teachings. Tibetan Buddhist scholars hold various views regarding which sūtras and treatises belong to which level. According to Kongtrul, only the third cycle of the Buddha's teachings comprises sūtras of the consummate definitive meaning.

presentations of the Victor and his successors, but it is also directly perceptible that the meaning of the profound is gradually established more and more clearly and completely.

Even though the middle cycle teaches with respect to the mode of appearance of the relative that what is nonexistent does not exist, and the last cycle says regarding the type of emptiness of the absolute that what is existent exists, Śāntipa and others are of the opinion that the final intention of the middle and the last cycles as well as of the two great pioneers[10] come down to the same.

Based on the twenty sūtras on the essence of the definitive meaning of the last cycle of teachings, the five works of Maitreya, and the teaching traditions of Nāgārjuna and Asaṅga and their successors, including those here in Tibet as well, from the time of the two translators Zu [Gawai Dorjé] and Tsen [Khawoché] up to the present day, the teaching and study tradition known as shentong Madhyamaka arose according to circumstances in slightly different ways. The three great pioneers of the shentong teaching tradition—the all-knowing Rangjung Dorjé, the all-knowing Dölpopa, and the all-knowing Longchen Drimé Öser—and in addition the Seventh Gyalwa Karmapa Chödrak Gyatso, Śākya Chokden Silung Panchen, Tāranātha, and Situ Tenpai Nyinjé, who definitely were on the spiritual levels of noble ones and who, being spiritual friends of the teachings in their entirety, possessed the eye of the Dharma that does not fall into sectarianism, ascertained the shentong teachings by way of the three: studying, teaching, and meditating. All of their excellent works support this tradition. Furthermore the ultimate intention of noble individuals who unmistakenly see the authentic mode of abiding by merging studying, reflecting, and meditating into one inseparable unity must flow solely into it.

As specific guidance for the profound view, there is on the one hand the general way of instruction for the view as emphasized by Maitrīpa (the master of the meaning and the intention of the *Uttaratantra*) and transmitted by Ratnavajra (the great pillar of the center), the Kashmiri Sajjana, and others. On the other hand, there is the extraordinary mahāmudrā instruction, which unites the sūtras and tantras and for which the Kagyü tradition is known far and wide. It was given to the master of Lhodrak by way of empowerment that transmits blessing. Among these two, it is the first that is presented here.

---

10. Nāgārjuna and Asaṅga.

II. The Actual Instruction for the View

The actual instruction for the view is also twofold, consisting in (A) the sūtra tradition that stands on its own and (B) the sūtra tradition combined with the profound tantra tradition.

A. The Sūtra Tradition

The first, the sūtra tradition, is divided into (1) the view, or what is to be understood, and (2) how this is to be put into actual practice.

1. Sūtra: View

Based on having stabilized the trust in the infallibility of causes and effects which is taught as the worldly correct view, it is necessary to rely on a flawless profound view by means of which the three realms of existence will be transcended.

Moreover, the śrāvakas establish the essencelessness of the person, the pratyekabuddhas the unreality of the apprehended, the Yogācāras (*naljor chöpa*) inherently real wisdom free from duality, and the ordinary Mādhyamikas that all phenomena are inherently empty. All of them meditate on the object determined by them and thereby have experiences. As, however, they are entangled in a threefold way in their mental processes, ideations, and views, they do not ascertain the nondual wisdom and are therefore far remote from buddhahood.

Who then experiences this nondual wisdom? The actual nondual wisdom is cognized by the noble ones' wisdom and the concordant one by those ordinary individuals who have purified their mindstream by a special way of studying, reflecting, and meditating.[11] Among the latter there are two types: the proponents of essencelessness (*ngowo nyi mepar mawa*) and the Yogācāras.

The Niḥsvabhāvavādas, Proponents of Essencelessness

By way of the five great reasonings, the proponents of essencelessness arrive at the conviction that all phenomena, from matter up to omniscience—in

---

11. Ordinary individuals who have purified their mindstream are capable of having a correct conceptual understanding that serves as a basis to develop the nonconceptual, actual nondual wisdom.

the same way that neither a hare's horn nor a barren woman's child is in the slightest nature perceptible—are not established as anything and that this emptiness appears as unimpeded manifestations of interdependence.

Subsequently, in the actual practice, first the conceptual ideas are examined by distinct analysis, and then even the knowledge of the distinct analysis as such is ascertained as nonreferential, just as fire finally comes to an end by itself when the flames have consumed both the wooden rubbing stick and the wooden support. If without any conceptualizing, without any mental engagement (*yila mijepa*), essencelessness is realized and meditation is done in a manner of no-meditation and in a state that resembles space, numerous gates of samādhi of the unity of calm abiding and deep insight, such as the one of the light of jewels,[12] are accessed. If at that time, having received a good introduction by means of pure authoritative explanations and profound instructions, the mistaken ways of clinging are purified, insight unfolds quickly, and the view of the specific Great Madhyamaka is realized. Yet, the *Samādhisambhāraparivarta* explains:

> The samādhi might be unwavering. However, if one clings to it,
> this is deemed a foolish ritual. Nirvāṇa will not be attained by this.

Thus some who take the experiences of emptiness as they arise by examining and analyzing to be dharmatā presumptuously think, "The Great Madhyamaka is exclusively as experienced by myself while everything else is flawed," and thereby they lose the path of emptiness. And some, having stable experiences of calm abiding, misconstrue the counting of what arises and ceases as mahāmudrā. Instead of liberating these thoughts by their own nature beyond the intellect, they lose the essence of emptiness.

Apart from the extent of the conceptual discernment, these two flaws are similar in that they make it impossible to transcend the three types of existence. Therefore, in order to enter through the gate of all-knowing wisdom, it is necessary to unmistakenly and precisely understand, experience, and realize by way of authoritative explanations, argumentations, and profound instructions and thereby arrive at an accuracy in view, meditative training, and conduct that—not being in contradiction with anything—is more supreme than all else.

---

12. Samādhis are referred to with different names, highlighting their special character. The "light of jewels" is one such name or image.

The Yogācāras

For the Yogācāras—those who rely on the works of Maitreya—it is best to preliminarily put an end to the illusory perceptions of the subject (i.e., the adventitious proliferations) by means of the teaching tradition of the treatises of the middle cycle of the Buddha's words and the explications of their meaning. If, however, this is too much to cope with, by all means one should study the Five Treatises by Maitreya or at least the *Uttaratantra*. In case this is also not possible, the *Mahāyānasūtrālaṃkāra* states:

> Having intellectually understood that there is nothing but mind,
> the mind as well is realized to be nonexistent.
> A wise person who has realized the nonexistence of both
> abides in the dharmadhātu without dualism.[13]

Accordingly, since beginningless time, one's own mind appears as manifold things to a noninvestigating, nonanalyzing perception, like delusions in a dream, due to adventitious stains—the aspect of ignorance. Yet if analyzed, all appearances are nothing but manifestations of mind because, not existing in any way, they are empty of their own respective entities. Therefore the true mode of abiding of relative truth is that grasped objects appear as if they were outer things, yet resembling the moon in water, they are empty of a self-nature in their manifestation; the grasping mind as well abides nowhere, neither outside nor inside. It is not established as an entity with shape and color. With its eightfold aspects of consciousness that arise from the continuum of self-clinging, mind—mistaking what is nonexistent as existent—is primordially empty like a sky flower. Yet it is wisdom empty of the two, grasped and grasping, dharmatā, encompassing everyone, from a buddha to an ordinary sentient being. This is the mode of abiding of absolute truth, *sugatagarbha*,[14] natural luminosity, primordially uncontaminated by adventitious stains. Having correctly recognized this—that is, the mode of abiding of relative and absolute truth—to settle in this state in meditative concentration is the intent of Maitreya's works. Just that much analysis must definitely be traversed in preparation.

Having thus ascertained the freedom from extremes, one trains in what is called the "practice of unity." This has been described as "abiding in self-arisen

---

13. *Mahāyānasūtrālaṃkāra*, 6.8.
14. This term is used as a synonym for *tathāgatagarbha*.

wisdom, the natural mode of abiding. The mode of emptiness is being empty of concepts of clinging to the extremes of proliferations, and the mode of realization is the realization by distinct self-aware wisdom."[15]

2. Sūtra: Actual Practice

Secondly, the actual practice of the sūtra tradition consists of three sections: (a) the preparation, (b) the main part, and (c) the postmeditation.

a. The Preparation

As to the preparation, sugatagarbha can be compared to a wish-fulfilling gem that is to be cleansed from coarse, fine, and superfine impurities. In this sequence one should contemplate and meditate in correspondence with the first cycle according to the synopsis of Dharma. Birth ends in dying, gathering in separating, accumulating in dispersing, and rising in falling. All of these conditioned phenomena are even more ephemeral than lightning or bubbles in water. Conditioned by the appropriation of karma and afflictions, one circles and falls into the three types of existence with the five physical-mental constituents, the body, and so on, like bees locked in a pot. This is suffering by nature. One is agitated by suffering, imprisoned in the net of suffering.

All relative phenomena, from matter up to omniscience, are empty because they are not truly established. The substrate, which is without the identity of either the grasped or the grasping, and is empty of all phenomena, free from the suffering of adventitious delusion, the great perfect nature, is permanent, constant, peaceful, and supreme. While contemplating this, repeatedly recite:

> Everything conditioned is impermanent.
> What is contaminated entails suffering.
> All phenomena are empty and essenceless.
> Nirvāṇa is peace.

The general preparations as they are presented in detail in works on the graded path should definitely be looked at from all perspectives.

b. The Main Part

The main part of the practice consists again of three sections: (i) refuge and

---

15. Śākya Chokden 2008, 390.

bodhicitta, (ii) the instructions for the meditation that unites *śamatha* and *vipaśyanā*, and (iii) the precise distinction and introduction into buddha nature.

i. Refuge and Bodhicitta

As by this type of refuge and bodhicitta the practice is transformed into the specific path of the Mahāyāna, while contemplating the profound meaning, recite for the taking of refuge:

> The mind, being by nature luminous, is tathāgatagarbha, is virtuous,
> yet sentient beings grasp to it as a self.
> Mind is free from finiteness and infinity.
> Just as sentient beings see golden color
>   once pure gold and bronze are polished,
> likewise they see reality through the ground of the *skandhas.*
> Buddha is neither an individual nor the skandhas. He is pure
>   wisdom.
> Knowing that he is permanent peace, I take refuge therein.[16]

And for the development of bodhicitta:

> The mind, being by nature luminous, is associated with afflictions,
> consciousness, and so on, and with the self.
> This was perfectly taught by the most supreme teacher.
> To purify myself from that, I train on the sublime path.[17]

ii. The Instructions for the Meditation That Unites Śamatha and Vipaśyanā

Abiding according to the middle cycle in meditative concentration without concepts and free from proliferations, one cultivates a transcendent certainty regarding the profound true nature of phenomena.

On a comfortable seat take a position according to the usual physical points and cultivate fervent devotion. If you have previously ascertained the view by studying and reflecting, recollect that view and abide in it in meditative concentration. If you did not properly study and reflect, generate the

---

16. *Laṅkāvatāra Sūtra*, 10.750–52.

17. Ibid., 10.753.

understanding of the essencelessness of the individual by ascertaining that this, your own mind, has no essence whatsoever. Generate the understanding of the essencelessness of phenomena by gaining the conviction that all objects of appearances are not established as anything other than appearing aspects of one's own mind, and then also generate the understanding of the sameness of the grasped and the grasping, that appearances and the mind are inseparable from each other, just as waves in water are nothing but water. Then abide as open as space, without being distracted toward the outside, without withdrawing inside, without grasping in between, and without going astray into indeterminate states or indifference.

When the mind does not abide but is in motion, and when—knowing that whichever appearance of the six collections arises, it is emptiness—you do not do anything, that is, neither abolish nor adopt, neither expect nor fear, neither negate nor establish, but cultivate a state of mind where whatever appears comes to an end on its own accord and is thus self-liberated, then the signs of the abiding mind will gradually occur.

Then, having in accordance with the instruction texts for meditation searched for the mind, there arises certainty that its nature has always been free from proliferations. Other than just realizing this mode of abiding, which is freedom from proliferations, there is nothing else to meditate on. Therefore cultivate constant mindfulness of it.

This has also been taught as being unfabricated, as freshness, as the innate in whatever arises. Therefore remain unfabricated in the clarity and emptiness of your own mind, without grasping, in whichever way it appears, whether as stillness or movement, joy or sadness. Not being fettered by the search for what is to be relinquished or an antidote, place yourself in no-training,[18] in a state of awareness that is without support. Thereby perfect calm abiding, and perfect deep insight according to the Mahāyāna will arise. In the process of these, whatever experiences and perceptions may occur and whatever qualities of the path may arise, the profound key point is to recognize their self-nature without attachment and clinging. Moreover, while recollecting the meaning, recite with your speech:

> The ground is emptiness, the path is freedom from characteristics, the fruition is wishlessness.

---

18. "No-training" refers to a state of mind that is uncontrived and effortless. Without meditating in a particular way on an object and without applying remedies to counteract unfavorable states of mind, one allows the mind to simply and directly settle in its own true nature.

iii. The Precise Distinction and Introduction into Buddha Nature

Upon the arising of the appropriate samādhi of calm abiding and deep insight follows the introduction by way of which existence, nonexistence, and so on are precisely distinguished in accordance with the last cycle and the Vajrayāna.

It is sufficient if there is a coarse understanding of the Buddha's excellent scriptures and the authoritative treatises. If this is not the case, you should receive instructions at least in the *Mountain Dharma Ocean of Definitive Meaning*[19] and reflect on its view as well as possible. In this way, untouched by the flaw of contradiction, the essence of mind will be comprehended despite it being called by various terms such as "emptiness endowed with all the supreme aspects," "natural luminosity," "tathāgatagarbha," "suchness," "emptiness," "mahāmudrā," "*aham*," and so on. Thus there is freedom from the error with regard to which it is said:

> All of the Buddha's teachings elucidate emptiness and essence-lessness. Simple-minded people, not knowing the meaning of emptiness and essencelessness, fail.[20]

Thus, based on the two truths and the four reliances, the Victor's excellent scriptures on the ultimate, definitive meaning and the wisdom that is to be experienced by oneself reciprocate by way of which the practice of the path fulfills its purpose.

In this way all phenomena that are subsumed in imaginations or adventitious mental processes are empty as cloud formations; yet dharmatā, sugatagarbha—the uninterrupted clear awareness as such—is the self-arisen wisdom. The practice follows upon having been introduced to this.

Refuge and bodhicitta should be generated as explained above. Then, as stated in the excellent scriptures of the noble Tāranātha, a meditation session is practiced where the teacher is recollected as the Buddha. Subsequently, while continuously remembering the absolute level of the Three Jewels, recite again and again:

> The Tathāgata is not showable; eyes cannot see him.
> The Dharma is not expressible; ears cannot hear it.
> The Saṅgha is not conditioned; body, speech, and mind cannot
> venerate it.

---

19. See Hopkins 2006 for a translation of this treatise, composed by Dölpopa.

20. *Mahāberīkaparivarta Sūtra*, Kangyur D222, Sūtra, *dza*, 108a.

And:

> The nature of the Buddha is not conditioned and is thus called
>   "permanent";
> "space" is the nature of the Buddha.
> The nature of the Buddha is the Tathāgata.
> The Tathāgata is not conditioned. What is not conditioned is
>   permanent.
> Permanence is the Dharma. The Dharma is the Saṅgha.
> The Saṅgha is not conditioned. What is not conditioned is permanent.[21]

In the *Laṅkāvatāra Sūtra* it is stated:

> Relying on mind only, the yogins do not conceive of phenomena
> as outer; relying on there being no appearances, they go beyond
> mind only; relying on the perfect ground, they go beyond there
> being no appearances; the yogins who remain in there being no
> appearances do not see the Mahāyāna.[22]

Accordingly one must remove the concept that relative illusions are "mind only" by means of the Madhyamaka without appearances. Then, having gone beyond that, one must penetrate into the unmistaken way of suchness through the Madhyamaka with appearances. What is meant here by the "perfect ground"? Just as among the four elements there is none that is not encompassed by space, there is no object of knowledge that is not encompassed by the dharmakāya of buddhahood. Concerning the suchness of buddhas, of the self, and of all sentient beings, there is no distinction between good and bad, big and small, high and low, and so on. The capacity to produce the buddha qualities—that which has been there since beginningless time, obtained through the nature of phenomena, dharmatā, which is the naturally present potential (*rangshin nepai rik*) or buddha element—precisely this exists in all sentient beings, in all those who are endowed with life force and breath. Therefore all sentient beings are endowed with buddha nature. In order to confirm this, recite:

> Because the perfect buddha *kāya* pervades,
> because suchness is undifferentiated, and

---

21. *Mahāparinirvāṇa Sūtra*, Kangyur D120, Sūtra, *tha,* 217b.
22. *Laṅkāvatāra Sūtra*, 10:256–57.

because they have the potential,
all sentient beings are always endowed with buddha nature.[23]

That which is the dharmakāya in the pure ones, suchness in the pure and
impure ones, and the potential in the impure ones[24] exists in the latter as
follows:

> Like the Buddha in a withered lotus, like honey surrounded
> by bees, like kernels of grains covered by the husk, like gold in
> filth, like a treasure under the ground, like a sprout grown from
> a small fruit, like an image of the Buddha wrapped in a tattered
> garment, like a king in the womb of a destitute woman, and like
> a precious statue in the earthen mold; in such a way, there abides
> the buddha element in living beings obstructed by the stains of
> adventitious afflictions.[25]

While you recite this, reflect on the meaning. Actions, causes and results,
effects of maturations, afflictions, physical-mental constituents, sense constituents and sense spheres, dependent arising, and so on, everything that
is separable from buddha nature never exists in an absolute sense. But not
just that: whereas within the relative scope it is endowed with all of that,
buddha nature is present without being contaminated. The unsurpassable
buddha qualities—the number of which exceeds the sand grains of the
river Ganges—that are not separable from buddha nature, such as the self-
arisen marks and signs, the powers, the fearlessnesses, the threefold close
abiding in mindfulness, great love and compassion, the vajra-like and the
other samādhis, immeasurable wisdom such as the one of the dharmadhātu,
and so forth, have been intrinsically present since beginningless time.
Thus buddha nature is not empty. While engendering confidence in the
ground of all freedom from stains and the potential arising of qualities,
contemplate:

---

23. *Ratnagotravibhāga*, 1.28.

24. According to *Ratnagotravibhāga*, 1.47, for example, buddha nature, which as such
never changes, manifests in three phases. It can be unpurified; in this phase, which is
the state of ordinary sentient beings, it is referred to as "potential." It can also be partly
purified so that it is both pure and impure; this is the phase of realized bodhisattvas, when
buddha nature is referred to as "suchness." And it can be fully purified, which is the case
with perfect buddhas; then it is referred to as "dharmakāya."

25. *Ratnagotravibhāga*, 1.96–97.

> The buddha element is empty of the adventitious that has the characteristic of being separable; but it is not empty of the unsurpassable qualities that have the characteristic of not being separable.[26]

> The buddha element is endowed with all the qualities of buddhahood, the number of which exceeds the sand grains in the river Ganges; they are luminous, unconditioned, and inseparable from it.[27]

Moreover, śrāvakas and pratyekabuddhas view joy as suffering, permanence as impermanence, selfhood as selfless, and pure as impure. Thus, even though they know the Victor's words, they do not comprehend their meaning. In this regard, the sense is as follows:

> Selflessness is that which is called *saṃsāra*; so-called selfhood is the Tathāgata. Impermanent are the śrāvakas and pratyekabuddhas; permanent is the Tathāgata's dharmakāya. Suffering are all the teachings of the tīrthikas; joy is the complete nirvāṇa. Completely impure are conditioned phenomena. Completely pure are the pure qualities of the buddhas and bodhisattvas.[28]

Contemplating that the true nature of one's own mind, sugatagarbha, is endowed with these four pure qualities that are beyond error, call to mind:

> It is pure because it is immaculate by nature and because tendencies are relinquished. It is genuine selfhood because elaborations of a self and of selflessness are fully pacified. It is joy as such because the physical-mental constituents, which are mind by nature, and their causes are brought to an end. It is permanence because saṃsāra und nirvāṇa are realized as sameness.[29]

The ground for such specific features is sugatagarbha. The specific features, such as being endowed with the various buddha qualities of freedom, are now, in the impure state, coemergent with self-aware wisdom, a clear, unimpeded,

---

26. Ibid., 1.155.

27. Ibid., 2.5.

28. *Mahāparinirvāṇa Sūtra*, Kangyur D120, Sūtra, *tha*, 34a.

29. *Ratnagotravibhāga*, 1.37–38.

and natural innateness, which is experienced by way of studying, reflecting, and meditating. Precisely this is abiding in the ground of purification. When the adventitious stains that are to be purified are removed, the result of purification, the mode of abiding that is present within, becomes manifest. This is called the "dharmakāya free from stains." Even though it appears with all the aspects of the entirety of saṃsāra and nirvāṇa, this mere appearance does not deviate from the ground, just as in a stainless crystal ball various reflections appear, but in this mere appearance, the crystal and the reflections do not mingle together. Likewise, whichever appearances of the three—saṃsāra, nirvāṇa, and the path—may arise in self-aware direct clarity and emptiness, in the self-manifest, self-liberated essence, there is never any contamination. Therefore there are not the slightest tendencies of views or deficiencies to remove, nor is it necessary to newly add any specific feature that was not there before. Thus having made the wisdom of the noble ones the actual substrate of the meditative concentration of emptiness, meditation is cultivated in sessions as appropriate. Sometimes, by way of the vajra verses, one calls to mind:

> There is nothing to be removed from it and nothing to be added.
> The real should be seen as real, and seeing the real, you become
>   liberated.[30]

Recite this or contemplate the meaning. This is what the noble master Tāranātha gave as profound essential instruction by saying:

> When the two, meditation regarding the nature of sugatagarbha
> and the contemplation as to the specific features—the qualities of
> the Victor—are brought together by a mind free from concepts,
> this is the supreme sugata-path of definitive meaning.

At the end, after such meditative concentration, according to the statement "it is of an unchangeable nature, as it is before, so it is after,"[31] this very sugatagarbha that is inherently present, the natural luminosity in its true identity, becomes evident. By way of meditative training, the right view has conquered the adventitious stains. When this has happened, it is called by the term for the fruition, *perfect awakening*. Generate the confident certainty that the cause and the result are endowed with precisely this fruit:

---

30. Ibid., 1.154.

31. Ibid., 1.51cd.

That which has been described as being luminous by nature and that resembles the sun and the sky is obscured by the thick veils of hosts of clouds of adventitious obstructions of afflictions and objects of knowledge. Yet it is immaculate and endowed with buddha qualities, permanent, everlasting, and changeless. It is achieved on the ground of nonconceptual and analytical realization of phenomena.[32]

Without beginning, middle, and end, without separation, free from the two, free from the three, stainless and nonconceptual—such is the dharmadhātu seen by the yogin who strives for that in meditation.[33]

Having developed this certainty, rise from meditative absorption.

c. The Postmeditation

When engaging in activities of postmeditation between the sessions, the following should be done. Generate dharmakāya devotion to the teacher who has excellently given the essential instructions. Have an all-encompassing pure view based on the knowledge that all sentient beings are endowed with tathāgatagarbha and that, apart from temporarily lacking the insight into their own nature, they ultimately have the essence of the sixty-four qualities. Generate unbearable compassion for all those who wander continuously in their illusory projection circle in the cycle of suffering. Among these infinite sentient beings, who in this way do not possess realization, there is not a single one who has not been one's own mother or father.

Therefore, with the Mahāyāna bodhicitta of aspiration and of application, relinquish nonvirtue regarding oneself and others in its twofold way.[34] Realize that it is primordially empty so that all sentient beings obtain the dharmakāya, the fruit of freedom that is inherent to the individual substrate.

Free from pride and arrogance, practice virtue as it is to be practiced, by engaging in the perfections such as giving and everything that goes in this direction. Do whatever is of direct or indirect benefit for sentient beings

---

32. Ibid., 2.3.

33. Ibid., 2.38.

34. The twofold way of nonvirtue pertains on the one hand to that which is nonvirtuous by nature and on the other hand to nonvirtuous actions involved in transgressing commitments.

without being too attached to oneself or to sentient beings. Know that all outer and inner dependent phenomena, which are entirely constituted by imaginary projections, appear yet are empty of inherent reality and thus resemble dreams and illusions.

Especially in those who have not accumulated merit, many faults such as wrong views arise. As it is taught that one must generate the accumulations to realize the right view, in general dedicate virtuous actions that are free from negativity and based in Mahāyāna bodhicitta, and in particular practice prostrations and circumambulations, make *tsatsas*, and offer lights to cause tathāgatagarbha to be seen.

With faith in the permanent Three Jewels, erect supports, make offerings and praises that please them, and in particular practice as much as possible the sevenfold practice without limiting it to a certain amount.

From time to time, by reading the twenty sūtras of definitive meaning, by reciting them and thinking about their sense and explaining them to others, and by striving to comprehend the *Uttaratantra* as well as authentic explications of its content such as the *Mountain Dharma Ocean of Definitive Meaning*, one should—without reducing the meditative training by studying and reflecting, and without suppressing the studying and reflecting by the meditative training—unite the two accumulations: the accumulation of wisdom in meditative concentration so that the naturally present potential becomes manifest, and the accumulation of merit in postmeditation so that the unfolding potential (*gyegyur gyi rik*) develops further and further.

The spiritual development achieved by the arising of even a minor insight that unmistakenly realizes the profound view covers so much more ground than inconceivable amounts of virtue arisen from conditioned phenomena. Thus emphasize meditative concentration. Yet compared to the arising of a seeming samādhi, when you study and reflect on the Victor's excellent scriptures, the long-term benefit for others is a hundred times, a thousand times, greater. Therefore one should not obstruct one with the other.

All conduct should be embraced by the two types of bodhicitta[35] without ever being separated from mindfulness and introspection.

---

35. Khenpo Ngawang 2004, 155, describes the two types of bodhicitta, relative and absolute, as follows: "Relative bodhicitta is aroused and dissolves with our thoughts, whereas absolute bodhicitta is that state of primal wisdom in which all the movements that are conceptual thought have subsided into the absolute space. Relative bodhicitta has two aspects: intention and application. Bodhicitta in intention is to pledge ourselves to the result. Bodhicitta in application is to pledge ourselves to the cause, that is, to wish to accomplish the six transcendent perfections that are the cause or means for attaining that result."

One day, at the time of death, it will be necessary to transfer the consciousness into the luminosity of the ground as pointed out in the extraordinary noble "instructions for transference" by the all-knowing Dölpopa. Therefore familiarize yourself with that from now on. Then the yogin's awareness of the emptiness endowed with all the supreme aspects dissolves in luminosity, whereby the primordially present dharmakāya is liberated from the sheath of adventitious stains. This leads to a state where the very nature—the wonderful kāyas, wisdom, the qualities and activities—becomes as vast as space and just like the wish-fulfilling jewel or tree, the source for the accomplishment of sentient beings' needs. As long as saṃsāra continues, there is uninterrupted activity that is permanent, encompassing, and spontaneous. For this to be accomplished swiftly, practice the common Mahāyāna dedications and aspirations, such as the *Perfect Conduct* and so forth. Do this also between the meditation sessions.

> From the Buddha comes the Dharma; from the Dharma, the community of noble ones; from the community the buddha nature, the element of wisdom.

> Ultimately wisdom is accomplished, supreme awakening with the qualities to act for the benefit of sentient beings.[36] May I be endowed with these qualities. Self-benefit and benefit for others are the kāyas of the absolute and the kāyas of the relative relying on it: the sixty-four qualities of fruition—of freedom and maturation.[37] May this swiftly be accomplished.

> The all-embracing ones are always spontaneous in their acts with respect to the constitution of students, the means for guiding them, and the guiding that is suited to their constitutions; they act at the appropriate places and the right time.[38] May this take place.

> Whatever virtue I obtained through reflecting and meditating on the seven points, the jewels, the perfectly pure element, immaculate enlightenment, the qualities, and activity, may beings through this see the *ṛṣi* Amitāyus, who is endowed with limitless light; having seen him, may the stainless Dharma eye arise, and may they then achieve supreme enlightenment.[39]

---

36. *Ratnagotravibhāga*, 1.3.

37. Ibid., 3.1.

38. Ibid., 4.1.

39. Ibid., 5.25.

Therefore recite aspirations without expectations or doubts and seal them with a dedication that does not conceptualize the three spheres.

B. The Tantra Tradition

When this view is practiced in association with the tantra tradition, there is also a twofold distinction into (1) that which is to be understood and (2) the actual practice.

1. Tantra: View

What appears in the shape of the three types of existence[40]—the outer world, the vessel, and its content—is just like the transference of a face in a mirror: the appearance is an expression of the inner—the channels, winds, and drops. Moreover, it is these three (the channels, winds, and drops) that—in the shape of the cycle of the other, supreme maṇḍala—abide together with the support and the supported.[41] All of this in turn is supreme, unchanging wisdom—suchness, the self-illumination, self-radiance of sugatagarbha, the dharmakāya as such—which appears as all of these aspects and is described as follows: The absolute dharmadhātu, which is accomplished through cultivating the unity of bliss and emptiness, is unchanging as to its nature and thus has an uninterrupted continuum. Therefore it is called *tantra*, "the continuum." Moreover, wisdom, in the sense of stained suchness[42] in the phase of the ground, is called the "continuum of the cause." In the sense of the gradual appearance of the actuality of dharmatā during the path, it is called the "continuum of methods" on the spiritual levels and paths. And in the sense of perfect purity, when the two types of purity have become manifest, it is called the "continuum of the fruit." It goes without saying that those who cling to a type of relative emptiness as supreme do not see this extraordinary view even partially.

The path of the independent sūtra tradition described above takes a long time. If, however, the meditative concentration of the sixfold *vajrayoga*, which is the most supreme of all the tantra paths characterized by empowerment and samaya, is applied, realization comes easily in a short time and with little effort.

---

40. The desire realm, form realm, and formless realm.

41. "Support" refers to the pure world of Kālacakra, "supported" to the physical appearance of Kālacakra, and "cycle of the other" to the nature of mind.

42. Stained suchness pertains to the state of sentient beings, when the mind, which as such is always pure, is obscured by adventitious defilements.

2. Tantra: Actual Practice

One engages in the actual practice in accordance with the statement of the *Great Commentary*:

> Fire is always present in wood but is not seen by the methods of cutting or discerning. If the wooden rubbing stick and the wooden support are rubbed by hand, what abides therein is seen. Likewise, mind's luminosity is not seen by the methods of conceptual meditation. Yet it is there and becomes visible when *rasanā* and *lalanā*[43] are fully purified.

Likewise natural luminosity, the unchanging highest wisdom as such, in the aspect of its essence, is the emptiness endowed with all the supreme aspects, and as to its nature, it is present as the supreme unchanging great bliss. However, it is not seen through conceptual meditation, regardless of its many types. Yet by means of nonconceptual samādhi and the specific methods of dividing and binding, it becomes visible, just like reflections in the case of a divination.

So first smoke, mirages, light, and the flame of a butter lamp are seen by means of the yoga of darkness, which relies on *pratyāhara* and *dhyāna*. Then a cloudless sky, radiance, the moon, the sun, the *vajra-rāhula* up to the supreme types, such as lightning and essential drops, are seen by the yoga of daytime. In this way, these completely empty forms, the ten signs, are made into the object. By way of meditative concentration during the day and the night, an experience is generated such that the emptiness of all aspects appears as the three types of existence endowed with all aspects. Then, based on the limbs of *prāṇāyāma* and *dhāraṇā*, the joy of melting is drawn up. Through *anusmṛti* and *samādhi* the ultimate, highest unchanging joy is achieved, which brings the movements of the tendencies of transference to an end.[44] Thereby relative, unreal perceptions stop abruptly, and the pure perceptions expand incessantly,

---

43. The right and left channels. This refers to the process of purifying the winds from these channels by directing the winds into the central channel (*avadhūti*).

44. *Pratyāhara* pertains to the withdrawal from common sense perceptions, a process that brings about the understanding that appearances are empty by nature. *Dhyāna* pertains to stable concentration in the awareness of empty forms. *Prāṇāyāma* involves manipulating the inner energies. *Dhāraṇā* entails holding the inner energies in the central channel, *anusmṛti* includes the practice of inner heat, and *samādhi* pertains to meditative concentration in the nonconceptual experience of the unity of bliss and emptiness. These are the six yogic practices of the completion phase of Kālacakra.

limitlessly, and boundlessly. The immaculate dharmakāya that encompasses space—the transcendence of purity, selfhood, bliss, and permanence that is the primordial inherent buddha—becomes manifest. During this time samayas and a perfectly pure conduct are required as support. This is the tradition of the teachings of the Dharma master and his successors and is to be internalized according to the profound instructions of a teacher and then to be practiced one-pointedly.

III. The Benefit

When the age of strife ends, the five types of degeneration spread, which leads to the twenty-eight types of degenerated views. Since the merit of sentient beings diminishes, they do not respect the essential sūtras of definitive meaning. Because they are lazy, they do not meditate on the meaning taught in them. Not only that, it is said that some who develop false views because they do not trust the sūtras about buddha nature will for this reason fall into the great abyss of the lower states of existence and thereby sever the rope of rescue for their liberation.

The opposite of that is the benefit. The *Uttaratantra* says that the benefit of listening to these profound teachings is much greater than that which derives from eons of the especially noble practices of giving, ethics, and meditation. A sūtra about the benefit of respecting the Mahāyāna says:

> Those who have given rise to a deep respect for the Mahāyāna will not go into the lower states of existence for one thousand eons. For five thousand eons they will not be born as a hungry ghost, and for twenty-five thousand eons they will be reborn in the worlds of the gods and the world of *brahmā*.

In the Prajñāpāramitā sūtras, it is said:

> Those who have studied *prajñāpāramitā* will upon death go to a Buddha world. Until their death they will be honored with all enjoyable things that sentient beings have. It is said that the merit that arises when one meditates on prajñāpāramitā is even greater than that which comes from dedicating oneself to study for four hundred eons, even if one does so for just a moment—the time of a finger snap.

Especially, the *Saṃdhinirmocana Sūtra*:

Compared to the dust particles of a fingernail or the water in a cow's hoof imprint, there are a hundred, a thousand, a hundred thousand times more dust particles on the vast earth or water in the four oceans. No illustration or calculations are adequate.[45]

Likewise it is said with respect to the sūtras of provisional meaning that the amount of merit that derives from respecting them up through practicing their meditations is far less than the amount of merit created by respecting the sūtras of definitive meaning up through practicing their meditations. No description of examples or causes is adequate.[46]

In another sūtra it is said:

If after my nirvāṇa some people can develop pure confidence in the statement "in all types of sentient beings there is sugatagarbha," they are deputies of the Buddha's kindness.

In the *Aṅgulimālīya Sūtra* it is said:

As far as teaching about tathāgatagarbha is concerned, this may be done by anyone—someone with afflictions or without afflictions. In either case, this person is called a perfect buddha.[47]

And:

Due to knowing that the permanent tathāgatagarbha exists in each sentient being, the highest types of joy and everything that is perfect is achieved in this world. Having studied the teachings about the permanent tathāgatagarbha, one will always achieve everything that is excellent in the three times and achieve every well-being in the higher states and on this earth.[48]

---

45. Counting the dust particles of a fingernail or measuring the water in a cow's hoof imprint is not an adequate way to learn how many dust particles there are on the earth or how much water there is in the ocean.

46. Respecting and practicing meditations from the sūtras of provisional meaning yields far less merit than does respect for and practice of the sūtras of definitive meaning. See *Saṃdhinirmocana Sūtra*, Kangyur D106, Sūtra, *ca*, 25b (where a slightly shorter version appears).

47. *Aṅgulimālīya Sūtra*, Kangyur D213, Sūtra, *tsha*, 158a.

48. Ibid., 156b.

And:

> Due to the merits that come from studying tathāgatagarbha, there
> will be freedom from illness, freedom from harm, and longevity,
> and all sentient beings will feel affection toward you. Someone
> who comes to learn that the tathāgata is permanent, constant,
> lasting, and unchanging and that the *parinirvāṇa* is also immortal
> will achieve everything and will be steadfast and constant for a
> long time.[49]

In the *Mahāparinirvāṇa Sūtra* it is taught in detail:

> Those sentient beings who teach that the tathāgatagarbha exists in
> all sentient beings have immeasurable qualities. Those successors
> of the noble family who strive for the perfect Dharma are purified
> from countless negative deeds just by getting headaches or conta-
> gious diseases, suffering from pain, or being exposed to slander.

And:

> A person who has the trust that the Tathāgata possesses the quality
> of permanence is very rare, as rare as the *udumbara* flower. You
> should know that those who after my parinirvāṇa study these
> very profound Mahāyāna sūtras and give rise to a mind of trust
> will in the future not fall into the lower types of existence for a
> hundred thousand eons.[50]

And:

> Sons and daughters of the noble family: the Tathāgata is perma-
> nent. The perfect Dharma will not disappear. The Saṅgha will not
> come to an end. Those who persevere in contemplation will, just
> as myself, see the abode of the Buddha.[51]

And:

> For example, the rising sun eliminates the night. Likewise, just

---

49. Ibid., 156b.

50. *Mahāparinirvāṇa Sūtra*, Kangyur D120, Sūtra, *tha*, 89b.

51. Ibid., 140b.

by studying this sūtra regarding buddha nature, one will swiftly be purified of the host of negativity, from completely abandoning one's vows to actions whose result ripens immediately after death. Just studying this sūtra about buddha nature becomes a cause for enlightenment—which pervades each pore of the body just like dust particles in the sun in summer. This also holds true even if, thinking, "I do not need enlightenment," bodhicitta is not developed, or when one has studied only out of competition with others or out of encouragement from others, or when one has composed verses only for gain and recognition.

If in the past one has given rise to bodhicitta in the presence of as many buddhas as there are sand grains on the bank of the Ganges, one will not disdain this Dharma in bad times but feel respect for it. If one has given rise to bodhicitta in the presence of as many buddhas as there are sand grains on the banks of eight Ganges, one will take hold of this sūtra in bad times, maintain it, read it, recite it, and write it down for others; encourage others to take hold of it, maintain it, and read it; and also explain it to others.

In short, the all-knowing Dölpopa says:

If already just hearing the term *sugatagarbha* brings about attainment of buddhahood, what need is there to mention the benefit for someone who, having developed trust and respect, has developed a clear understanding of sugatagarbha and is cultivating the realization of it.

Therefore wise and compassionate people should—even at the cost of their lives—teach about sugatagarbha, and those who strive for liberation should, even if they were to cross a great pit of fire, search for these teachings on sugatagarbha and listen to them.

This instruction should be held to be quintessential.

The transmission lineage: Up until the all-knowing Tāranātha, the transmission lineage of these teachings corresponds with the one appearing in the shentong prayer of transmission.[52] After the noble Tāranātha, the holders of

_____

52. See the lineage prayer in Tāranātha n.d., vol. 18, 484–88: The names given prior to Tāranātha are Maitreya, Asaṅga, Vasubandhu, Gaṅgamaitrī, Ānandakīrti, Śāntikāra, Brahman Sajjana, Gawai Dorjé, Darma Tsöndrü, Yeshé Jungné, Jangchup Kyap, Shönu

these teachings were Gyaltsap Narthangpa Lodrö Namgyal, Ngawang Trinlé, Kunsang Wangpo, Rikdzin Tsewang Norbu, Situ Tenpé Nyinjé, Karmapa Düdul Dorjé, and Maitreyanātha, the perfect Buddha, known as Situ Pema Nyinjé Wangpo, from whom I have received the perfect stream of blessing as well as the methods of ripening and liberating of Kālacakra[53] based on the instruction text for the view of the thirteenth master.[54] There are also other pure traditions.

The excellent scriptures of the profound view
are indeed of definitive meaning,
yet only few understand this.
As the regent Maitreya is without any delusion,
teach and study the *Mahāyānottaratantra*!
This is the ultimate practice of the vajrayoga,
yet the associated meditation is rare.
Trust buddha nature, the king of continua, and
do not allow a yearning for what is lower!
The excellent conduct in every regard involves but few hindrances,
and the spiritual development achieved is great,
yet to practice it correctly is difficult.
Therefore take the hagiographies of the forefathers as witnesses,
and with the ethics of the vows for individual liberation
and the vow of a bodhisattva strive for good training.
If view, meditation, and conduct are completely pure,
one's own benefit and that of others will be swiftly achieved.
This is the assertion of wise people; it is not self-made.

May the virtue, the quintessence of
the intent of the Buddha's words and the treatises,
lead to all sentient beings and myself relinquishing the five great flaws,[55]

Jangchup, Mönlam Tsultrim, Chomden Raldri, Kyitön Jampaiyang, Kunkhyen Dölpopa, Nyabön Chöjé, Chöpal Gönpo, Lodrö Sangpo Gyatso, Jamgön Nyipar Drak, Śākya Chokden, Dönyö Drupa, Jamgön Drupai Pawo, Kunga Gyaltsen, and Drakden Drupa Chok.

53. "Ripening" pertains to empowerment, "liberating" to the instructions for meditation.

54. The Thirteenth Karmapa Düdul Dorjé (1733–97).

55. See *Ratnagotravibhāga,* 1.157. The five great flaws are faintheartedness, disparaging inferior sentient beings, holding on to what is unreal (the adventitious stains), deprecating the true buddha qualities, and maintaining affection for oneself.

obtaining the five great qualities,[56]
and then manifesting the ultimate dharmadhātu.

This was composed by me, the idle monk Yönten Gyatso, at the great Dharma abode Pal Dzamtang. I wrote it after I achieved confidence based in the understanding of sugatagarbha as the ground for emptiness, in accordance with the assertions of the holder of the Jonang teachings called Khedrup Ngawang.[57] In all my lives may I have the great fortune to study, reflect, and meditate on the teachings regarding the essence of the definitive meaning.

---

56. Ibid., 1.166. The five great qualities are happiness, appreciating sentient beings, insight, wisdom, and great loving-kindness.

57. Khedrup Ngawang is one of Tāranātha's names.

Translated Work

Kongtrul Lodrö Thayé (Kong sprul Blo gros mtha' yas). 2002a. *Gzhan stong dbu ma chen po'i lta khri rdo rje zla ba dri ma med pa'i 'od zer.* Collected Works, vol. 5 (*ca*), 735–65. Delhi: Shechen Publications.

Suggested Readings

Baker, Willa. 2005. *Essence of Ambrosia: A Guide to Buddhist Contemplations by Taranatha.* Dharamsala: Library of Tibetan Works and Archives.
Hopkins, Jeffrey. 2006. *Mountain Doctrine: Tibet's Fundamental Treatise on Other-Emptiness and the Buddha Matrix by Döl-bo-ba Shay-rab-gyel-tsen.* Ithaca, NY: Snow Lion Publications.
Jackson, David. 1990. *Enlightenment by a Single Means.* Vienna: Verlag der Österreichischen Akademie der Wissenschaften.
Lhalungpa, Lobsang. 2006. *Mahāmudrā: The Moonlight—Quintessence of Mind and Meditation.* Boston: Wisdom Publications.

Additional References

Callahan, Elizabeth, trans. 2007. Jamgön Kongtrul Lodrö Thayé. *The Treasury of Knowledge: Book Six, Part Three, Frameworks of Buddhist Philosophy, A Systematic Presentation of the Cause-Based Philosophical Vehicles.* Ithaca, NY: Snow Lion Publications.
Dakpo Tashi Namgyal (Dwags po Bkra shis rnam rgyal). 2009. *Zla ba'i 'od zer nges don phyag rgya chen po'i sgom rim gsal bar byed pa'i legs bshad chen zla ba'i 'od zer.* In *Nges don phyag rgya chen po'i bod gzhung*, vol. 9. Chengdu: Si khron mi rigs dpe skrun khang.
Gö Lotsawa Shönu Pal ('Gos Lo tsā ba Gzhon nu dpal). 2003. *Theg pa chen po rgyud bla ma'i 'grel pa de kho na nyid rab tu gsal ba'i me long.* Critically edited by Klaus-Dieter Mathes (Nepal Research Centre Publications 24). Stuttgart: Franz Steiner Verlag.
Khenpo Ngawang Pelzang. 2004. *A Guide to the Words of My Perfect Teacher.* Translated by the Dipamkara Translation Group and the Padmakara Translation Group. Boston: Shambhala Publications.
Kongtrul Lodrö Thayé. 1982. *Theg pa'i sgo kun las bdus pa gsung rab rin po che'i mdzod bslab pa gsum leg par ston pa'i bstan bcos shes bya kun khyab*, 3 vols. Beijing: Mi rigs spe skrun khang.
———. 2002b. *Nyams mgur.* Collected Works, vol. 6 (*cha*), 977–87. Delhi: Shechen Publications.
———. 2002c. *Ris med chos kyi 'byung gnas mdo tsam smos pa blo gsal mgrin pa'i mdzes rgyan.* Collected Works, vol. 5 (*ca*), 859–90. Delhi: Shechen Publications.
Mathes, Klaus-Dieter. 2008. *A Direct Path to the Buddha Within: Gö Lotsāwa's Mahāmudrā Interpretation of the Ratnagotravibhāga.* Boston: Wisdom Publications.

Śākya Chokden (Shākya mchog ldan). 2008. *Phyag rgya chen po'i shan 'byed.* Collected Works, vol. 17. Kathmandu: Sachen International.

Stearns, Cyrus. 2010. *The Buddha from Dölpo, Revised and Expanded: A Study of the Life and Thought of the Tibetan Master Dölpopa Sherab Gyaltsen.* Ithaca, NY: Snow Lion Publications.

Tāranātha, Jonang Jetsun (Jo nang rje btsun). n.d. *Zab mo gzhan stong dbu ma'i brgyud 'debs.* Collected Works, vol. 18, 3–8. 'Dzam thang dgon.

van der Kuijp, Leonard W. J. 1983. *Contributions to the Development of Tibetan Buddhist Epistemology—From the Eleventh to the Thirteenth Century.* Alt-Neu-Indische Studien 26. Wiesbaden: Franz Steiner Verlag.

13. Instructions on the Great Perfection

Jamgön Kongtrul
Translated by Marc-Henri Deroche

The Contemplation of Pure Awareness

Especially revered within the broad Tibetan oral literature of spiritual instructions (*damngak, mengak*) and oral advice (*shaldam, shalung*) are instructions on mind (*semtri*) and direct introductions to the nature of mind or direct introductions to pure awareness (*semnyi ngotrö, rikpa ngotrö*). Such instructions constitute the treasured words of an experienced master, who points out the essence of the Buddhist view and practice to his qualified disciples. In Tibet, these direct presentations are most often found in the traditions of the Great Seal (Mahāmudrā) of the Kagyüpas and the Great Perfection (Dzokchen) of the Nyingmapas.

For many centuries, Tibetan meditators have combined Mahāmudrā and Dzokchen views and practices. The confluence of these two traditions formed a precedent for the work of the rimé masters of nineteenth-century Tibet and deeply influenced their approach. In particular, the Dzokchen view—of an all-encompassing enlightened mind that embraces all phenomena and is the pinnacle of all spiritual paths—provided a philosophical basis for ecumenically minded adepts as they engaged with the diverse spiritual lineages of Tibet.[1] The present chapter focuses on this Dzokchen view by offering a translation of Jamgön Kongtrul Lodrö Thayé's instructions for the direct

---

1. See, for example, Samten Karmay's comments on this subject and on the Dzokchen link between Bön and Buddhism (Karmay 2007, 13–14 and 216–23).

introduction to the nature of mind, extracted from a manual of instructions (*triyik*) that he assembled. The words themselves are largely a compilation of preexisting teachings, but their arrangement makes for a unique presentation.

Born in eastern Tibet in a family belonging to the Bön tradition, Kongtrul (1813–99) became a monk in the Nyingma monastery of Shechen. There he was first introduced to the nature of mind by Shechen Paṇchen Gyurmé Thutop Namgyal (b. 1787). Later, he came to the Karma Kagyü monastery of Palpung, directed at the time by the Ninth Situpa, Pema Nyinjé Wangpo (1798–1868). After completing his studies he devoted his life to solitary contemplation in a hermitage close to Palpung called Tsadra Rinchen Drak and wrote extensive works known as the Five Great Treasuries.[2] These writings consisted in large part of compilations from various teaching and practice lineages, brought together in order to transmit and preserve them.

Jamgön Kongtrul had a large number of spiritual teachers belonging to the different schools of Tibetan Buddhism. His association with Jamyang Khyentsé Wangpo (1820–92) was central to the emergence of the so-called "impartial" (*rimé*) movement. Together with the treasure-revealer (*tertön*) Chokgyur Dechen Lingpa (1829–70), they formed the core of the "movement." Khyentsé, a visionary and a pilgrim who had traveled all over Tibet and collected many lineages, was an inspirational figure to his peers. Kongtrul, who embraced the life of a hermit, was a prolific writer and compiler. Chokgyur Lingpa made an important contribution by revealing hidden treasures (*terma*). Their work should not to be understood as a formal organization, however. It was rather a series of trans-sectarian activities: the revelation, collection, compilation, and transmission of Tibetan Buddhist lineages, all supported by a network of Degé's Nyingma, Kagyü, and Sakya monasteries.

In his autobiography Kongtrul labels himself with the terms *chokmé* and *rimé*, which both convey the fundamental virtue of impartiality: the absence (*mé*) of bias (*chok, ri*). E. Gene Smith interpreted these terms to refer to religious tolerance and translated them as "nonsectarianism." The English term *nonsectarianism* implies the overcoming of political and religious conflict. In a broader sense, *chokmé* and *rimé*, understood as virtues of impartiality or neutrality, are deeply connected to Buddhist ideals of detachment and

---

2. For more details about the Five Great Treasuries, see Smith 2001, 262–67, and the translation of Kongtrul's autobiography by Richard Barron (Jamgön Kongtrul Lodrö Thayé 2003).

contemplation. The adjective *rimé* is used in the Dzokchen text presented here, as it is in other Dzokchen and Mahāmudrā sources, in order to describe a state of pure awareness: an open presence or choiceless awareness that is neutral, without bias or inclination, that avoids conceptualizing any extreme and transcends all pairs of opposites. I propose that we call the social virtue of religious tolerance "relative rimé." This is particularly appropriate since the rimé movement was only *relatively* nonsectarian, given that it was, in a sense, a blend of non-Geluk traditions reaffirming themselves in Kham far from Lhasa's Geluk government. Whereas in contrast, we might call the inner contemplation described in Kongtrul's manual "absolute rimé." I would argue that it is only through an inner effort to transcend one's own partiality and egocentrism that the social virtues of religious tolerance and nonsectarianism can naturally and authentically manifest. There is an important connection between the contemplative spirit of the rimé movement and its pluralist approach toward different traditions of practice.[3]

The text translated here is found in the section on the Nyingma lineage in Kongtrul's *Treasury of Spiritual Instructions*, which is itself a collection of particular importance for understanding the intent of the impartial movement. According to Smith, by collecting spiritual instructions from distinct lineages and schools, Kongtrul was implicitly pointing out their common ultimate goal.[4] The organization of the *Treasury of Spiritual Instructions* is based on a classification of eight lineages of practice, a model attributed to Prajñāraśmi (Trengpo Tertön Sherab Öser, 1518–84), who defines the common and principal teaching of all eight lineages to be the direct introduction to "primordial gnosis" (*yeshé, jñāna*).[5]

The full title of the manual of instructions can be translated into English as *Immaculate Advice: A Manual of Instructions on the Heart Essence of the Secret Great Perfection That Gathers the Streams of Mother and Child Traditions*. The combination of mother and child traditions refers to the main tradition of Vimalamitra (eighth century)—the mother—and its continuation and revival

---

3. As this chapter was being submitted, I was also preparing a full study of the various uses of the terms *chokmé* and *rimé* (and their Sanskrit equivalents) to be published in another publication.

4. Smith 2001, 263–64.

5. For a study of Prajñāraśmi's life, works, and contribution to the revival of the Nyingma school and the emergence of the rimé movement, see Deroche 2011. For further discussion, see Deroche (forthcoming).

by Longchen Rabjam Drimé Öser (1308–64)—the child.[6] Kongtrul also includes in this compilation the Third Karmapa Rangjung Dorjé's (1284–1339) special transmission, among others.[7] The entire manual belongs to the heart-essence (*nyingthik*) subcategory of Dzokchen trainings. Dzokchen teachings are traditionally classified into three series: the mind series (*semdé*), space series (*longdé*), and spiritual instructions series (*mengakdé*). The heart-essence teachings, and therefore the segment of Kongtrul's instruction manual that I translate here, belong to the spiritual instructions series, considered to be the most profound in the classification of three series.[8] Kongtrul reports that he himself received the whole confluence of Dzokchen's heart-essence lineages from Karma Shenphen Thayé and Jamyang Khyentsé Wangpo, the latter being especially revered by Kongtrul for his direct spiritual guidance. The manual is thus an excellent example of Khyentsé and Kongtrul's close collaboration. It is the fruit of their great effort to collect and compile instruction lineages and to provide written support to guarantee their preservation, transmission, and practice.

In its introduction, Kongtrul describes the manual's content as the summit of all teachings of the Buddhas, the quintessence of all teachings from every cycle, the ultimate among all the swift paths of Vajrayāna, and the heart of the 6.4 million tantras of Dzokchen. He boasts that it includes a complete set of meditative and yogic practices that form the entire path of Dzokchen, and specifies that the instructions are only to be followed under the

---

6. Longchenpa is famous for having combined the various Dzokchen lineages of the heart essence (*nyingthik*) in his compilation the *Heart Essence in Four Parts*, to which Kongtrul often refers in his manual of instructions. In the current redaction of the *Heart Essence in Four Parts*, there are actually five parts: the *Heart Essence of Vimalamitra* by Vimalamitra (and others); its commentary, the *Quintessence of the Master* by Longchenpa; the *Heart Essence of the Sky Dancer* by Padmasambhava; its commentary, the *Quintessence of the Sky Dancer* by Longchenpa; and finally the *Quintessence of the Profound* by Longchenpa, which comments on both the *Heart Essence of Vimalamitra* and the *Heart Essence of the Sky Dancer*. See Longchen Rabjam Drimé Öser 1975.

7. Longchenpa and the Third Karmapa Rangjung Dorjé shared a master in Kumārāja (1266–1343), from whom they received Dzokchen transmission. The Third Karmapa, after also obtaining a direct visionary transmission from Vimalamitra, later composed his own systematization of instructions called the *Heart Essence of the Karmapa* (*Karma Nyingthik*). In addition to elements of Rangjung Dorjé's instructions, Kongtrul also includes transmission from the *Heart Essence of Vairocana* (*Vairo Nyingthik*) lineage in his manual.

8. In the translated extract that follows, Kongtrul draws upon references and quotations from the Seventeen Tantras of the *mengakdé* series. He also quotes from Longchenpa's *Heart Essence in Four Parts*.

guidance of an expert teacher. Its implementation requires empowerments, performance of preliminary practices (*ngöndro*), and receiving of reading transmissions and oral instructions. Traditionally a manual such as this one would be transmitted to people spending several years in spiritual retreat, such as the three-year and three-fortnight retreat traditional to Nyingma and Kagyü schools. The manual would therefore be studied in meditation colleges rather than in scholastic institutions. In fact, the text likely acts as a written foundation for the Dzokchen section of the contemplative curriculum followed in meditation colleges established under the guidance of Kongtrul.[9] Its style and content is systematic, as shown in the outline below. But it is less speculative than descriptive of meditation experience. In fact, its descriptive tone is what is meant by "direct introduction." It primarily addresses lineage holders for the purpose of aiding them in their teaching responsibilities, and secondarily advises their disciples for the purpose of helping their practice and progression.

The outline of the entire manual of instructions is as follows, with the section translated in this chapter listed under 2.3.1.2.1.3—namely, "the instructions on the view without reference points":

1. The entrance into the frame of the instructions by gathering suitable conditions
    1.1. The qualifications of the master
    1.2. The qualifications of the disciple
    1.3. The manner of how to teach
    1.4. The establishment of the basis of suitable conditions
2. The main exposition of the system of guidance and its instructions
    2.1. The lineage history that increases conviction
    2.2. The maturing empowerments
    2.3. The liberating instructions
        2.3.1. The instructions liberating those of higher diligence in this life
            2.3.1.1. The instructions on the preliminary practices that make an appropriate receptacle for the meditation of the path
            2.3.1.2. The main practice: instructions of the meaning of the heart essence of radiant light that bring certainty concerning mind and pure awareness

---

9. According to Kongtrul's manual for spiritual retreat translated by Ngawang Zangpo (1994), Dzokchen acted as the culminating subject of a contemplative curriculum that integrated the eight lineages of spiritual instructions. On these lineages see Deroche (forthcoming).

Our selected extract comes from the main practice of the cycle, and of this central practice's two parts, it is drawn from the first, called *breakthrough* (*trekchö*). This form of meditation entails recognizing and remaining in the primordial purity (*kadak*) of the nature of mind. The second part of the cycle's main practice is *direct transcendence* (*thögal*). It is constituted by visionary practices that bring attention to the spontaneous presence (*lhundrup*) of pure awareness. The twofold practice of breakthrough and direct transcendence is meant for individuals of higher acumen who are capable of practicing with remarkable diligence. The manual later offers instructions to those of lesser capacity who may be liberated at the moment of death in the intermediate state (*bardo*). Those of even lower capacity may aim to be reborn into a pure spiritual realm where they could more easily progress further. The manual thereby provides diverse methods for different disciples.

The section on breakthrough contains four subsections on conduct, meditation, view, and fruit. It is the section on the view that I translate in this chapter. This section deals with the direct introduction to the nature of mind. As such, it includes the famous "three statements hitting the essence" taught by Garab Dorjé, the first human teacher of Dzokchen, accompanied by Kongtrul's commentary. Preceding sections focus on the purification of body, speech, and mind through different exercises. These preceding sections also explain how to analyze the mind: by searching for its origin, its endurance, and its disappearance. This manner of analysis leads to the discovery of the essence of mind. But Kongtrul properly describes the essence of mind in the section on the view that I translate. He directly addresses the fundamental topics of self-recognition and self-knowledge—pure contemplation that integrates the depth and breadth of all possible experience into pure awareness.

The term *view* (*tawa*, *dṛṣṭi*) refers, in much Buddhist discourse, to philosophical understanding. Such a view is not only a conceptual abstraction but also a transformative insight. In Kongtrul's text, *view* refers to a contemplation (in the sense of the Latin *contemplatio*, meaning "the activity of looking at") that he defines as "without reference points," meaning one that transcends subject and object. As he explains, it is "the mode of being that completely transcends meditation object and meditating subject." In this ultimate form of contemplation, where one does not fixate on anything, pure awareness simply contemplates itself, encompassing everything that arises as its own dynamic power. It is, in this way, contemplation without an object. Mind perceives directly its original nature: all-pervading presence that is beyond limitations and manifests its own qualities, free from delusion. According to Dzokchen terminology, mind's essence is emptiness, its nature is clarity, and its compassionate energy is unobstructed. In this way the Dzokchen view integrates negative and positive approaches to the absolute (what we call in the Western tradition *apophatic* and *cataphatic*, respectively). The negative approach is expressed through the notion of primordial purity—the emptiness or absence of intrinsic nature of all phenomena. The positive approach is represented by the description of spontaneous presence—the clear knowing and vivid experience of the manifold manifestations of perception.

In terms of the first aspect—emptiness, or primordial purity—the text insists on the negation of all fixations, oppositions, and duality. It is in this context that we find two occurrences of the term *rimé*, here best translated as "without bias," which means being free from a perspective of duality, at either one extreme or at its opposite. Its first occurrence reads: "Gain confidence in self-arising, without bias (*rimé*), without grasping, effort, rejection, adoption, or antidote." Its second occurrence is in the same vein: "Without bias (*rimé*) that differentiates meditative sessions and postmeditative sessions, without interruption between day and night, avoiding the perilous paths of eternalism and annihilation, without points to accept or to reject." Kongtrul instructs practitioners to reintegrate all of their conscious experiences into the primordial state that transcends all pairs of opposites. Rimé, in this context, is a description of pure awareness.

In reference to the second, positive aspect—luminosity or spontaneous presence—Dzokchen literature uses unique terminology to express the vibrancy of pure awareness, such as "dynamic power" (*tsel*) or "play" (*rölpa*). Pure awareness is further described as "brilliant" (*salé*), "pristine" (*sang-ngé*), and "clear" (*walé*). These terms generally do not appear in isolation but rather in lists describing a whole spectrum of contemplative experience. The difficulty is that there is no single, strict English equivalent for any of these Tibetan words. I have tried to solve this problem by translating them as sets of complementary terms, sometimes overlapping in meaning with one another, in order to render the original Tibetan's colorful portrait of an especially vivid, lively experience.

Another peculiar feature of Dzokchen discourse is its rhetoric of naturalness. The Tibetan word for "self" (*rang*) is used in a variety of compounds like "self-arising" (*rangshar*), "self-abiding" (*rangné*), and "self-liberation" (*rangdröl*). When used to describe the "nature" (*rangshin*) of experience, it is sometimes better translated as "natural," as in "natural rest" (*rangbab*), and "natural gnosis" or "self-existing gnosis" (*rangjung yéshé*). Other translators also use words such as "auto-" or "intrinsic" to convey the idea of unfabricated, spontaneous experience. Because *rikpa*, pure awareness, is primordially pure and spontaneous, it is beyond any artifice, intervention, fabrication, antidote, effort, or constraint. Traditional comparisons referring to natural elements, like the sky, a mountain, or the ocean, also evoke the natural immensity, grandeur, stability, and profundity of pure awareness. It has no limitations in terms of space. It is infinite. Similarly, it is timeless. The attention to the instant (a central topic of Kongtrul's direct introduction) leads to the sense of an eternal present, the so-called fourth time, free from past, present, and future: an all-transcending, all-embracing presence.

Kongtrul's language in our selected extract makes clear that the recognition and cultivation of the central view of Dzokchen—pure awareness—emerges within a traditional setting infused with devotion and sacred inspiration. The blessings and inspirational power, bestowed by a practitioner's lineage and master and accessed through *guru yoga*, are considered to be decisive on the Dzokchen path.[10] Whereas the nature of mind is said to be ineffable, beyond

---

10. Guru yoga ("union with the master") is the last of the common preliminary practices that Kongtrul teaches in a preceding section of the manual. Its practice is central to the path of Dzokchen. It consists of invoking the master (*lama, guru*), who is visualized as the primordial Buddha Samantabhadra. By enhancing faith and devotion in the disciple, guru yoga is the means for opening the disciple to the blessings of the lineage and the master. It further enables the disciple's mind to ultimately be united with the master's enlightened state. See section 2.1 in the translation: "The direct introduction through the power of blessing." This section illustrates the correlation between devotion, inspiration, and objectless meditation in Dzokchen practice.

language and discourse, the heartfelt words of its direct introduction from an experienced master has a psychagogic function that can provoke what French philosopher Pierre Hadot has called, in reference to Western quests for wisdom, the "conversion of the interest and the attention."[11] Dzokchen oral instructions should therefore be understood as "inspired advice."

Acknowledgments

I am grateful to Chögyal Namkhai Norbu Rinpoché for his teachings and explanations on the entire Dzokchen manual presented here, and for the same reason as well to Denys Rinpoché, who is currently directing an annotated French translation of the same manual (and to which I am a contributor). I have also greatly benefited from the expertise of translator Thierry Lamouroux for the clarification of some passages. All mistakes or imprecisions that might remain are nevertheless my sole responsibility

---

11. Hadot 2002, 222.

Instructions on the View without Reference Points

by Jamgön Kongtrul Lodrö Thayé

This teaching has two parts: the experience of the ultimate and the direct introduction to the naked nature of mind.

1. The experience of the ultimate

This is also subdivided: the understanding and the actual experience.

1.1. The understanding

The understanding will be gained according to texts such as *Supportive Teachings of Breakthrough: The Immaculate Space*[12] and *Clouds of Nonconceptual Space.*[13]

1.2. The actual experience

Having accomplished guru yoga as a preliminary, one's own awareness is realized as the immaculate body of reality (*chöku*) according to the *Three Words That Strike the Crucial Point* taught by the body of emanation (*tulku*) Garab Dorjé.

1.2.1. Immediate introduction to one's own nature

The present cognition, free from alterations or remedies, beyond grasping an entity, pure awareness not established as any characteristic, empty and clear

---

12. This text (*Trekchö kyi Gyapyik Namkha Drimé*) belongs to *Quintessence of the Master*, in the *Heart Essence in Four Parts* compiled by Longchenpa (Longchen Rabjam Drimé Öser 1975, 1:388–421).

13. This text (*Tokmé Namkhai Trinphung*) also belongs to *Quintessence of the Master* (Longchen Rabjam Drimé Öser 1975, 2:135–43).

natural gnosis, the great transcendence of thought and conceptuality; this very awareness, which rests in a state of brilliance, limpidity, and equality, is to be recognized as the natural gnosis, the body of reality, the intention of primordial purity.

1.2.2. Deciding upon the unique conclusion

One is to remain immobile in the state of the fourth time free from past, present, and future, which is the wisdom mind beyond discursivity—the body of reality. Do not stop former thoughts nor generate those to come. The present cognition, in the state free of artifices and alterations, the radiance of pure awareness, is without obstructions. In this state similar to limpid water where impurities have dissolved, there is no veil of striving for a goal. Without being lost in distraction, one is to remain in the ordinary pure awareness, natural rest, unique, lucid, limpid, open, and brilliant.

1.2.3. Gaining confidence in the immediacy of liberation

At the moment of dwelling in such a state, pure, free from mental constructs, similar to a limpid ocean, the ordinary cognition radiates in the immediate perception of sense objects. Yet they are self-manifested and self-liberated in the manner of waves emerging from water and dissolving into it. When they appear, you relax into the state without distractions or alterations, without following thoughts, and they vanish. They go and dissolve into the basis of perception. This is called "self-liberation" (*rangdröl*). Gain confidence in self-arising, without bias (*rimé*), without grasping, effort, rejection, adoption, or antidote.

2. The direct introduction to the naked nature of mind

With two parts: the direct introduction through the power of blessing and the direct introduction through the cultivation of experience.

2.1. The direct introduction through the power of blessing

In a remote place, arrange vast feast offerings and sacrificial cakes. Disciples sit straight in meditation posture. The master giving the direct introduction is taken as the basis for meditation. His person constitutes the object that has been explained previously in the section on guru yoga.[14] He has exhausted all faults. He has all of the complete qualities. He bestows all of what is needed or desired. A supreme conviction arises that he is the essence unifying all aspects of the refuge. With the idea "whatever you do, you know best!" disciples totally surrender to the master, thinking:

> Root master and lineage masters, with your enlightened mind of infinite compassion, may you bless me. May you inspire me such that in this very present moment the realization of the profound path arises.

Give birth to fervent devotion and longing until the eyes are filled with tears. Incense and fragrant resin are burnt. Accompanied by the master playing the drum and the bell, inspiration comes from the supplication to the lineage and the succession of masters:

> Body of reality Samantabhadra, we address our prayer to you. May you inspire the experience and realization of the profound path to arise in us.

Then the infinite compassion of the master himself dissolves into light, which is absorbed into the top of the disciples' heads. The mind relaxes. It enters into and remains in the inseparable three gates of the disciples and three vajras of the master, without mental constructs.[15] An intense inspiration will then arise. As the appearances of the three gates of the disciples have melted with the master, thoughts emerge as vivid devotion. The basic nature, without grasping, is naturally liberated into openness. Remaining in this state, without fabrication, at ease and relaxed, is called the liberation of self-awareness into the sphere of the body of reality: primordial purity. This direct introduction is not found within Dzokchen root teachings. But the precious and great treasure-revealer Orgyen Terdak Lingpa (1646–1714) performed this practice in order to generate and advance the contemplative experience of his disciples. Thus it constitutes a very great blessing.

---

14. Guru yoga is taught in a preceding section of Kongtrul's manual as one of the preliminary practices. See the outline in the introductory essay to this translation.

15. The three gates of the disciples are their ordinary body, speech, and mind, while the three vajras of the master are his enlightened body, speech, and mind. The latter are said to be like a vajra (a diamond, scepter, or thunderbolt). They are conceived to be adamantine, clear, pure, and indestructible.

2.2. The direct introduction through the cultivation of experience

There are three direct introductions to the nature of mind: at rest, in movement, and in the conjunction of rest and movement.

2.2.1. At rest

Having resolved that the absolute is unborn, the immediate basis of rest is introduced as the mode of being without bondage or liberation. It is the meaning of the primordial purity of the exhaustion of phenomena. As previously, disciples dispose their bodies in the seven-point posture of Vairocana.[16] The key point of speech and vital energy is to remain naturally. The key point of mind is that former thoughts are not stopped and subsequent thoughts are not generated. The nature of present awareness, the fourth time free from past, present, and future, is not established as anything. But radiating as great bliss, it is unobstructed. Although its dynamic power appears as the variety of phenomena, its essence is indescribable, inconceivable, and inexpressible. It transcends the objects of conceptual mind. This pure awareness is clear, open, lucid, naked, and immaculate. It is the natural gnosis, the body of reality, the great transcendence of conceptual mind. Recognizing it directly, remain for a while in this state like space free from extremes. This is the direct introduction with signs. Remaining in this way, the fabrications of discursive thoughts having been entirely pacified, all activities and thoughts emerge as the play (*rölpa*) of bliss, clarity (*salwa*), and nonconceptual gnosis. Without bias (*rimé*) differentiating meditative sessions and postmeditative sessions, without interruption between day and night, avoiding the perilous paths of eternalism and annihilation, without points to accept or to reject, settle finally in the wisdom mind of primordial purity, the exhaustion of phenomena, the mode of being that completely transcends meditation object and meditating subject. According to the *Secret Sound Tantra*:[17]

> Without thoughts of before and after,
> in this very cognition of the present,

---

16. The seven points of this classical meditative position are as follows: (1) legs disposed in the full (or half) lotus, (2) spine straightened, (3) shoulders opened, (4) neck delicately bent, (5) hands placed in the gesture of equanimity, (6) tip of the tongue touching the palate, and (7) gaze directed toward the nose.

17. Possibly an alternative title for the *Penetration of Sound Tantra* (*Dra Thalgyur*), belonging to the Seventeen Tantras.

wakeful, pristine, and clear,
recognize the body of reality endowed with four qualities.[18]

At this moment, what remains free from the fabrications of mind is the body of reality. Clear and without fixation is the body of enjoyment. The basis of the emergence of manifold appearances and unobstructed is the body of emanation. Essence (*ngowo*), nature (*rangshin*), and compassion (*thukjé*) are inseparable.[19] According to the *Inlaid Jewels Tantra*:[20]

The perfect Buddha is self-awareness itself.
Its essence is immutable in the three times.
Its nature is continuously unobstructed.
Its compassion is self-appearing everywhere.

Regarding the three substances of any object whatsoever, such as the three substances of a pillar: what it is in the three times—the past, present, and future pillar. In a unique moment of simultaneity, rather than experiencing their general aspects but by focusing the mind with care on their subtle particularities in one instant, there is a special mode of emergence. On this basis the master introduces directly the fourth time free from the three others. As it is said, the fourth time, which is shown, is devoid of any concrete basis. This is the intended meaning.

---

18. In *Quintessence of the Profound* (Longchen Rabjam Drimé Öser 1975, 12:211–12), Longchenpa gives a commentary on the same quotation. The four qualities of the body of reality are said to be (1) "the coemergent gnosis without elaborations" (*trömé lhenchik kyepai yeshé*), (2) "primordial purity not sullied by the veils of conceptuality" (*loyi drimé ma göpai kadak*), (3) "primordial liberation not bound by the attachment to experience" (*nyamkyi shenpé ma chingpai yedröl*), and (4) "absolutely primordial buddhahood" (*tené yé sangyé*).

19. These are the three inseparable qualities, or "gnosis," of the primordial basis, as explained in the Seventeen Tantras. Essence which is empty, nature which is clarity, and compassion which is unobstructed are here equated to the three buddha-bodies, respectively: essence to the body of reality (*chöku*), nature to the body of enjoyment (*longku*), compassion to the body of emanation (*tulku*). The underlying idea is that the three bodies of the *fruit* of buddhahood with their qualities are already present within the *basis* of buddha nature. They have to be recognized and integrated on the path in order to be fully actualized.

20. The *Inlaid Jewels Tantra* (*Norbu Trakö*) is one of the Seventeen Tantras.

2.2.2. In movement

Having reached the conclusion that the dynamic power of appearances is unobstructed, the direct introduction to the nature of mind in movement, the self-liberation without abandonment or remedy, is as follows: The nature of mind is bliss, clarity, and nonconception. In this state, the unobstructed dynamic power of appearances, the occurrence and dissolution of thoughts, however they appear, are not obstructed externally and not bound by the antidotes coming from grasping and attachment internally. Remain in natural rest, in the radiance of awareness and clarity, in pure awareness, naked, wakeful, and unadorned, not distorted or corrupted by the notions of before or after, welcoming or following, accepting or rejecting, stopping or cultivating. It is similar to the waves in the ocean, which although they appear do not differ from the very water of the ocean. Like this, whatever thoughts may appear, not being rejected, not being adulterated, do not go beyond or differ from the play of reality (*chönyi*). Thus while a variety of phenomena emanate externally, the mind remains unmoved by appearances, like an illusory person who is free from the calculations of attachment and desire. While a variety of phenomena appear internally, remain without grasping or becoming attached, like in the cognition of an infant, not identifying anything with "this is it." In this way all perceptions and conceptions are like salt dissolving into water. Being self-pacified, self-purified, they vanish. Thus it is called the self-liberation of all appearances. According to the *Penetration of Sound Tantra*:

> The awareness of whatever appears
> is self-liberated like a snake's knot.
> Because there is no antidote, effort falls away.
> This is the primordial liberation by the essence itself.

2.2.3. In the conjunction of rest and movement

Having resolved that rest and movement are in essence inseparable, regarding this conjunction the introduction to the naked awareness of all appearances is as follows: In the state in which the three gates are relaxed in their natural character, remaining in natural rest without stopping or cultivating, adopting or rejecting whatever thoughts may arise uninterruptedly from the manifestation of the dynamic power of pure awareness, one rests in the state of reality without moving. The self-expression of rest is liberated uninterruptedly. Thus the nature of rest and of manifestation are not dual, they are inseparable. According to the point that rest and movement do not have an essence posited in relation to each other, whatever arises in the six spheres of consciousness remains as the naked awareness, without falling into either direction of rest or of movement. All thoughts, coarse or subtle, arise and disappear suddenly. Like ice melting into water or fog vanishing in the sky, they do not go beyond the play of reality or move from it. As it is said in the *Marvel*:[21]

> Like the waves of the ocean,
> all the moving waves of mind
> dissolve into the ocean of the primordial basis (*döma shi*).

In this way, if mind rests, it rests in the primordial state. If it moves, it appears as the play of primordial gnosis. If it is equal, being free in the state of nonduality of rest and movement, whatever may arise does not go beyond the natural radiance of reality. Equality is not accomplished, movement is not blocked, and rest is not awakened. Whatever appears does not go beyond the magical display of one's own pure awareness. According to a scriptural quotation:

> The pure and immaculate Buddha
> is self-awareness, the immutable body of reality.
> Brilliant, pristine, and clear,
> it is like an autumn sky without clouds.[22]
> Rest immutable and stable like a mountain.
> Rest immobile and limpid like an ocean.
> Rest vast and without constriction like space.
> Rest in whatever state may be: it is the state of pure awareness.
> Rest in movement or at calm in self-awareness, limpid, brilliant, and
>   open.
> All actions, even flying in the sky,
> do not go beyond space.
> Similarly with rest: the natural clarity of phenomena does not move
>   from the state of pure awareness.

---

21. A Dzokchen tantra that I have not been able to identify, as several of them bear this same term in their title.

22. Within the Indian context to which this text refers, autumn follows the rainy season. The sky is then particularly clear.

As it is said above, without fabrication or artifice, in natural rest, relaxed, without stopping or cultivating, adopting or rejecting, hoping or fearing, an immediate peace emerges. Understand it to be the meditative absorption of self-abiding pure awareness. If this is recognized, knowledge in the three times, at rest or in movement, with negation or affirmation, good thoughts or bad thoughts, is seen wide-eyed as the natural rest of self-luminous self-awareness. Self-abiding meditative absorption without any grasping appears nakedly and uncovered. It is maintained by remembrance and attention, which proceed like the flow of a river. These instructions directly introduce whatever phenomena appear or are experienced as beyond stopping or cultivating, adopting or rejecting, hoping or fearing, transcending fixation on ordinary characteristics.

Moreover, instead of the last direct introduction, it is also very good to transmit two methods of direct introduction according to the *Essential Instructions on Breakthrough: Naturally Resting in the Primordial Nature*:[23] (1) introduction to the self-abiding wisdom mind and (2) introduction to the absence of apparitions and disappearance of mindful awareness. The master confers the direct introduction directly into the heart of fortunate persons who experience the ultimate. Doubts concerning the profound mode of being are cut. Its continuity being maintained without deterioration, stability is quickly obtained. For those who have not developed an experience of the meaning of meditation and who are lost in conceptual understanding, even if the direct introduction were transmitted, it would be useless. Thus they should practice with effort the steps of meditation with an object until the development of experience. Following the progressive generation of experience and realization, the transmission of direct introduction causes the end of meditation to be progressively attained.

---

23. This text (*Trekchö Yé Babsor Shagi Döntri*) belongs to the *Quintessence of the Master* (Longchen Rabjam Drimé Öser 1975, 1:371–88).

Translated Work

Jamgön Kongtrul Lodrö Thayé ('Jam mgon Kong sprul Blo gros mtha' yas). 2013. *Rdzogs pa chen po gsang ba snying thig ma bu'i bka' srol chu bo gnyis 'dus kyi khrid yig dri med zhal lung*. In *Blo gros mtha' yas pa'i mdzod*, vol. 15, 97–102. Kalimpong: Rigpe Dorje Institute.

Suggested Readings

Jamgön Kongtrul Lodrö Thayé. 1994. *Jamgön Kongtrul's Retreat Manual*. Translated by Ngawang Zangpo. Ithaca, NY: Snow Lion Publications.
——. 2003. *The Autobiography of Jamgön Kongtrul: A Gem of Many Colors*. Translated by Richard Barron. Ithaca, NY: Snow Lion Publications.
——. 2007. *The Treasury of Knowledge: Book Eight, Part Four: Esoteric Instructions*. Translated by Sarah Harding. Ithaca, NY: Snow Lion Publications.
Smith, E. Gene. 2001. "'Jam mgon Kong sprul and the Nonsectarian Movement." In *Among Tibetan Texts: History and Literature of the Himalayan Plateau*. Edited by Kurtis Schaeffer, 235–72. Boston: Wisdom Publications.

Additional References

Arguillère, Stéphane. 2007. *Vaste Sphère de Profusion: La vie, l'œuvre et la pensée de Klong-chen rab-'byams (Tibet, 1308–64)*. Louvain: Peeters.
Deroche, Marc-Henri. 2011. "Sherab Wozer (1518–1584)." In *The Treasury of Lives: Biographies of Himalayan Religious Masters*. New York: Rubin Foundation. Accessed May 7, 2013, http://treasuryoflives.org/biographies/view/Sherab-Wozer/8964.
——. (forthcoming). "Along the Middle Path, in Quest for Wisdom: The Great Madhyamaka in Rimé Philosophy." In *The Other Emptiness: Perspectives on the Zhentong Buddhist Discourse in India and Tibet,* edited by Klaus-Diether Mathes and Michael Sheehy. New York: State University of New York Press.
Germano, David F. 1992. "Poetic Thought, the Intelligent Universe, and the Mystery of Self: The Tantric Synthesis of rDzogs chen in Fourteenth Century Tibet." PhD Diss., University of Wisconsin.
Hadot, Pierre. 2002. *What Is Ancient Philosophy?* Translated by Michael Chase. Cambridge, MA: Belknap Press.
Karmay, Samten. 2007. *The Great Perfection (rDzogs chen): A Philosophical and Meditative Teaching of Tibetan Buddhism*. Leiden/Boston: Brill.
Longchen Rabjam Drimé Öser (Klong chen rab 'byams 'Dri med 'od zer). 1975. *Snying thig ya bzhi*, 13 vols. A 'dzom chos sgar par khang edition. Delhi: Lama Sherab Gyaltsen.
The Seventeen Tantras (Rnying ma'i rgyud bcu bdun), 3 vols. 1973–77. A 'dzom chos sgar par khang edition. New Delhi: Sanje Dorje.

Glossary

Abhidharma. See *ngönchö.*

abu (*a bu*). A term of endearment for a young boy.

Akaniṣṭha. A heavenly abode or pure realm.

akhu (*a khu*). An honorific term for a monk in the Amdo dialect.

Amitāyus. Buddha of infinite life.

amṛta. Nectar, elixir.

anusmṛti. Meditation, recollection.

ātman. Individual self.

avadhūti. Central channel of the subtle body.

bardo (*bar do*). Intermediary state between life, death, and rebirth.

Bhagavān. An epithet for the Buddha.

bhūmis. Levels or stages of attainment according to the Mahāyāna.

bodhicitta. See *jangchup kyi sem.*

Bön (*bon*). Indigenous religion of Tibet.

brahman. Great self or absolute in a non-Buddhist framework.

bṛhatī. In prosody, a class of meter with nine syllables.

bumku (*bum sku*). The vase body.

cakravartin. A wheel-turning king.

chakchen (*phyag rgya chen po, mahāmudrā*). The Great Seal.

chakgya (*phyag rgya, mudrā*). Seal, symbol.

chegom (*dpye sgom*). Analytic meditation in which one actively investigates the nature of mind.

cherdröl (*gcer grol*). Liberating perception.

chi dar (*phyi dar*). Later spreading, or propagation, of Buddhism in Tibet.

chö (*chos*). Dharma.

chö (*gcod*). Severence. A lineage of practice instruction traced to Machik Labdrön.

chöchen (*chos can, dharmin*). Conditioned phenomena.

chok lhung dralwa (*phyogs lhung bral ba*). Devoid of partiality.

chokgi ngödrup (*mchog gi dngos grub*). The supreme *siddhi* or accomplishment, that is, enlightenment, buddhahood.

chokmé (*phyogs med*). Impartial, without bias.

chokshak sum (*cog bzhag gsum*). Threefold freely resting: freely resting mountain, freely resting ocean, and freely resting awareness.

chöku (*chos sku, dharmakāya*). Body of truth or reality.

chöluk (*chos lugs*). Dharma lineages, religion.

chöné (*mchod gnas*). Basis of offering, someone worthy of receiving religious offerings.

chönyi (*chos nyid, dharmatā*). Reality, basic nature, ultimate nature, true being.

chösé (*chos zad*). Dharmas' exhaustion, the fourth vision of *thögal*.

chöying (*chos dbyings, dharmadhātu*). Sphere of reality.

chudrulü (*chu gru lus*). Slang from Degé meaning "nothing." Made up of three syllables: *chu* (*chu*), water; *dru* (*gru*), boats; and *lü* (*lus*), body.

ḍāka. Hero, male counterpart to *ḍākinī*.

ḍākinī. See *khandroma*.

dakmé (*bdag med*). Without self, nonself.

daljor (*dal 'byor*). Freedoms and fortunes; see also *dalwa gyé* and *jorwa chu*.

dalwa gyé (*dal ba brgyad*). The eight freedoms.

damngak (*gdams ngag*). Spiritual instructions, advice.

damtsik (*dam tshig, samaya*). Tantric vow or commitment.

deshek (*bde gshegs, sugata*). One who has gone to bliss; epithet for a buddha.

deshek nyingpo ('*bde gshegs snying po, sugatagarbha*). Buddha nature.

deshin shekpai nyingpo ('*de bzhin gshegs pa'i snying po, tathāgatagarbha*). Buddha nature.

dharāṇā. Retention, holding the inner energies in the central channel.

dharmadhātu. See *chöying*.

dharmakāya. See *chöku*.

dharmatā. See *chönyi*.

dhyāna. Meditative absorption, stable concentration.

do (*mdo, sūtra*). Discourse.

dodé (*mdo sde, sūtra piṭaka*). The Sūtra basket of the Buddhist canon.

dokpa (*ldog pa*). To reverse, to turn around.

dölpa (*gdol pa*). Outcast, low-born.

döma shi (*gdod ma gzhi*). Primordial basis.

dönchi (*don spyi*). An abstract concept.

dorjé (*rdo rje, vajra*). Scepter; indestructible.

dorjé thekpa (*rdo rje theg pa*). Vajrayāna, indestructible or diamond vehicle.

dra (*dgra*). Enemy.

dra (*sgra*). Sound.

drachi (*sgra spyi*). The general sense of what has been heard.

drangdön (*drang don, neyārtha*). Provisional truth or meaning.

drang-ngé (*drang nges*). Provisional and definitive teachings.

drilen (*dris lan*). Dialogues.

drupdra (*sgrub grwa*). Retreat center.

drupgyü shingta gyé (*sgrub brgyud shing rta brgyad*). Eight chariot-like practice lineages: Nyingma, Kadam, Marpa Kagyü, Shangpa Kagyü, Sakya, Kālacakra, Chöd and Shijé, and Orgyen Nyendrup.

druptha (*grub mtha'*). School, tradition, or philosophical system.

drupthop (*sgrub thob, siddha*). Accomplished one, realized practitioner, adept.

drupthop chenpo (*sgrub thob chen po, mahāsiddha*). Great adept.

dulwa ('dul ba). The Vinaya basket of the Buddhist canon containing rules of monastic conduct.

dzo (mdzo). Hybrid of yak and domestic cattle.

Dzokchen (rdzogs chen; rdzogs pa chen po). Great Perfection or Completion.

dzokrim (rdzogs rim). Completion stage.

gaṇacakra. Tantric feast.

Ganden Phodrang (dga' ldan pho brang). Name of the Tibetan government under the Dalai Lama incarnation line, with its capital in Lhasa.

gar (sgar). Encampment.

gelong (dge slong, bhikṣu). Fully ordained monastic.

genyen (dge bsnyen, upāsaka). Buddhist layperson who takes up to five precepts—to avoid killing, stealing, lying, engaging in sexual misconduct, and consuming intoxicants.

geshé (dge bshes). Highest monastic degree in the Geluk tradition.

gom (goms). Familiarization, one of the five meditative experiences of absorption.

gomé (sgom med). Nonmeditation, the fourth level of Mahāmudrā.

gomrim (sgom rim). Graduated meditation.

gongdré ('gong 'dre). A type of ghost known for its ability to take away wealth.

gongphel (gong 'phel). Increasing, the second vision of *thögal.*

gongpo ('gong po). A type of ghost, a synonym for *gongdré.*

gur (mgur). Song or spiritual song.

gurlu (mgur glu). See *gur.*

gyegyur gyi rik (rgyas 'gyur gyi rigs). Unfolding potential.

gyepa (dgyes pa). Joy; to enjoy.

gyü (rgyud, tantra). Continuum; esoteric scriptures of the Vajrayāna.

gyuma (sgyu ma, māyā). Illusion.

gyumai naljor (sgyu ma'i rnal 'byor). Yoga of illusion.

gyumai palmo (sgyu ma'i dpal mo). Queen of illusion.

jalü ('ja' lus). Rainbow body.

jangchup kyi sem (*byang chub kyi sems, bodhicitta*). The mind set on enlightenment; the commitment to attain enlightenment in order to liberate all sentient beings from saṃsāra.

jengak (*rjes bsngags, anuṣṭubh*). In prosody, a class of meter with eight syllables.

jetsun lama (*rje btsun bla ma*). Venerable master.

jñāna. See *yeshé*.

jödral (*brjod bral*). Inexpressible.

jokgom (*'jog sgom*). Placing the attention in meditation.

jorwa chu (*'byor ba bcu*). The ten fortunes.

jorwai yenlak (*sbyor ba'i yan lag*). The application element of a complete act.

jung né dro sum (*'byung gnas 'gro gsum*). The three things: arising, remaining, going. An analytical practice in the Great Perfection.

ka (*bka'*). Command, words of the Buddha.

kachuwa (*dka' bcu ba*). A type of monastic degree.

kadak (*ka dag*). Primordial purity.

Kagyé (*bka' brgyad*). Eight Dispensations.

Kālacakra (*dus kyi 'khor lo*). A cycle of tantric practices.

kama (*bka' ma*). The oral transmission of canonical teachings in the Nyingma tradition.

kāvya. See *nyen ngak*.

khandroma (*mkha' 'gro ma, ḍākinī*). Sky-goer; realized female adept.

Khecara (*mkha' spyod*). A celestial realm.

khyimpa (*khyim pa*). Householder.

kusum (*sku gsum, trikāya*). Three bodies of a buddha. See *chöku, longku,* and *tulku*.

kyakshor (*skyag shor*). Cowardly (in the Labrang Amdo dialect).

kyerim (*bskyed rim*). Creation stage.

kyongtsul (*skyong tshul*). Way to maintain.

lalanā. Left channel of the subtle body.

lama (*bla ma, guru*). Master. Spiritual master.

lamrim (lam rim). Progressive stages of the path.

lapja (bslab bya). Advice, practical advice.

lenté jokpa (glan te 'jog pa). Placement of attention on a single object.

lhachö (lha chos). Spiritual virtue or teachings; Buddhism.

lhakgé (lhag ge). Vivid.

lhakthong (lhag mthong, vipaśyanā). Superior or deep insight, special seeing.

lhangé (lhang nge). Total.

lhenchik kyepa (lhan cig skyes pa). Coemergent.

lhöpo (lhod po). Idle and carefree.

lhundrup (lhun grub). Spontaneous presence.

lodok namshi (blo ldog rnam bzhi). Four thoughts that turn the mind.

longchö kyi khorlo (longs spyod kyi 'khor lo). The wheel of enjoyment, formed by the subtle channels at the throat cakra.

longdé (klong sde). Space series, one of three subcategories of Dzokchen teachings.

longku (longs sku, saṃbhogakāya). Body of enjoyment.

lopön (slob dpon). A master or preceptor, usually monastic.

loyi drimé ma göpai kadak (blo yi dri mas ma gos pa'i ka dag). Primordial purity not sullied by the veils of conceptuality.

luk (lugs). A system or tradition of practice.

lung (lung). Scripture, doctrine.

lung (rlung). Wind.

luntam (blun gtam). Babble of a foolish man.

Madhyamaka. See *uma*.

Mādhyamika (dbu ma pa). A proponent of the Madhyamaka view.

Mahāmudrā. See *chakchen*.

Mahāsiddha. See *drupthop chenpo*.

Mahāyāna. See *thekpa chenpo*.

Mañjuśrī. The bodhisattva of wisdom.

Mantrayāna. See *sangak kyi thekpa*.

marikpa (*ma rig pa, avidyā*). Ignorance.

mengak (*man ngag, upadeśa*). Esoteric or spiritual instructions; secret method.

mengakdé (*man ngag sde*). Spiritual instructions series, one of three subcategories of Dzokchen teachings.

michö (*mi chos*). Human virtue.

mudrā. See *chakgya*.

mutekpa (*mu stegs pa, tīrthika*). Proponent of a non-Buddhist view.

naljor chöpa (*rnal 'byor spyod pa, yogācāra*). Followers of Yogācāra.

naljorpa (*rnal 'byor pa, yogin*). Adept, practitioner of yoga.

namsum dakpai sha (*rnam gsum dag pa'i sha*). The rule of threefold purity for meat found in the Vinaya or monastic code.

nga dar (*snga dar*). The earlier spreading, or propagation, of Buddhism to Tibet.

ngakpa (*sngags pa, tāntrika*). A nonmonastic tantric practitioner.

ngedön (*nges don, nītārtha*). Definitive truth or meaning.

ngepai tsik (*nges pa'i tshig, nirukti*). Etymology.

ngödrup (*dngos grub, siddhi*). Accomplishment; see *chokgi ngödrup* and *tunmongi ngödrup*.

ngoma (*ngo ma*). Genuine, true; the real thing.

ngönchö (*mngon chos, abhidharma*). The Abhidharma basket of the Buddhist canon.

ngöndro (*sngon 'gro*). Preliminary practices.

ngöndu tön (*mngon du ston*). To demonstrate.

ngönshé (*mngon shes*). Actual knowing, clairvoyance.

ngotrö (*ngo sprod*). Introduction; pointing-out instructions.

ngowo (*ngo bo*). Nature, essence.

ngowo nyi mepar mawa (*ngo bo nyid med par smra ba, niḥsvabhāvavāda*). Proponent of essencelessness.

Niḥsvabhāvavāda. See *ngowo nyi mepar mawa*.

nirmāṇakāya. See *tulku*.

nyamgur (*nyams mgur*). Spontaneous song of realization, song of experience.

nyamjuk gi samten gu (*mnyam 'jug gi gsam gtan dgu*). The nine concentrations of equilibrium.

nyamkyi shenpé ma chingpai yedröl (*nyams kyi zhen pas ma bcings pa'i ye grol*). Primordial liberation not bound by the attachment to experience.

nyen ngak (*snyan ngag, kāvya*). Poetry.

nyentö (*nyan thos, śrāvaka*). Hearer; a follower of the Buddha.

nyingjé (*snying rje*). Compassion.

Nyingma (*rnying ma*). Old school of Tibetan Buddhism; those practice lineages that emerged during the earlier spreading of Buddhism in Tibet.

nyingtam (*snying gtam*). Heart advice.

nyingthik (*snying thig*). Heart essence, a subset of teachings and practices in Dzokchen.

nyongtri (*myong khrid*). Guidance based on personal experience.

nyönmong (*nyon mongs, kleśa*). Negative emotion, affliction.

nyungné (*bsnyung gnas*). Fasting practice.

ösal (*'od gsal*). Clear light, luminosity.

paṇḍita. Scholar, learned master.

pāramitā. Perfection.

parinirvāṇa. Final *nirvāṇa* at the time of death of a buddha.

phochen (*pho chen*). Great transference, an abbreviated form of *pho ba chen po*.

popa (*spobs pa, pratibhāna*). Confident eloquence.

prajñāpāramitā. Perfection of wisdom.

prāṇāyāma. Regulation of the breath in yogic exercises.

prātimokṣa. Code of conduct for monks and nuns in the Vinaya.

pratyāhara. Withdrawal from sense perceptions.

pratyekabuddha. Solitary buddha.

pungpo (*spung po, skandha*). The aggregates.

rabga (*rab dga', uṣṇih*). In prosody, a class of meter with seven syllables.

rabjampa (*rab 'byams pa*). A type of monastic degree.

rabjung (*rab byung*). Renunciate.

rang (*rang*). A prefix meaning self, auto, intrinsic, natural.

rangbab (*rang babs*). Natural rest.

rangdröl (*rang grol*). Self-liberation.

rangi sem la tawa (*rang gi sems la blta ba*). Looking at your own mind.

rangjung yeshé (*rang byung ye shes*). Natural gnosis, self-existing wisdom.

rangné (*rang gnas*). Self-abiding.

rangshar (*rang shar*). Self-arising.

rangshin (*rang bzhin*). Character, nature.

rangshin nepai rik (*rang bzhin gnas pa'i rigs*). Naturally present potential.

rangtong (*rang stong*). Self-empty, empty of self.

rasanā. Right channel of the subtle body.

rikpa (*rig pa*). Awareness.

rikpa ngotrö (*rig pa ngo sprod*). Direct introductions to pure awareness.

rimé (*ris med*). Ecumenism, nonsectarian; impartial, without bias.

risu mepa (*ris su med pa*). See *rimé*.

rochik (*ro gcig*). Single flavor, one taste, the third level of Mahāmudrā.

rölpa (*rol pa*). Play, display.

ṛṣi. Hermit, sage.

rushen (*ru shan*). Separation, the name of a Dzokchen exercise.

sa chenpo kyong (*sa chen po skyong*). Governing a great land.

sakyong (*sa skyong*). Earth protector, title for the rulers of Degé.

salé (*gsal le*). Brilliant.

salwa (*gsal ba*). Clarity.

Samantabhadra (*kun tu bzang po*). The name of a primordial Buddha.

śamatha. See *shiné*.

samaya. See *damtsik*.

sambhogakāya. See *longku*.

sampai yenlak (*bsam pa'i yan lag*). The intention element of a complete act.

saṃsāra. (*'khor ba*). Cyclic existence.

samten (*bsam gtan, dhyāna*). Meditative concentration.

sangak kyi thekpa (*gsang sngags kyi theg pa, mantrayāna*). The vehicle of secret mantra.

sang-ngé (*sang nge*). Pristine.

sangthal (*zang thal*). Interpenetrating, unobstructed, unimpeded.

sangtsen (*gsang mtshan*). Secret name; the name one receives in an empowerment.

sangyé (*sangs rgyas*). A buddha, an awakened being.

sapché (*sa bcad*). Textual outline.

Sarma (*gsar ma*). New schools of Tibetan Buddhism; those practice lineages that emerged during the later spreading of the Dharma in Tibet.

sem (*sems*). Mind, ordinary dualistic mind.

semdé (*sems sde*). The mind series, one of three subcategories of Dzokchen teachings.

semné gu (*sems gnas dgu*). The nine stabilizations of the mind.

semné sumpa (*sems gnas gsum pa*). The third stage of stabilizing the mind, referring to repeated placement of attention on a single object, without distraction.

semnyi (*sems nyid*). Mind-as-such, the true being or nature of mind.

semnyi ngotrö (*sems nyid ngo sprod*). Direct introductions to the nature of mind.

semtri (*sems khrid*). Instructions on mind.

semtsöl (*sems 'tshol*). Searching for mind.

shal (*zhal*). Mouth.

shalchem (*zhal chems*). Final testament.

shaldam (*zhal gdams*). Personal advice or instructions.

shalgyun (*zhal rgyun*). Oral transmission.

shalkö (*zhal bkod*). Direct advice.

shalung (*zhal lung*). Oral advice.

shalshé (*zhal shes*). Personal direction.

shalta (*zhal ta*). Pith advice.

shé (*shes*). To know.

shedra (*bshad grwa*). Academy, monastic college.

shegé ki tam (*gzhad gad kyi gtam*). Humorous discourse.

shentong (*gzhan stong*). Empty of other.

sherab (*shes rab, prajña*). Knowledge, wisdom, transcendent intelligence.

shi (*gzhi*). Ground, the most fundamental dimension of the mind.

shi yenlak (*gzhi'i yan lag*). The ground element of a complete act.

shijé (*zhi byed*). Pacification, a lineage of practice associated with Pha Dampa Sangyé.

shiné (*zhi gnas, śamatha*). Calm abiding.

siddha. See *drupthop*.

siddhis. See *ngödrup*.

sing-ngé (sing nge). Sharp.

sipa (*srid pa, bhāva*). Existence, becoming, saṃsāra.

skandhas. See *pungpo*.

so so yangdak par rikpa (*so so yang dag par rig pa, pratisaṃvid*). Thorough, perfect knowledge.

so sor tokpa (*so sor rtog pa, pratyavekṣā*). Distinct analysis.

söpa (*bzod pa)*. Forbearance.

śrāvaka. See *nyentö*.

sugata. See *deshek*.

sugatagarbha. See *deshek nyingpo*.

sūtra. See *do*.

svābhāvikakāya. A fourth buddha body uniting the other three; see *kusum*.

tam (*gtam*). Discourse.

tantra. See *gyü*.

tathāgatagarbha. See *deshin shekpai nyingpo*.

tatri (*lta khrid*). Instruction for the view.

tawa (*lta ba, dṛṣṭi*). Philosophical view, insight.

ten (*brtan*). Stability, one of the five meditative experiences of absorption.

tené yé sangyé (*gtan nas ye sangs rgyas*). Absolutely primordial buddhahood.

terchö (*gter chos*). Treasure collection, treasure teachings.

terma (*gter ma*). Treasure texts or revelations.

tersar (*gter sar*). Title used to refer to a recently discovered treasure revelation.

tertön (*gter ston*). Treasure-revealer.

thamal gyi shepa (*tha mal gyi shes pa*). Ordinary mind.

thangka (*thang ka*). A hanging scroll painting.

thar (*mthar*). Consummation, one of the five meditative experiences of absorption.

thartuk gi yenlak (*mthar thug gi yan lag*). The completion element of a complete act.

thekpa chenpo (*theg pa chen po, mahāyāna*). The Great Vehicle.

thögal (*thod rgal*). Direct transcendence, crossing over; one of two categories of Dzokchen practice from the *mengakdé* series of instructions.

thop (*thob*). Attainment, one of the five meditative experiences of absorption.

thukjé (*thugs rje*). Cognitive potency. Compassion.

tingedzin (*ting nge 'dzin, samādhi*). Meditative absorption.

tokgewa (*rtog ge ba*). A philosopher.

topshi (*stobs bzhi*). Four powers (necessary for confession practice).

torma (*tor ma*). Dough offerings, made by mixing tsampa and butter, for ritual purposes.

trekchö (*khregs chod*). Breakthrough, cutting through; one of two categories of Dzokchen practice from the *mengakdé* series of instructions.

tringyik (*springs yig*). Epistle.

triyik (*khrid yig*). Written advice, instruction texts.

trödral (*spros bral*). Unembellished, the second level of Mahāmudrā.

trömé lhenchik kyepai yeshé (*spros med lhan cig skyes pa'i ye shes*). The coemergent gnosis without elaborations.

tröpa (*spros pa, prapañca*). Mental elaboration or proliferation.

tsatsa (*tsha tsha*). Clay figurines.

tsawai lama (*rtsa ba'i bla ma*). Root lama, principal teacher.

tsechik (*rtse gcig*). One-pointed, the first level of Mahāmudrā.

tsephep (*tshad phebs*). Reaching culmination, the third vision of *thögal*.

tsulmin (*tshul min*). How things are not.

tsulshin (*tshul bzhin*). The way things are.

tsulyin (*tshul yin*). How things are.

tsulyinmin (*tshul yin min*). What is real and unreal.

tulku (*sprul sku, nirmāṇakāya*). Emanational body; a reincarnated master.

tulshuk (*brtul zhugs*). Comportment, yogic conduct; tantric observance.

tummo (*gtum mo*). Heat-generating yogic practice.

tunmongi ngödrup (*mthun mong gi dngos grub*). Common *siddhis* or accomplishments.

uma (*dbu ma*). Madhyamaka, teachings on the Middle Way.

uma chenpo (*dbu ma chen po*). Great Madhyamaka.

umai lam (*dbu ma'i lam, madhyamā pratipad*). The middle path.

upāsaka. See *genyen.*

vajra. See *dorjé.*

Vajradhāra. A primordial Buddha.

Vajrayāna. See *dorjé thekpa.*

Vidyādhara. A wisdom-holder; level of realization.

vinaya. See *dulwa.*

vipaśyanā. See *lhakthong.*

walé (*wa le*). Clear.

yenlak shi (*yan lag bzhi*). The four elements of a complete act: ground, intention, application, and completion.

yeshé (*ye shes, jñāna*). Primordial gnosis or wisdom.

yidak (*yi dwags*). Hungry ghosts.

yidam (*yi dam*). A tantric deity.

yila mijepa (*yid la mi byed pa*). Mental nondoing or disengagement.

yo (*g.yo*). Wavering, one of the five meditative experiences of absorption.

Yogācāra. Practice of yoga, a Mahāyāna philosophical school.

yongdzin (*yongs 'dzin*). Master.

yulmé (*yul med*). Without objectivity.

Tibetan Proper Names

Abu Lhöpo. A bu lhod po.

Abum. A 'bum.

Adzom Drukpa Pawo Dorjé. A 'dzom 'brug pa Dpa' bo rdo rje.

Amdo. A mdo.

Aro Yeshé Jungné. A ro Ye shes 'byung gnas.

Atiśa (Dīpaṃkaraśrījñāna). Jo bo rje A ti sha, Dpal mar me mdzad dpal ye shes.

Bamda Thupten Gelek Gyatso. 'Ba' mda' Thub bstan dge legs rgya mtsho.

Bara Kagyü. 'Ba' ra bka' brgyud.

Barawa Gyaltsen Palsang. 'Ba' ra ba Rgyal mtshan dpal bzang.

Bodong Choklé Namgyal. Bo dong Phyogs las rnam rgyal.

Bön. Bon.

Chamdo. Chab mdo.

Chokdrup. Mchog grub.

Chokgyur Dechen Lingpa. Mchog 'gyur Bde chen gling pa.

Chomden Raldri. Bcom ldan ral gri.

Chöpal Gönpo. Chos dpal mgon po.

Dakpo Kagyü. Dwags po bka' brgyud.

Damngak Dzö. Gdams ngag mdzod.

Darma Tsöndrü. Dar ma brtson 'grus.

Degé. Sde dge.

Dilgo Khyentsé Tashi Paljor. Dil mgo mkhyen brtse Bkra shis dpal 'byor.

Do. Rdo.

Do Drimé Siji. Mdo dri med gzi brjid.

Do Khyentsé Yeshé Dorjé. Mdo mkhyen brtse Ye shes rdo rje.

Do Sermik. Mdo gzer mig.

Dodrupchen. Rdo grub chen. See Jikmé Tenpai Nyima and Jikmé Trinlé Öser.

Dodrupchen Monastery. Rdo grub chen dgon.

Dölpopa Sherab Gyaltsen. Dol po pa Shes rab rgyal mtshan.

Dönyö Drupa. Don yod grub pa.

Dra Thalgyur. Sgra thal 'gyur.

Drakden Drupa Chok. Grags ldan grub pa mchog.

Dratön Kalsang Tenpai Gyaltsen. Dbra ston Skal bzang bstan pa'i rgyal mtshan.

Drepung Monastery. 'Bras spungs dgon.

Dromtön Gyalwa Jungné. 'Brom ston rgyal ba 'byung gnas.

Drowé Palmo. 'Gro ba'i dpal mo.

Drukpa Kagyü. 'Brug pa bka' brgyud.

Drung Mipham Chokdrup. Drung Mi pham mchog grub.

Dudjom Lingpa. See Trakthung Dudjom Lingpa.

Dulgyü. 'Dul rgyud.

Dulwa Gyüdruk. 'Dul ba rgyud drug.

Dulwa Kunlé Tü. 'Dul ba kun las bstus.

Dungkar Losang Trinlé. Dung dkar Blo bzang 'phrin las.

Dza Patrul Orgyen Jikmé Chökyi Wangpo. Rdza Dpal sprul O rgyan 'jigs med chos kyi dbang po.

Dza Patrul Rinpoché. See Dza Patrul Orgyen Jikmé Chökyi Wangpo.

Dzachuka. Rdza chu kha.

Dzagyal Monastery. Rdza rgyal dgon.

Dzamling Wangyal. 'Dzam gling dbang rgyal.

Dzamtang. 'Dzam thang.

Dzokchen Guru Shiwa. Rdzogs chen Gu ru zhi ba.

Dzokchen Monastery. Rdzogs chen dgon.

Gampopa Sönam Rinchen. Sgam po pa Bsod nams rin chen.

Ganden Monastery. Dga' ldan dgon.

Ganden Phodrang. Dga' ldan pho brang.

Gangteng Tulku Pema Namgyal. Sgang steng sprul sku Pad ma rnam rgyal.

Garab Dorjé. Dga' rab rdo rje.

Gawai Dorjé. Dga' ba'i rdo rje.

Gelongma Palmo. Dge slong ma Dpal mo.

Geluk. Dge lugs.

Gemang Monastery. Dge mang dgon.

Getsé Gyurmé Tsewang Chokdrup. Dge rtse 'Gyur med tshe dbang mchog grub.

Getsé Mahāpaṇḍita. *See* Getsé Gyurmé Tsewang Chokdrup.

Golok. Mgo log.

Gongyal Monastery. Gong rgyal dgon.

Gönlung Monastery. Dgon lung dgon.

Götsangpa Gönpo Dorjé. Rgod tshang pa Mgon po rdo rje.

Gungru Khandroma. Gung ru Mkha' 'gro ma.

Guru Rinpoché. Gu ru rin po che. *See* Padmasambhava.

Gyaltsap Narthangpa Lodrö Namgyal. Rgyal tshab Snar thang pa Blo gros rnam rgyal.

Gyaltsen Pal. *See* Yangönpa Gyaltsen Pal.

Gyalwa Götsangpa. *See* Götsangpa Gönpo Dorjé.

Gyalwa Yangönpa. *See* Yangönpa Gyaltsen Pal.

Hashang Moheyan. Hwa shang Ma hā yā na.

Jamgön Drupai Pawo. 'Jam mgon Grub pa'i dpa' bo.

Jamgön Kongtrul Lodrö Thayé. 'Jam mgon Kong sprul Blo gros mtha' yas.

Jamgön Nyipar Drak. Byams mgon Gnyis par grags.

Jampaiyang Kengrü Chewa Tsikpai Phodrang. 'Jam pa'i dbyangs keng rus mche ba gtsig pa'i pho brang.

Jamyang Gyatso. 'Jam dbyangs rgya mtsho.

Jamyang Khyentsé Wangpo. 'Jam dbyangs Mkhyen brtse'i dbang po.

Jamyang Loter Wangpo. 'Jam dbyangs blo gter dbang po.

Jangchup Kyap. Byang chub skyabs.

Jetsun Jangpa. Rje btsun Byang pa.

Jetsun Milarepa. Rje btsun Mi la ras pa.

Jikjé Düdrai Wangpoi Phodrang. 'Jigs byed dus dgra'i dbang po'i pho brang.

Jikmé Damchö Gyatso. 'Jigs med dam chos rgya mtsho.

Jikmé Gyalwai Nyugu. 'Jigs med rgyal ba'i myu gu.

Jikmé Lingpa Khyentsé Öser. 'Jigs med gling pa Mkhyen brtse 'od zer.

Jikmé Tenpai Nyima. (Rdo grub chen) 'Jigs med bstan pa'i nyi ma.

Jikmé Trinlé Öser. (Rdo grub chen) 'Jigs med phrin las 'od zer.

Jonang. Jo nang.

Ju Mipham Gyatso. 'Ju Mi pham rgya mtsho.

Kadam. Bka' gdams.

Kagyü. Bka' brgyud.

Kama Shintu Gyepa. Bka' ma shin tu rgyas pa.

Kangyur. Bka' 'gyur.

Karma Ngedön Chökyi Gyatso. Karma nges don chos kyi rgya mtsho.

Karma Shenphen Thayé. Karma gzhan pan mtha' yas..

Karmapa Chödrak Gyatso. Karma pa Chos grags rgya mtsho.

Karmapa Düdul Dorjé. Karma pa Bdud 'dul rdo rje.

Kathok Monastery. Kaḥ thog dgon.

Kathok Situ Chökyi Gyatso. Kaḥ thog si tu Chos kyi rgya mtsho.

Kham. Khams.

Khamtrul Tenpai Nyima. Khams sprul Bstan pa'i nyi ma.

Khangsar Tenpai Wangchuk. Khang sar Bstan pa'i dbang phyug.

Khedrup Ngawang. Mkhas grub ngag dbang. *See* Tāranātha.

Khenpo Jikmé Punstok. Mkhan po 'Jigs med phun tshogs.

Khenpo Shenga. *See* Shenphen Chökyi Nangwa.

Khenpo Tsewang Döngyal. Mkhan po Tshe dbang don rgyal.

Khenpo Yeshe Gyaltsen. Mkhan po Ye shes rgyal mtshan.

Khenpo Yönten Gyatso. Mkhan po Yon tan rgya mtsho.

Khepa Śrī Gyalpoi Kyechö. Mkhas pa sri rgyal po'i khyad chos.

Khotsé Village. Kho tshe sde.

Khyemé Dorjé. Khyad med rdo rje.

Könchok Thapkhé. Dkon mchog thabs mkhas.

Kongtrul Lodrö Thayé. Kong sprul Blo gros mtha' yas.

Kunga Drölchok. Kun dga' grol mchog.

Kunga Gyaltsen. Kun dga' rgyal mtshan.

Kunsang Wangpo. Kun bzang dbang po.

Kyitön Jampaiyang. Skyi ston 'Jam pa'i dbyangs.

Labrang Tashikhyil. Bla brang bkra shis 'khyil.

Langdarma (Tri Darma Udumtsen). Blang dar ma (Khri dar ma U dum btsan).

Lhatho Tori Nyenshal. Lha tho tho ri nyan shal.

Lhathok. Lha thog.

Lhawang Tashi. Lha dbang bkra shis.

Lhodrak. Lho brag.

Lodrö Sangpo Gyatso. Blo gros bzang po rgya mtsho.

Longchen Nyingthik. Klong chen snying tig.

Longchen Rabjam Drimé Öser. Klong chen rab 'byams 'dri med 'od zer.

Longchenpa. *See* Longchen Rabjam Drimé Öser.

Losang Tsultrim Gyatso. Blo bzang tshul khrims rgya mtsho.

Machik Labdrön. Ma gcig lab sgron.

Manga Wershi. Mangga wer zhi.

Mar. Smar.

Marpa Chökyi Lodrö. Mar pa chos kyi blo gros.

Marpa Kagyü. Mar pa bka' brgyud.

Mé. *See* Yorpo Mepal.

Menri Monastery. Sman ri dgon.

Metön Sherab Öser. Me ston Shes rab 'od zer.

Michö Nekyi Trengwa. Mi chos gnad kyi phreng ba.

Milarepa Thöpaga. Mi la ras pa Thos pa dga'.

Mipham Rinpoché. *See* Ju Mipham Gyatso.

Mitrayogin. Mi tra dzo ki, Mi pham Sbas pa'i bshes gnyen.

Mönlam Tsultrim. Smon lam tshul khrims.

Mutik Tsenpo. Mu tig btsan po.

Namkha Öser. Nam mkha' 'od zer.

Ngangtsul Jangchup Gyalmo. Ngang tshul byang chub rgyal mo.

Ngawang Trinlé. Ngag dbang phrin las.

Ninth Situpa. *See* Situpa Pema Nyinjé Wangpo.

Norbu Trakö. Nor bu phra bkod.

Nyabön Chöjé. Nya dbon chos rje.

Nyakrong. Nyag rong.

Nyamé Sherab Gyaltsen. Mnyam med Shes rab rgyal btsan.

Nyingma. Rnying ma.

Okmin. 'Og min (Akaniṣṭha).

Önpo Sherab. Dbon po Shes rab.

Orgyen Chenpo. O rgyan chen po. *See* Guru Rinpoché; Padmasambhava.

Orgyen Menla. O rgyan Sman bla.

Orgyen Nyendrup. O rgyan bsnyen sgrub.

Orgyen Terdak Lingpa. O rgyan gter bdag gling pa.

Padmasambhava. Padma 'byung gnas. *See* Guru Rinpoché.

Palpung Monastery. Dpal spungs dgon.

Patrul Rinpoché. Dpal sprul rin po che. *See* Dza Patrul Orgyen Jikmé Chökyi Wangpo.

Pha Dampa Sangyé. Pha Dam pa sangs rgyas.

Phakpa Lodrö Gyaltsen. 'Phags pa Blo gros rgyal mtshan.

Phurtsa Khenpo Akön. Phur tsha Mkhan po a dkon.

Prajñāraśmi. *See* Trengpo Tertön Sherab Öser.

Rangjung Dorjé. Rang byung rdo rje.

Repkong. Reb gong (or Reb kong, Re skong).

Rikdzin Gargyi Wangchuk. Rig 'dzin Gar gyi dbang phyug.

Rikdzin Jangchup Dorjé. Rig 'dzin Byang chub rdo rje.

Rikdzin Tsewang Norbu. Rig 'dzin Tshe dbang nor bu.

Rimé Chöjung. Ris med chos 'byung.

Rinchen Terdzö. Rin chen gter mdzod.

Sachen Kunga Nyingpo. Sa chen Kun dga' snying po.

Sakya. Sa skya.

Śākya Chokden. Shākya mchog ldan.

Sakya Paṇḍita Kunga Gyaltsen. Sa skya Paṇḍita Kun dga' rgyal mtshan.

Śāntideva. Zhi ba lha.

Sawang Sangpo. Sa dbang bzang po.

Ser. Gser.

Sera Monastery. Se ra dgon.

Shabkar Tsokdruk Rangdröl. Zhabs dkar Tshogs drug rang grol.

Shangpa Kagyü. Shangs pa bka' brgyud.

Shangshung. Zhang zhung.

Shangtön Tenpa Gyatso. Zhang ston Bstan pa rgya mtsho.

Shardza Ritrö. Shar rdza ri khrod.

Shardza Tashi Gyaltsen. Shar rdza Bkra shis rgyal mtshan.

Shechen Monastery. Zhe chen dgon.

Shechen Paṇchen Gyurmé Thutop Namgyal. Zhe chen paṇ chen 'Gyur med mthu stobs rnam rgyal.

Sheja Dzö. Shes bya mdzod.

Shenphen Chökyi Nangwa. Gzhan phan Chos kyi snang ba.

Shönu Jangchup. Gzhon nu byang chub.

Sindrang Yab Gomchen Dorlop Chewang Rindzin. Sin drang Yab sgom chen rdo slob Tshe dbang rig 'dzin.

Situ Tenpai Nyinjé. Si tu Bstan pa'i nyin byed.

Situpa Pema Nyinjé Wangpo. Si tu pa Padma nyin byed dbang po.

Śrī Siṃha. Shrī sing ha.

Śrī Siṃha Shedra. Shrī sing ha bshad grwa.

The Supreme Incarnation Yungdrung. Mchog sprul G.yung drung.

Tāranātha. Tā ra nā tha.

Tengchen Monastery. Steng chen dgon.

Tengyur. Bstan 'gyur.

Thayé Gyatso. Mtha' yas rgya mtsho.

Third Dodrupchen. *See* Jikmé Tenpai Nyima.

Third Karmapa. *See* Rangjung Dorjé.

Thupal. Mthu dpal.

Tokden Śākya Śrī. Rtogs ldan Śākya shrī.

Tokmé Namkhai Trinphung. Rtog med Nam mkha'i sprin phung.

Tönpa Shenrab. Ston pa gshen rab.

Trakthung Dudjom Lingpa. Khrag 'thung Bdud 'joms gling pa.

Trekchö Kyi Gyapyik Namkha Drimé. Khregs chod kyi rgyab yig Nam mkha' dri med.

Trekchö Yé Babsor Shagi Döntri. Khregs chod ye babs sor Bzhag gi don khrid.

Trengpo Tertön Sherab Öser. 'Phreng po gter ston Shes rab 'od zer.

Tri Ralpachen. Khri ral pa can.

Trisong Detsen. Khri srong lde'u btsan.

Tsadra Rinchen Drak. Tsā 'dra Rin chen brag.

Tsari. Tsa ri.

Tsen Khawoché. Btsan Kha bo che.

Tseshung. Rtse gzhung.

Tseten Zhabdrung Jikmé Rikpai Lodrö. Tshe tan zhabs drung 'Jigs med rigs pa'i blo gros.

Tsewang Lhamo. Tshe dbang lha mo.

Tsiksum Nedek. Tshig gsum gnad brdegs.

Tsongkhapa Losang Drakpa. Tsong kha pa Blo bzang grags pa.

Vairocana. Nampar Nangzé. Rnam par snang mdzad.

Yadzi. Yar dzi (Chinese: Jishi zhen).

Yangchen Drölma. Dbyangs can sgrol ma.

Yangönpa Gyaltsen Pal. Yang dgon pa Rgyal mtshan dpal.

Yarlung Pemakö. Yar lung Padma bkod.

Yeshé Jungné. Ye shes 'byung gnas.

Yilhung Lharu. Yid lhung lha ru.

Yönten Gyatso. Yon tan rgya mtsho. *See* Kongtrul Lodrö Thayé.

Yorpo Mepal. G.yor po me dpal.

Yungdrung Tri Ö. G.yung drung Khri 'od.

Zu Gawai Dorjé. Gzu Dga ba'i rdo rje.

Contributors

Geoffrey Barstow is assistant professor in the School of History, Philosophy, and Religion at Oregon State University. He has been studying Tibetan culture, religion, and language for seventeen years, including several extended stays in India, Nepal, and the eastern Tibetan region of Kham. As a scholar, he focuses on the history and practice of vegetarianism in Tibet. His book on this topic is *Food of Sinful Demons: Meat, Vegetarianism, and the Limits of Buddhism in Tibet* (Columbia University Press, 2017).

John Canti trained as a doctor in Cambridge and London and while still a student met his teachers, Kangyur Rinpoché, Dudjom Rinpoché, and Dilgo Khyentsé Rinpoché. He worked in eastern Nepal in the late seventies and then moved to the Dordogne area of France, where he has been based ever since. After a period of study and practice in traditional long retreats, he helped found the Padmakara Translation Group, of which he is currently president and an active member. He was a Tsadra Foundation fellow from 2001 to 2014 and since 2009 has been the editorial chair of 84000: Translating the Words of the Buddha.

Marc-Henri Deroche is associate professor at Kyōto University (GSAIS, Shishu-Kan), Japan, where he teaches Buddhist studies and cross-cultural philosophy. His doctoral dissertation (École Pratique des Hautes Études, Paris, 2011) and a series of articles have investigated the life, works, and legacy of Tibetan author Prajñāraśmi (Tertön Sherab Öser, 1518–84) in the successive revivals of the Nyingma school and the nineteenth-century ecumenical (*rimé*) movement. He is also the coeditor of *Revisiting Tibetan Religion and Philosophy* (AMI, 2012). Recent research has focused on Dzokchen, including "The *Dzogs chen* Doctrine of the Three Gnoses" (with Akinori Yasuda, RET, No. 33, 2015) and a current project on its specific philosophy of vigilance.

Having traveled extensively in Tibet and the Himalayas, and having lived in Kyōto since 2008, his work centers on the philosophical and transcultural significance of the Buddhist paradigm of the development of wisdom according to "listening, reflection, and meditation."

Tina Draszczyk studied Indology and Tibetology at the University of Hamburg. For many years she acted as an interpreter at the Karmapa International Buddhist Institute in New Delhi as well as in Buddhist centers throughout Europe. She trained in Buddhist philosophy and meditation with both Tibetan Buddhist and Theravāda teachers. In 2012 she completed her doctoral thesis on tathāgatagarbha and shentong at the Department for South Asian, Tibetan, and Buddhist Studies of the University of Vienna, Austria, where she currently works as a Tibetan-language instructor and on research projects focusing on Mahāmudrā and buddha nature in the framework of the Bka' brgyud tradition. She also teaches courses on Tibetan Buddhism at the Akademie für Buddhismus und Christentum and courses on mindfulness at various institutes in Vienna.

Douglas Duckworth is associate professor in the Department of Religion at Temple University. He is the author of *Mipam on Buddha-Nature: The Ground of the Nyingma Tradition* (SUNY, 2008) and *Jamgön Mipam: His Life and Teachings* (Shambhala, 2011). He also introduced and translated *Distinguishing the Views and Philosophies: Illuminating Emptiness in a Twentieth-Century Tibetan Buddhist Classic* by Bötrül (SUNY, 2011).

Wulstan Fletcher studied in Oxford and Rome (modern languages, patristic studies). He made the traditional three-year retreat in Dordogne, France (1986–90), and has since lived there, working as a member of the Padmakara Translation Group. He became a fellow of the Tsadra Foundation in 2001. His translations with Helena Blankleder include *The Way of the Bodhisattva* (Shambhala, 1997), *Food of Bodhisattvas: Buddhist Teachings on Abstaining from Meat* (Shambhala, 2004), *The Nectar of Manjushri's Speech* (Shambhala, 2010), *Treasury of Precious Qualities: Book One* (Shambhala, 2010), *Treasury of Precious Qualities: Book Two* (Shambhala, 2013), and many more.

Holly Gayley is associate professor of Buddhism in the Department of Religious Studies at the University of Colorado Boulder. Her current research explores an emerging ethical reform movement in eastern Tibet, spearheaded by cleric-scholars at Larung Buddhist Academy in Serta. Recent articles on the topic include "Reimagining Buddhist Ethics on the Tibetan Plateau" (*Journal* *of Buddhist Ethics*, 2013), "Controversy over Buddhist Ethical Reform: A Secular Critique of Clerical Authority in the Tibetan Blogosphere" (*Himalaya Journal*, 2016), "Nonviolence as a Shifting Signifier on the Tibetan Plateau," coauthored with Padmatso (*Contemporary Buddhism*, 2016), and "The Compassionate Treatment of Animals: A Contemporary Buddhist Approach in Eastern Tibet" (*Journal of Religious Ethics*, 2017). Her first book, *Love Letters from Golok: A Tantric Couple in Modern Tibet* (Columbia University Press, 2016), explores the lives and letters of the treasure-revealers Khandro Tāré Lhamo and Namtrul Jikmé Phuntsok (locally known as Namtrul Rinpoché), who played a significant role in the revitalization of Buddhism in the region of Golok during the post-Mao era.

Sarah Harding undertook training in the traditional three-year retreat under Kyapjé Kalu Rinpoché in 1976, after which she began working as a translator and teacher. She is currently associate professor of religious studies at Naropa University, where she has been teaching since 1992. She spent 1996–97 in Bhutan translating for Gangteng Tulku. She has also been a fellow of the Tsadra Foundation since 2000. Her published translations include *Creation and Completion: Essential Points of Tantric Meditation* (Wisdom, 1996), "The Special Teaching of the Wise and Glorious Sovereign" in *Lion's Gaze* (Sky Dancer, 1998), *Machik's Complete Explanation: Clarifying the Meaning of Chöd* (Snow Lion, 2003), *The Life and Revelations of Pema Lingpa* (Snow Lion, 2003), *The Treasury of Knowledge: Esoteric Instructions* (Snow Lion, 2008), and *Niguma: Lady of Illusion* (Snow Lion, 2011). Her translations from Jamgön Kongtrul's *The Treasury of Precious Instructions: Essential Teachings of the Eight Practice Lineages of Tibet*, sponsored by the Tsadra Foundation, include volume 13 on the Pacification tradition (in progress) and volume 14 on the Severance tradition, published by Shambhala Publications as *Chöd: The Sacred Teachings on Severance* (2016).

Amy Holmes-Tagchungdarpa is an associate professor in the Department of Religious Studies at Occidental College. She is the author of *The Social Life of Tibetan Biography: Textuality, Community, and Authority in the Lineage of Tokden Shakya Shri* (Lexington, 2014), which explores the trans-Himalayan lineage of Tokden Śākya Śrī that spanned communities in eastern Tibet, western China, Bhutan, Sikkim, Nepal, Ladakh, and beyond. Her current research focuses on Buddhism, book culture, language, and community formation across the Himalayas.

Gedun Rabsal works as a senior lecturer at Indiana University Bloomington, where he teaches Tibetan language and culture within the Department of Central Eurasian Studies. Before moving to the United States, Gedun Rabsal worked in Dharamsala, India, as a Tibetan-language teacher at Tibetan Children's Village, as a researcher at the Central Institute of Higher Tibetan Studies, as a reporter for Radio Free Asia, and as an editor for the *Tibet Times*. His publications include his autobiography *Let's Go Into Exile!* (*'Gro skyabs bcol la 'gro*), *A Comprehensive History of Tibetan Literature* (*Bod kyi rtsom rig gi byung ba brjod pa rab gsal me long*), and Tibetan-language translations of English works such as Ernest Hemmingway's *The Old Man and the Sea* and Mikel Dunham's *Buddha's Warriors: The Story of the CIA-Backed Tibetan Freedom Fighters, the Chinese Communist Invasion, and the Ultimate Fall of Tibet*.

Jann Ronis is a lecturer in the Tibetan Language Program at the University of California, Berkeley. His early research focused on innovations in scholastics, liturgical practices, and administration spearheaded by the lamas of Kathok Monastery and the widespread adoption of those innovations in the region. He is currently investigating the twelfth- and thirteenth-century formation of an important ritual tradition in Tibetan Buddhism called the *Kagyé*, or Eight Dispensations, in an effort to better understand the domestication of Buddhism in Tibet.

Joshua Schapiro is a lecturer in the Theology Department at Fordham University, where he teaches undergraduate courses on Asian religion. His current research explores conceptions of skillful teaching in religion, with a special focus on Tibetan Buddhist advice literature and the life and writings of Dza Patrul Rinpoché.

Michael R. Sheehy is the director of programs at the Mind & Life Institute, where he leads interdisciplinary dialogues and educational programs in the contemplative sciences. Concurrently, he is a faculty member in the Department of Religious Studies at the University of Virginia, where he is affiliated with the Contemplative Sciences Center and Tibet Center. Before joining Mind & Life, he was a Visiting Scholar at Harvard Divinity School. He has spent extensive periods conducting fieldwork and collaborating with monastic communities inside Tibet, including three years training in a Buddhist monastery in Golok. For eight years, Michael directed research at the Tibetan Buddhist Resource Center, where he worked closely with the late Tibetologist E. Gene Smith (1936–2010) to digitally preserve rare manuscripts in monasteries and private archives across the Tibetan plateau and build an encyclopedic digital library of Tibetan literature. His interests abide in Tibetan Buddhism and its philosophical and literary contributions in dialogue with broad issues in the humanities about contemplative experience, consciousness and its transformations, and the Buddhism/science interface.

Nicole Willock is an assistant professor of Asian religions at Old Dominion University in Norfolk, Virginia. She is currently a 2017 Research Fellow through the Robert H. N. Ho Family Foundation Program in Buddhist studies for her book project, *Lineages of the Literary: Tibetan Buddhist Scholars Making Modern China.* This project analyzes the writings of three Tibetan Buddhist intellectuals (Tseten Zhabdrung, Dungkar Rinpoché, and Mugé Samten) through the lens of postcolonial and poststructuralist theories to challenge normative assumptions on religious subjects, state-driven secularization, and moral agency in China. Her publications include "The Revival of the Tulku Institution in Modern China: Narratives and Practices" (*Revue d'Etudes Tibétaines*, 2017) and "Dorjé Tarchin, the Mélong, and the Tibet Mirror Press: Negotiating Discourse on the Religious and the Secular in Tibet" (*Himalaya Journal*, 2016). Since 2011, she has served as a Tibet and Himalaya Panel Steering Committee member for the American Academy of Religion (AAR) and as an Academic Advisory Board member for the *Treasury of Lives: Biographical Encyclopedia* digital project.

About Wisdom Publications

Wisdom Publications is the leading publisher of classic and contemporary Buddhist books and practical works on mindfulness. To learn more about us or to explore our other books, please visit our website at wisdompubs.org or contact us at the address below.

Wisdom Publications
199 Elm Street
Somerville, MA 02144 USA

We are a 501(c)(3) organization, and donations in support of our mission are tax deductible.

Wisdom Publications is affiliated with the Foundation for the Preservation of the Mahayana Tradition (FPMT).